TARGET ZERO

TARGET ZERO

A LIFE IN WRITING

ELDRIDGE CLEAVER

EDITED BY **KATHLEEN CLEAVER**

FOREWORD BY **HENRY LOUIS GATES, JR.**

AFTERWORD BY **CECIL BROWN**

First published in hardcover in 2006 by
PALGRAVE MACMILLAN™
175 Fifth Avenue, New York, N.Y. 10010 and
Houndmills, Basingstoke, Hampshire, England RG21 6XS.
Companies and representatives throughout the world.

PALGRAVE MACMILLAN is the global academic imprint of the Palgrave
Macmillan division of St. Martin's Press, LLC and of Palgrave Macmillan Ltd.
Macmillan® is a registered trademark in the United States, United Kingdom
and other countries. Palgrave is a registered trademark in the European Union
and other countries.

ISBN-13: 978-1-4039-7657-4 paperback
ISBN-10: 1-4039-7657-0 paperback

Library of Congress Cataloging-in-Publication Data is available from the
Library of Congress.

A catalogue record of the book is available from the British Library.

Design by Letra Libre, Inc.

First PALGRAVE MACMILLAN paperback edition: January 2007

10 9 8 7 6 5 4 3 2 1

Printed in the United States of America.

CONTENTS

FOREWORD

HENRY LOUIS GATES, JR.

I first encountered Eldridge Cleaver during my senior year of high school through the pages of *Soul on Ice*. For my generation, *Soul on Ice* was one of the three classic works of the Black Power era, along with *The Autobiography of Malcolm X* and Claude Brown's *Manchild in the Promised Land*. *Soul on Ice*, however, was especially titillating—I know no more appropriate word to use—both because of Cleaver's bold advocacy of the uses of Fanonian armed resistance in the next phase of the civil rights struggle, and in particular his somewhat obsessive fascination with black male and white female sexual encounters. (I have to confess that I never understood, or accepted, his justifications of rape as an act of revolution, but even then I believed that we took this to be some sort of metaphor for radical self-assertion, but a metaphor run wild.) We read *Soul on Ice* against the backdrop of Black Panther politics, leather jackets, berets, and all the other trappings of a late sixties mythos of black revolution.

I could not possibly imagine, then, in 1968, that I would ever meet Eldridge Cleaver, a man whom some claimed to be the legitimate heir to Malcolm X. But I did: I met him in Paris, in December 1973. I had learned through poet Ted Joans that the rumors circulating around Europe were true: Eldridge and Kathleen *were* indeed living underground in Paris—"underground" in the imaginative French euphemism for political exile: "illegal," unsanctioned entry, but with the full knowledge and complicity of the French government. In return for a small loan, Ted gave me Cleaver's phone number; those were my terms. I hoped to launch my career as a journalist, which I had begun at the London bureau of *Time Magazine* in the summer of that year, with an exclusive interview with Eldridge Cleaver, revolutionary warrior, underground on the Left Bank.

We met at Shakespeare and Company, the historic English-language bookstore, nestled in the shadow of Notre Dame. He was three hours late; I was petrified. I wandered through the stacks, worrying that he would blow off our rendezvous. Truth be told, I wasn't certain that I wanted him to materialize. Alternating between fear that he would show, and fear that he wouldn't, I found myself thinking about a young James Joyce. I wondered if he ever was forced to wait here for the lofty T. S. Eliot for hours on end, just as I was waiting for Big Eldridge. My apprehension intensified the longer I waited in those dusty stacks of unsold, out-of-print American and English paperbacks. Huckleberry Finn just doesn't look the same staring up at you from a dust jacket near the banks of the Seine. I realized that I, too, longed to be a writer.

I nearly fainted when Eldridge Cleaver placed his huge right hand firmly but invitingly on my right shoulder. He had been watching me, apparently, for a long time, suspicious of my motives.

As we talked over the next two weeks in Eldridge's study—he sat in a barber's chair in the center of the room while I interviewed him—it turned out that "Over My Shoulder" was the tentative name he had given to a novel he was writing. In time, as he relaxed, growing ever more reflective, I realized that Eldridge was far more of a *writer*, an essayist, than he was an activist, and that he was exceptionally intelligent and funny. I also realized that he was lonely in exile, despite his intellectual companionship with his wife, Kathleen, and that he was homesick and would rather be living in Babylon. It also became clear to me that his periods of asylum in Cuba and Algiers had convinced him that socialism, at least as practiced in Cuba, China, North Korea, and Russia, would not obliterate racism, a palpable presence on its own, even if inextricably intertwined with class relations.

Eldridge phoned me frequently when I returned to my graduate studies at the University of Cambridge. He even invited me on the now famous road trip during which he claimed to have had a road-to-Damascus conversion to Christianity. During that time, the great African American historian John W. Blassingame and I were negotiating to acquire his papers for the Beinecke Rare Book Library at Yale. We both were stunned to learn that Eldridge had arrived at an agreement to return to the United States from exile. We were even more shocked when he announced his conversion, *à la* Charles Colson, to a born-again variety of Christianity, including eventually a sojourn with the Mormons. I saw him occasionally at Yale, where he would come to visit Kathleen and their children Maceo and Joju while she completed her B.A. at Yale College and her J.D. at the Yale School of Law.

Even when I didn't understand Eldridge's opinions, I still admired him immensely. Here was someone who, through the power of his own words, had written himself out of prison, replaced a criminal past with an intellectual future, started a family with a remarkably brilliant woman, Kathleen, only to give himself up to the American justice system soon thereafter. Eldridge's peers from his Black Panther years resented his religious and political conversions, which caused an insurmountable ideological and personal rift between him and his friends. But he was always firm in his opinions and held on to his new beliefs despite the pain this rift inevitably caused him. Eldridge always had answers when I questioned him about his conversion to Christianity or his embrace of a most conservative approach to solving the problems of the black poor. He enjoyed debate, and debate we did!

Eldridge was an imposing man: he was very tall, handsome, and had a sharp wit that was delightfully challenging. His humor comes across in the writings Kathleen has ably collected here, just as his depth of knowledge, his passion and eloquence in expressing his beliefs come across in every line. This book is an enlightening testimony of a turbulent and controversial time, an essential historical record of the origins and development of Black Panther ideology, an exploration of the meaning of prison and exile, and ultimately the compelling saga of an unforgettable life.

These collected writings chart Eldridge's lifetime in his own words and thus, for the first time, the full arc of the intellectual transformation of this exceptional mind comes to light. In *Target Zero*, Eldridge Cleaver writes himself firmly and squarely and into the history of American letters.

—Henry Louis Gates, Jr.,
W. E. B. Du Bois Professor of the Humanities,
Harvard University

INTRODUCTION

KATHLEEN CLEAVER

The Eldridge Cleaver of national headlines—fugitive revolutionary, charismatic Black Panther, celebrated author of *Soul on Ice*—had faded from sight by 1998. I heard less and less about his life during the eleven years since our divorce. On the afternoon of May 1, 1998, I was at a human rights conference at the law school of the City University of New York. I was listening to a friend explain why she disagreed with the panelist speaking about a Supreme Court decision on prisoners of war when an emissary from the dean interrupted us. To my surprise, she asked me to come to the office for a phone call. I guessed there might be some plumbing emergency at home, and when asked if I were sitting down, answered "yes." The words "Eldridge just died" shocked me into silence. Then I went numb.

Eldridge had survived imprisonment, shootings, treachery, exile, getting trapped on a crumbling freeway during the earthquake of 1989, and even brain surgery. He seemed indestructible. The day before, his niece Madeleine learned that he'd been taken to a hospital in Pomona, California. When she went to visit him in the morning, she discovered he'd died a few hours earlier, apparently of a heart attack. She spent that first day of May notifying family members. My only memory after the telephone call is of the storming rain that blurred my vision while I plowed through the highway traffic to Brooklyn to let my son know about his father's death.

Maceo, who had come back to the United States after studying Arabic at the University of Kuwait, was a devout Muslim and student of the Qur'an. Always serious, his religious conversion four years earlier seemed to have intensified his somber view of life. Tears were streaming down my face as I walked into his apartment, but after I told him what had happened his expression barely changed. Back in 1994, Maceo rushed out to

California to be at his father's bedside days after he'd received a severe blow to his head on the streets of Berkeley and underwent emergency brain surgery. The doctors gave Eldridge a fifty percent chance of surviving the surgery. For months following his father's hospitalization, Maceo lived with him in Berkeley, and assisted his recovery and rehabilitation. Afterward, he confessed how appalled he felt about the disintegration he'd witnessed in his father's life. When he stood facing me that afternoon, wearing an Islamic style robe, he said, quietly, "I've been expecting to hear this for some time."

The project tentatively known as the Eldridge Cleaver Reader, for which he'd pulled together substantial portions of his writing, was left unfinished when he died. I became involved several years after his collection had failed to kindle any publisher's interest. I helped revise his book's conceptualization, picked a new title, expanded the range of material included, and finally took on the work of editing it. What emerged from the lengthy process of collaboration with potential publishers and his literary agent Claudia Menza was *Target Zero: A Life in Writing*. The compilation of essays, interviews, memoirs, letters, speeches, and poems in this book brings the broad spectrum of Cleaver's existence into focus. Divided into four parts that track the course of Eldridge's life, *Target Zero* opens with "Early Years," followed by "Revolution," then "Exile," and concludes with "Transition," which publishes work that clarifies the decades between his 1975 surrender and his death in 1998.

The path that Eldridge took from depression-era Arkansas through exile in Algeria and back to the Alameda county jail was strewn with pitfalls, illusions, and danger. Yet, at one time life showered him with international renown and intense personal happiness. His eloquent voice defined that tortured Vietnam War era Americans can neither forget nor accept. He was a man whose creative power burst the confines of poverty, prison, and violence with an energy born from that imaginative principle—that target zero—which lies within each of us, but so few hit. The genius of Eldridge Cleaver lay in never allowing his imaginative power to be extinguished.

Thanks in large part to the persistence of Anthony Bliss, Curator of Rare Books and Literary Manuscripts at UC Berkeley's Bancroft Library, in locating and collecting Cleaver's papers, *Target Zero* includes generous selections of his unpublished and presumably lost work. Significant excerpts have also been taken from three of the four books Cleaver published during his lifetime: *Soul on Ice,* the best selling collection of essays released in 1968, followed in 1969 by *Eldridge Cleaver: Post-Prison Writings and Speeches,* and the 1978 memoir *Soul on Fire,* which he wrote following his return to the United States explaining his conversion to Christianity. Starting with autobiographical writing about his childhood and ending with a talk Cleaver gave to a black church in Los Angeles months before his sudden death, *Target Zero* provides a narrative, in his words, of the world-changing times in which he lived.

Soul on Ice was praised in the *New York Times* as "brilliant and revealing." Eldridge composed it while serving time within California's worst prisons. He viewed his writing as a means of getting an attorney, and sent a stream of letters out to lawyers in hopes of finding someone to take his case. He caught the attention of Beverly Axelrod, a radical San Francisco attorney he read about in the newspaper. When prison censors blocked him from mailing his manuscript to publishers, Cleaver smuggled his work out as legal correspondence with Beverly Axelrod. She showed his impressive writing to her friend Edward Keating, who published the radical magazine *Ramparts.* The two of them persuaded famous American writers to campaign for Cleaver's parole from prison, a successful effort that launched his career as a writer.

"Early Years," which opens with several reflective chapters about young Eldridge's family life, features the novella "The Black Moochie," a captivating account of his adolescence in the Rose Hills section of Los Angeles, which he wrote in prison. Two classic essays from *Soul on Ice* are included, as well as chapters about his prison years taken from the unpublished *Autobiography of Eldridge Cleaver* and *Promises,* a book he started while exiled in France. All these pieces were written at different stages in the tumultuous course of the author's life. What unites them is the insight they provide about Cleaver's life before he emerged as one of the most compelling and creative black leaders during the late 1960s.

Released from prison in December 1966, Cleaver settled in San Francisco where he joined the staff of *Ramparts.* He reveled in the city's seductive mix of artists, musicians, labor organizers, free thinkers, black nationalists, communists and pot heads. His articles quickly attracted attention, and he was recruited by the leaders of a local revolutionary group named the Black Panther Party for Self-Defense. Eldridge began editing their newspaper out of his apartment, but the strict conditions of his recent parole made it essential to keep his affiliation with Black Panthers, an armed organization, unknown. Their early letterhead listed the minister of information as "underground."

Eldridge's black radical journalism nationally circulated in *Ramparts* made him welcome in revolutionary circles around the country. In the spring of 1967 he and I met at a conference held by the Student Non-violent Coordinating Committee (SNCC), the movement I'd dropped out of college to join. Cleaver was thrilled to be around those civil rights organizers whose courage had inspired him from afar, and the revolutionary atmosphere he encountered among us captivated him. Later, he admitted that he fell in love with me at first sight. Within ten days I was deliriously in love with him, and by July we were engaged. In early October Black Panther defense minister Huey P. Newton was arrested following an early morning shoot-out which left him wounded and an Oakland policeman dead. Newton was jailed on murder charges, and faced death in the gas chamber if convicted. Cleaver then decided that "helping Huey stay out of the gas chamber was more important than my staying out of San Quentin,"[1] and emerged publicly as a passionate Black Panther spokesman. Eldridge insisted I come help him. In November I left SNCC's Atlanta headquarters to join him in spearheading the "Free Huey" mobilization in the San Francisco Bay Area. We were married in the midst of launching a campaign that catapulted the Black Panthers into a statewide then national revolutionary movement that ultimately captured the imagination of black people around the world.

In describing the first time he ever met Eldridge, Warren Wells, then a tough eighteen year old convict in Soledad prison who later joined the Black Panthers, wrote "I was wild and reckless then, and my reputation preceded me. Eldridge spoke to me—'Warren Killer Wells, that's your name, young fool. If you slow down long enough to get out of here alive, we may need you in our army!'[2]

"'Army?' I said. 'What kind of army you talking about?' I didn't want nothing to do with any American army, I had just spent three years in the holes of Tracy and Soledad, beaten by racist guards, set up to be killed by racist convicts. I learned how to kill or die, I guess I was already a soldier.

"Eldridge said, 'A black liberation army!!! An army of angry niggas!! Bad ass m—f— just like you, Killer Wells.'"

"That was 1965, and there wasn't a Black Panther Party yet. Some-how, Eldridge knew there would be one. . . ."

Excerpts from a book Cleaver started writing in Algiers but never fin-ished, called *Uptight in Babylon* are published in "Revolution," the sec-ond part of *Target Zero*. In an early passage from *Uptight in Babylon*, Eldridge wrote:

> The bloods who flocked to join the Black Panther Party did so on the ex-plicit belief that they were joining that army, and that they were going to war. We were going to fight the war to liberate our people, against all who came. We would start with . . . the cops, who occupied our com-munities and rained down terror on the heads of our people. . . . That's why we were exasperated with those who looked upon Huey's deed as just a shoot out between a black brother and some cops and were glad that Huey had won. To us, that was just the opening round of fire. There would be more. . . .

Once paroled, Cleaver was free to experience in person the prelude to revolution that he'd been observing from behind prison walls for years. His 1967 essay "My Father and Stokely Carmichael" demonstrates that he was as deeply concerned about the role of intellectuals as soldiers in the black liberation movement. Discussing the revolutionary implica-tion of those students who had initiated direct action against segrega-tion, he wrote there was "a vast difference between Negroes who are willing to go South and all those generations whose ambition was to flee the South. A cycle has been completed," he said, concluding that "the real work for the liberation of black people in American has begun." Compared to black leaders like Marcus Garvey and Malcolm X, who had never finished high school, Cleaver saw the beginning of another cycle with Stokely Carmichael, "the first of his stature to receive a col-lege degree." He insisted that the success "of the struggle for liberation awaits the arrival of intellectuals who have thrown off the shackles of the slave and are willing to put their talents and genius selflessly to work for the masses." Eldridge Cleaver must be counted as one such intellectual, self-educated in prison, who did exactly that.

When *Ramparts* published "My Father and Stokely Carmichael," the magazine identified Cleaver as the chairman of the Bay Area's Malcolm X Afro American Society. The society was an organization he had started to continue the work of the African history and culture class he had taught in Soledad prison. Functioning as a political group for black convicts who followed Malcolm X after his expulsion from the Nation of Islam, the class attracted Alprentice "Bunchy" Carter, who like Cleaver, came from Los Angeles, where he'd been a feared leader of the Slauson gang. The class turned into a forum where Bunchy and Eldridge developed in embryonic form the political structure they envisioned to infuse a revolutionary consciousness among the dispossessed urban blacks once they were free. Cleaver got out of Soledad first. But his encounter with Huey Newton, at a meeting of the grass roots coalition organizing a commemoration of the assassination of Malcolm X, inspired him to adjust the ideas he'd formulated in Soledad. He vividly explains this experience in the essay "The Courage to Kill: Meeting the Panthers."

"Bunchy," an excerpt drawn from the book *Uptight in Babylon,* opens with the tension evoked by Cleaver's decision to align with the Black Panther Party instead of the organization he and Carter had envisioned in prison. It reveals how aggravated Newton felt by the way Cleaver expressed his identification with the ideas of Malcolm X, and how Carter flatly rejected Huey Newton as a leader when he first got out of prison. However, the power of this excerpt lies in its portrayal of the little known but intense political drama on the ground from which the Los Angeles chapter of the Black Panther Party arose. Bunchy Carter, a brilliant and charismatic leader, created and directed that chapter until he was murdered in January 1969 during a shootout instigated on the UCLA campus by agent provocateurs. Eldridge concludes this excerpt by acknowledging, "Bunchy and I both knew that we were living on borrowed time. We were both on parole and by now the pigs understood that we were working together in the Party." But it was the assassination of Martin Luther King on April 4, 1968, he wrote, that more than any other event, "changed all our calculations."

The assassination happened the week before Newton's murder trial was slated to begin in Oakland. King's murder unleashed torrents of mass violence in city after city, starting in Memphis, where he was shot. Washington, D.C. went up in flames. Two days later, on April 6, 1968, Cleaver was injured in a late night shoot-out that erupted between several Black Panthers and Oakland police. *Soul on Ice* had barely been on sale for a month. That night when Cleaver was wounded, and taken back to prison, several other Black Panthers (including Warren Wells) were arrested, and seventeen year-old Bobby Hutton was killed. Eldridge smuggled the narrative "Affidavit #1: I Am 33 Years Old," out of prison to aid his defense, which is reprinted here in "Revolution."

Witnessing that moment, *Ramparts* editor-in-chief Robert Scheer wrote, "Perhaps because of those two months in Vacaville, or because of his feeling of debit for Bobby Hutton's death when he himself had been the target, Cleaver came out . . . determined to confront white California from [Governor] Ronald Reagan on down. Cleaver was possessed, and the words came as readily as the invitations to speak."[3] On May 13 the recently established Peace and Freedom Party, a group started by disaffected Democrats, committed antiwar organizers, socialists, and other white radicals, which Cleaver had organized into a coalition with the Black Panthers, nominated him for their candidate for president of the United States. However, the symbolic campaign the Peace and Freedom Party anticipated he would be waging from behind bars didn't materialize. In a stunning move that June, Solano County Superior Court Judge Raymond Sherwin granted Cleaver's *habeas corpus* petition and released him on $50,000 bail. Judge Sherwin wrote in his court order that "the peril to [Cleaver's] parole status stemmed from no failure of personal rehabilitation, but from his undue eloquence in pursuing goals, goals which were offensive to many of his contemporaries."[4] Striding back into the firestorm of dissent, the provocative author of *Soul on Ice* and outspoken Black Panther Party leader actively pursued his presidential campaign.

Nineteen sixty-eight was a pivotal year. Both the white supremacist right and the antiwar left ran candidates for president, the Tet offensive demonstrated the prowess of the Viet Cong against the U.S. military in Vietnam, and torrents of paranoia, anguish, and violence flooded the land in the wake of the dual assassinations that spring of Reverend Martin Luther King, Jr. and Senator Robert Kennedy. It was the year, Eldridge Cleaver wrote, that the Black Panther Party spread like a "wild prairie fire." His leadership became critical to the radical alignments he inspired to bring about solidarity against racist domination among all peoples. The Asian Red Guards, the Puerto Rican Young Lords, the Chicano Brown Berets, and the American Indian Movement all adapted the Panther's ten point platform to their communities and modeled self defense and community empowerment activities after the work they witnessed the Black Panther Party doing. These dynamic movements inspired waves of young people, who worked enthusiastically building coalitions with each other and the Black Panther Party, which aligned itself closely with the Students for a Democratic Society (SDS) and other white radical organizations. The ghastly Vietnam War became the backdrop to exploding ghettos and tumultuous protest demonstrations, and a volatile mix of rage and fear burst across America. A revolution was beginning to ignite. During that chaotic summer best remembered for the Chicago riots outside the 1968 Democratic Presidential Convention, Cleaver traveled all over California and the United States. He addressed crowds urgently, passionately explaining his experiences, his hatreds, and his radical ideas of how people should transform America. "Either you're part of the solution, or part of the problem" became his trademark admonition.

Huey Newton's murder trial in the Alameda County courthouse facing Oakland's Lake Merritt began in July. Eldridge Cleaver had staked his life on keeping Newton out of the gas chamber. He had made that goal central to every chapter of the Black Panther Party, an organization drawing in thousands of new members in the wake of Martin Luther King's assassination. Accompanied by massive demonstrations, the trial proceedings became the focus of the national 'Free Huey' mobilization Cleaver had spearheaded. The case received worldwide media attention. As the summer of 1968 drew to a close, the jury trying Newton rejected the murder charge and convicted him on a lesser offense that did not carry the death penalty. That September, on the same day Newton was sentenced for involuntary manslaughter, the California Appellate Court reversed Judge Sherwin's ruling that freed Cleaver, but permitted a sixty-day period for an appeal. Unless he could win his case in the California Supreme Court, Eldridge's parole would be revoked and he would resume serving his old prison sentence that November.

Shortly after the court ruling was announced, Nat Hentoff—one of the writers who had helped win Eldridge's 1966 parole—flew out to San Francisco to interview him for *Playboy*. It became the longest and most far reaching interview Cleaver had given to date, and has been excerpted for this volume. Its extemporaneous format was conversational and timely. It permitted Eldridge to clarify, for example, what he thought made the Black Panther Party distinctive in the ongoing black empowerment struggle, pointing out that the election of black mayors was "not about basic changes in the system. . . . Let me make this very clear. We are demanding structural changes in society, and that means a real redistribution of power, so that we have control over our own lives. Having a black mayor in the present situation doesn't begin to accomplish that."

His *Playboy* interview was geared to a mainstream audience, not necessarily to Cleaver's comrades and supporters already determined to transform American society. It was to that much smaller audience that he directed "On the Ideology of the Black Panther Party," an analytical essay on the motivation and theoretical foundation animating the Black Panther Party. It challenged the racism he saw inherent within contemporary Marxist analysis, and tackled what he defined as the false assumption of the "existence of one All-American Proletariat, one All-American Working Class, and one All-American Lumpen Proletariat." Wherever he went—whether lecturing in a graduate course at UC Berkeley, campaigning for president, or speaking at an outdoor rally—Eldridge repeatedly proclaimed that he would never surrender to the police.

The second part of *Target Zero* concludes with the last public speech Eldridge gave in San Francisco only five days before he was ordered to turn himself over to prison authorities. By then, a crowd of demonstrators holding placards saying 'Free Eldridge' were camped out every day in front of our house on Pine Street, where armed Black Panthers constantly guarded every window and doorway. The California Hall auditorium where Eldridge spoke that evening was packed. He loved being among crowds. When he believed he would die during the shoot-out in Oakland, he wrote that his "mind seemed to dwell on crowds of people, masses of people . . . the people at the rally at the Oakland Auditorium, the surging, twisting sea of people at the Peace and Freedom Party Convention at the Richmond Auditorium . . . throngs of students at Merritt College, at San Francisco State College, and at UC Berkeley. . . ."[5] His last talk was more emotional, more personal than his typical speech, starting off softly with the offhand remark, "kind of stuck for words tonight. I don't know whether this is a hello or a good-bye." He spoke in detail about the California prison system, which he condemned, likening it to the political system, calling it "this piggish, criminal system . . . that is the enemy of the people." He left no doubt in the audience's mind that he had no intention of surrendering on November 27, 1968 as ordered by the court.

We had been married for only eleven months when my husband clandestinely left the country. On Christmas Day 1968, disguised as a Cuban soldier, he arrived in Havana on a freighter and whether or not he knew it at the time, began a seven-year journey of separation and exile that would indelibly mark his life.

Seven years after his last speech in San Francisco, Cleaver published an op-ed article in the *New York Times,* reprinted here in "Exile," that revealed an attitude radically at odds with his beliefs when he landed on the FBI's wanted list back in 1968. On November 18, 1975 he wrote, "Each generation subjects the world it inherits to severe criticism," and described his generation as "more critical than most, and for good reason. At the same time, at the end of the critical process we should arrive at some conclusions. We should have discovered which values are worth conserving." By then, the Watergate scandal had thrown President Richard Nixon out of the White House, the war in Vietnam had ended in victory for the Communists, the Black Panther Party had crumbled, *Ramparts* had gone out of business, and Eldridge Cleaver was no longer a firebrand of revolutionary change. The writings gathered in the third part of *Target Zero* illuminate the experiences that brought about his change.

In May 1969 the Reuters wire service published an unexpected news story that exposed Eldridge Cleaver's presence in Havana. The incident nearly wrecked Cleaver's rocky relationship with the Cuban government officials, according to the American photojournalist Lee Lockwood who was visiting Cuba at that time. Describing Eldridge shortly after the story broke, Lockwood wrote that Cleaver's voice was "grim with suppressed anger. The Cubans were upset over the publicity that was being given his presence. . . . They wanted him to fly to Algeria on the next plane, which was leaving in two days . . . in order to 'take the heat off Cuba,' in Cleaver's words. He would hold a press conference in Algiers, stay there for a while, and later on he would be allowed to return quietly to Havana."[6]

The turmoil triggered by the revelation of his presence in Havana erupted about the same time that Eldridge learned that I was finally on my way to Havana. My plan to join him had been plagued by delay; after five months of waiting, I decided I'd have to stop relying on his associates and make all my arrangements myself. By the time I left New York City—taking a circuitous route to Havana through Algeria—I was seven months pregnant, and anxious to be with my husband for the birth of our first child. Our communication had been hampered by the U.S. blockade which barred direct mail, phone contact or travel to Cuba, but since Lockwood was heading to the U.S. via Paris, Eldridge asked him to find me to let me know that he would meet me in Algiers instead of Havana. By late May 1969 I'd already reached Paris, where I was waiting for my visa to travel to Algeria, where I could catch a weekly flight to Havana. On the day Lockwood reached me and gave me Eldridge's message, I was getting reading to check out of my hotel and leave for the airport. Fortunately, when I arrived in Algiers instead of getting on the Aeroflot plane for Havana as planned, I contacted the Cuban Embassy. A diplomat arranged my reunion with Eldridge, who arrived clandestinely during the first week of June.

Eldridge remained in limbo in Algiers, traveling on a Cuban passport and not certain of where his life was headed for nearly a year. Some of the articles gathered in the third part of *Target Zero,* such as "Three Notes from Exile" which references his 'surfacing' at the 1969 Pan African Cultural Festival, were written as Eldridge's situation unfolded, but others, like the chapters taken from the *Autobiography of Eldridge Cleaver,* were composed decades later. By the summer of 1970 Cleaver's effort to win official authorization to set up an international office of the Black Panther Party in Algiers was successful. Speaking to an American journalist about the Black Panther activity in Algiers after they were installed in the villa that previously housed Vietnam's National Liberation Front, Eldridge said, "Of course, it's frustrating to live in exile. I'd much prefer to be there [in the United States]." But, he continued, "I have been able to do some meaningful work that helps carry on our struggle. All I do is towards the idea of going back, but not to surrender myself to those pigs. . . . Here in Algiers, we internationalize our struggle . . . make alliances with other movements . . . develop exchanges with other groups. . . . We are a liberation movement in every sense of the word. . . ."[7]

Our family grew during the years we spent in Algiers. Our son was born there in July 1969, and our daughter Joju was born the following July during a visit we made to North Korea in 1970. The international section also expanded, joined by more fugitive Black Panthers, their wives and children, as well as other revolutionaries, including AWOL black soldiers looking for a sanctuary.

During Cleaver's years of exile, the FBI and other government agencies accelerated their counter-intelligence operations aimed at sabotaging the Black Panther Party, which succeeded in fomenting a destructive level of internal distrust and dissension. By early 1971, the Central Committee of the organization was split following Newton's controversial expulsion of the entire international section that Eldridge had established, as well as leaders of the Black Panther Party on trial in New York City, and the popular Los Angeles Black Panther Elmer "Geronimo" Pratt. Panthers who aligned with the so-called 'Cleaver faction' in New York City soon began publishing an opposition newspaper briefly called *Babylon*. Eldridge loved to use the name "Babylon" to describe the United States, it evoked the excessive corruption and decadence denounced in the Book of Revelations of the Bible. He appropriated the term to symbolize what he saw happening within the United States. One article from *Babylon* Eldridge wrote in the wake of the killings of student protestors at Kent State and the crushing of the prison rebellion at Attica is included in "Exile." He wrote the essay "Culture and Revolution: Their Synthesis in Africa," following the visit of a Black Panther delegation he led from Algiers to the Peoples' Republic of the Congo, then known as 'Congo-Brazzaville' in May 1971. By the time that essay was published in *The Black Scholar,* the socialist government led by Marian Ngouabi, which had hosted our delegation, had been overthrown in a bloody coup d'etat. Being isolated in North Africa protected us from the brunt of the assault against our movement, but we were living in a highly unstable situation. When President Richard Nixon made his historic visit to Communist China in 1972, it signaled a major shift in global political dynamics. It changed the course of the war in Vietnam, and prepared the way for peace negotiations. Within the United States, repression against radical movements grew even more devastating. The same year the Algerian government, which was reconfiguring its diplomatic relationship to the United States, shut down the International Section of the Black Panther Party, and demanded that all our members leave the country. Eldridge secretly entered France in 1973. The French writer Jean Genet, an ardent Black Panther supporter, intervened to help him gain political asylum there. Henry Louis Gates, Jr., then a graduate student at Cambridge University, flew over to Paris to interview him in 1974. Reprinted in "Exile," that interview delves frankly into the experiences that dimmed Cleaver's admiration for Marxism and for the Third World.

For seven years he had lived on the run. He had traveled widely in the socialist world, and had become a father. He adored his children, and his awareness of life's spiritual dimension was stimulated as he watched them grow up. In a chapter from his *Autobiography,* Cleaver writes about witnessing a startling vision while in the south of France during the fall of 1975. The experience fundamentally reorganized his entire concept of life. All of a sudden, he decided to return to the United States, despite the fact that he would have to go back to prison.

It was a startling move. I'd devoted years to gaining the support of politicians and lawyers for Eldridge's attempt to come back without being sent to prison, and keenly felt how much his about-face would surprise people. I was surprised also, but relieved. His decision meant the stream of uncertainties that living at the mercy of a foreign government brings would come to an end. A friend visiting us from California agreed to accompany our two children on their flight back to Los Angeles, where they went to stay with Eldridge's mother pending his return.

Samuel Pisar, Eldridge's new attorney, took nearly a month to complete the arrangements for his surrender, since France lay outside the FBI's jurisdiction, and the relationship between the French and U.S. authorities was still rocky in 1975. The only condition Eldridge asked his attorney to ensure was that he would not be returned to San Quentin prison. But his sudden change of heart was so shocking that it fueled wild assumptions and rumors about a supposed "deal" he'd struck with the FBI in exchange for his surrender. Given the dark climate of deception and intrigue that cloaked that decade of war in Vietnam, no evidence was needed for these assumptions; suspicion became sufficient unto itself. After Eldridge left, I stayed behind in Paris for another month to pack up our belongings and negotiate with publishers to get the funds to return myself.

The world was changing. Francisco Franco, the formidable dictator of Spain since World War II, passed away that same November day Eldridge boarded a plane in Paris in the company of two FBI agents. Back in the United States, the Senate's Church Committee was holding hearings that exposed the covert and illegal operations intelligence agencies had carried out against American citizens, and particularly against the Black Panthers. Eldridge Cleaver was changing—but the reports of his salvation by Jesus Christ and his newfound faith in America were ridiculed, and he was denounced by his former friends and comrades. In the fall of 1976, after being released from the Alameda County jail on bail pending his trial, Eldridge appeared on the television show "Meet the Press." The late Carl Rowan, the show's only black panelist, asked him: "Mr. Cleaver, when you came back to this country, you announced a conversion to American patriotism and ideals. Some of your former revolutionary colleagues said that must represent some kind of deal with the government to stay out of jail. Is that true?" Eldridge replied, "The fact that I didn't stay out of jail should explain that very quickly, that it wasn't true. I had some very deep transformations in my own personal life and my outlook on life which they didn't understand."[8]

The writing in "Transition," the final part of *Target Zero*, deals with the years that followed Cleaver's surrender. The section opens with his poignant description of the rejection he suffered when the news of his conversion was first publicized, and also includes several of Eldridge's poems on themes of love, rejection and environmental destruction. His criminal case was not resolved until five years after his surrender, during which time his public role as a famous "born again Christian" put tremendous strains on our marriage. We grew distant from each other, no longer sharing the same aspirations and beliefs. By the time he ultimately pled guilty to weapons possession and was sentenced in Oakland in 1980, our relationship had fallen apart. During the late summer of 1981, we separated. I took our two children, then twelve and eleven with me when I moved to Connecticut, where I went back to college, and then entered Yale Law School. In 1987 we divorced. Years later, Eldridge admitted he would have divorced himself if he'd been in my position. Eldridge remained in the Bay Area, but suffered a decline in his health, a situation aggravated by the financial instability and personal isolation he experienced. The 1980s for him turned into years of disappointment, confusion, and decline.

Tens of thousands of people during that era sought some way to fill the void left after the destruction of those movements that had given meaning to their lives. Some joined religious cults while others turned to drugs, and although many navigated a transition into new careers and family lives, that proved elusive for Eldridge Cleaver. Personal letters he wrote to Bobby Seale and Timothy Leary, published here for the first time, reveal what he was feeling during those fragmented years. Eldridge tried his hand at writing screen plays, gave lectures from time to time, but his life seemed to unravel. A couple of topical essays written during the '90s that have contemporary resonance are included, such as "The Bushwhacking of America" about the ramifications of the Gulf War, and his piece entitled "Reflections on the Million Man March." Unfortunately, much of his writing was scattered, stolen or lost during that time. When he moved to southern California in 1996, where he settled in an artists' colony in Pomona, however, he began to regain balance in his life. The final part of *Target Zero* concludes with a talk he gave in 1998 during Black History

Month to a black church in Los Angeles. It conveys a sense of homecoming, for a man who had so vigorously repudiated, then later embraced the Christian faith, and defined it as the core of black people's ongoing struggle for justice and freedom to which he had devoted his life.

The last time I saw Eldridge alive was in 1997. Elmer "Geronimo" Pratt (now ji Jaga) had finally won a hearing on his habeas petition, the fifth one he filed, that was held in Orange County Superior Court.[9] Eldridge had consistently supported Geronimo, both prior to his sudden expulsion from the Black Panther Party back in 1970, and during the entire 27 years he'd been imprisoned for a murder he didn't commit. In fact, his defense of Geronimo had precipitated the so-called "split" in the Central Committee and factionalization of the Black Panther Party in early 1971. Despite his embracing of conservative Christianity, Eldridge had remained a staunch defender of his revolutionary comrade, who had become a legend during the decades he'd been shipped across the state of California to one maximum security prison after another. As the hearing drew to a close, Eldridge joined the throng of supporters who packed the courtroom.

Eldridge looked far older than his sixty-one years—his hair had turned white, his shoulders seemed stooped, and his mismatched, poorly fitting suit looked like one salvaged by Goodwill. By then, I was an attorney, working on Geronimo's legal team headed by Johnnie Cochran. It had been more than a decade since I'd seen Eldridge in person, and during those years most of our communication was mediated through our daughter Joju, who remained close to her father. While the halls outside the elevator doors were filling with supporters, friends, journalists and attorneys waiting for the proceedings to begin one morning, Eldridge walked up to me. Still a tall, imposing presence, I looked up as we greeted each other. Suddenly, as if he'd been holding his breath, he blurted out, "Kathleen, I love you!" His words evoked such intensely conflicting emotions, I didn't know what to say. I scurried away, mumbling something about getting back into the courtroom; seeing how he had deteriorated distressed me. When a friend later on remarked to me, "Eldridge looked terrible," what ran through my mind was: "You just have no idea of how lucky he is to be alive." He was tough—a difficult, visionary, sensitive man who'd risked his life for what he believed. Not everyone who took that path had survived.

Eldridge Cleaver's writings provide a literary prism for understanding the era that shaped his extraordinary life. Educated in prison, he became a provocative, brilliant and inconvenient critic, one who never stopped examining ideas or grew reluctant to question entrenched beliefs, including his own. He passed out copies of Robert Williams's *Negroes with Guns* to incoming Black Panthers during the party's early days and later enthusiastically promoted the ideological writings of Kim Il Sung following his visit to North Korea. After repudiating Marxism and violence, Eldridge's politics turned conservative and he was studying an interpretation of the Bible called *A Course in Miracles* toward the end of his life. During his height as a revolutionary leader, Cleaver spoke out loudly, his tone inspired by maroon ancestors escaping the chains of slavery who had to whisper to stay alive. His voice sent out a bold signal to thousands of restless youth to seize the moment, rise up and change the destiny of our country. That was a sin rarely forgiven by those in power, or forgotten by those they oppress. *Target Zero: A Life in Writing* defies the simplistic characterization our sound-bite culture relies upon. The range of Cleaver's work it presents invites you to expand and reconsider what you think you know about the most controversial era that convulsed America since the Civil War.

PART ONE EARLY YEARS

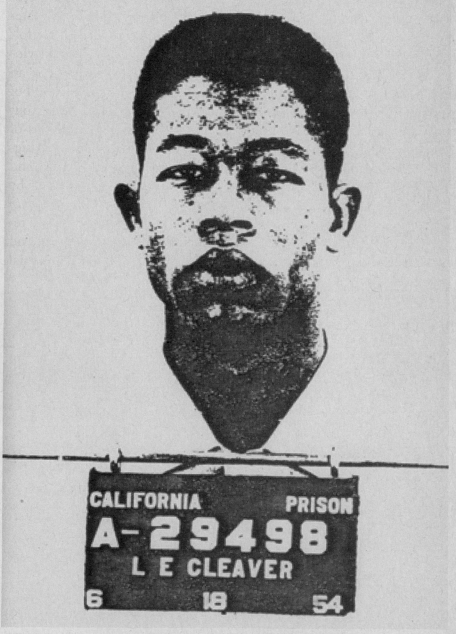

Leroy Eldridge Cleaver, Mug Shot, June 1954

Eldridge Cleaver called this excerpt from his 1978 memoir Soul on Fire a 'few hazy memories of Little Rock, Arkansas,' where he was born.

"Childhood Lessons." Reprinted by permission. From Soul on Fire *by Eldridge Cleaver. Copyright © 1978 by W. Publishing, a division of Thomas Nelson, Inc., Nashville, Tennessee. All rights reserved.*

CHILDHOOD LESSONS

Arkansas was a perpendicular cliff of red clay in our backyard. Our house straddled the edge of this cliff, with the back porch sticking out into empty space, resting on long stilt supporting timbers, rising up from the black dirt of our backyard below. I do not remember how high up the porch was, except that it was equal to the height of the cliff, all of it something happening over my head. I can peg these moments in time with images of my baby brother, Theophilus, five years my junior, wearing diapers and sucking on his bottle, marking me as five or six years old. Suddenly I was there, playing in the clay out of which mother said we had been formed. I still recall the vital, pungent odor of the soft clay, its cool texture. How good it felt when squeezed through fingers and toes.

Big black bumblebees, with yellow stripes across their backs, made their homes in holes in the clay. As they emerged from their holes, we sometimes trapped them in glass jars, watched them searching in confusion for a way out, and listened to their distressed buzzing through airholes punched in the tin lids. More than once I must have spied a lizard sneaking into the old water pipe sticking out of the clay at about the level of my eyes, and more than once I must have flushed him out with a long stick, or with a stiff stream of hot pee pee artfully directed, sending the lizard scurrying for higher ground.

When Theophilus, sitting on the back porch at the top of the stilts, fell off, landed in the clay, and never even stopped sucking his bottle, the value of the clay could only have been enhanced in my eyes. I remember neither when I started nor when I stopped eating the clay, only my mother's shrill voice prophesying doom if I didn't stop. I can still see the little dark hands, feet, and legs of brothers, sisters, and perhaps friends, as over the years we shaped the world with our hands.

Years later, long after we were gone from this house at the source, great tidal waves of red gooey muck rushed at me in a recurring bad dream. In the dream I was always fleeing, or flopping about, always on the verge of being overwhelmed.

We were five children then, two girls and three boys, offspring of Leroy Cleaver and Thelma Hattie Robinson united in Holy Matrimony in 1926. I list us in rank by birth:

Wilhelmina Marie	October 21, 1926
Helen Grace	May 3, 1932
Leroy Eldridge	August 31, 1935
James Weldon	October 10, 1937
Theophilus Henry	December 9, 1940

There was a great antagonism between the Cleavers and the Robinsons—going back, to my knowledge, at least to my grandfathers on both sides. They had been called, they said, by God Almighty, to preach the true gospel to their people. The difference between these two gentlemen was the classic dichotomy between black people in America, with roots that go back into slavery. Grandpa Robinson was a House Nigger and Grandpa Cleaver was a Field Nigger.

Grandpa Robinson was part of a great tribe of mulattos. They were proud of their gray-blue eyes and pointed noses, and alluded to the white and Indian blood in their veins. They ran rumors around in circles of cousins who were passing for white, about one who had married and disappeared into the white race, leaving not a trace behind, except them. Grandpa Robinson was the pillar in the Little Rock branch of his tribe. St. Andrews AME was an important church in town. He was the first to make Little Rock work for the Robinsons, and his success enabled others of his tribe to pluck up their roots in Hot Springs and Pine Bluff and migrate to Little Rock.

Grandpa Cleaver was the very opposite of Grandpa Robinson. Tall and black-skinned, he had a house that sat in the middle of a cotton farm, and he did his shopping at the company store. He raised hogs, chickens, and vegetables, and is said to have sired several families besides the one from whence my father came. The old lady I knew as Grandma is said to have been about his third wife. He lived to be 98 years old.

This old man, rooted in Malvern and Camden, had been a CC rider, a circuit-riding preacher who had traveled for years throughout the region, preaching the gospel as revealed to him. He had finally settled down in Wabbaseka, which must be one of the smallest dots on any map of Arkansas. As in our house my father's piano was untouchable, his father's holy of holies was an old typewriter, and if you touched it you would go directly to hell, with a broken tail.

Mother met father because both of their fathers were working the soul circuit, and there were conventions, picnics, and various other get-togethers. Perhaps. But my father was capable of running my mother to the ground under other circumstances, totally unrelated to church, because if there was anything my father hated, it was "a chicken eating preacher." It was well understood that my mother married my father over the objections of her family, first of all her father.

My father had no patience at all with churchgoing. If you asked him, he'd tell you in a minute, "No. There ain't no God. And I'm the only Santa Claus you ever gonna see."

Mother was different. Proverbs, parables, and principles poured out of her mouth in a constant stream. She had a quotation to fit every occasion, chief among them was, "Honor thy father and thy mother, that thy days may be long upon this earth."

When I hassled her in the kitchen as she prepared a meal, singing what came to be my song—"I'm huuuunnngrrryy!!"—Mother would retort, "Run around the house and catch Congry." Which would send me into spasms of frustrated rage.

"Get out of here, boy," she'd scat me. "Watch a pot and it'll never boil."

If her nose itched, mother would say, "Hmm! Nose itching. Company's coming." And someone was bound to show up.

She believed in God, dreams, luck, and intuition. Before she'd allow me to crawl into bed at night, I had to say my prayer, repeating it nightly down a misty string of years:

Now I lay me down to sleep,
I pray the Lord my soul to keep.
If I should die before I wake,
I pray the Lord my soul to take.
Amen.

Being the oldest boy, I was the apple of my daddy's eye, which set me at irreconcilable odds with Helen and Wilhelmina. Not so much Helen as Wilhelmina, who was my active antagonist, my implacable foe. Being neither the oldest girl nor the oldest boy, Helen played the classic neutral, wishing a plague upon both our houses. With stony objectivity, she'd tell the pure truth on either of us if we lied about who hit whom first. The rub between Wilhelmina and me wasn't any lightweight sibling rivalry. It was closer to war. This was made forever clear to me one day when Wilhelmina, crying and fussing because she had to wash dishes, threw a fork—I had patted my fanny at her, all the while tauntingly intoning, "Ha, ha, ha. You have to do the dishes"—which plunged deeply into my arm just as I ran out of the kitchen. For years thereafter, I wore the marks of the four prongs on my left forearm and remembered the incident as my first encounter with a witch.

Daddy had two jobs—waiting tables during the day in a big hotel restaurant, playing the piano in a club at night. We didn't see much of him; he was always either going or coming. When he was home, if he was not digging in the ground, he was sawing and nailing planks of wood, in a constant struggle to keep our house from collapsing. I liked helping him work, handing him the hammer or nails, or helping him shovel the dirt he dug up with the pick. Once I thought my daddy was magic. He drove the pick deep into the ground, and when he pulled it out there was a brand new penny stuck to the dirt clinging to one of the points of the pick. He gave me the penny. He repeated this magic feat five times, each time coming up with a brand new penny, giving it to me.

Daddy had a piano in a room of our house. We called it the Piano Room. Anybody who fooled around in the Piano Room was just begging for a whipping. The only person who could have her way in the Piano Room was Wilhelmina, whom Daddy was teaching how to play.

Mother had the uncanny ability to smell snakes. She said they smelled like watermelon rinds. One day she said some snakes were around somewhere close because she smelled them. Daddy said she was crazy, but agreed to have a look. He found two big blacksnakes under our house. He chopped off their heads and nailed their bodies to a tree stump in our backyard. They wiggled and thrashed around, seemingly more full of life without their heads than with them. Daddy said they'd keep it up until the sun went down, then they'd die. I watched them, glued to the spot, until mother made me come inside for dinner and bed. The next morning, I ran outside to see. The snakes were strangely stilled. I watched them for hours. Not a twitch.

Getting an education was a religion in our house. Mother was the high priestess of its doctrine. According to her, the worst thing in life was to miss an education. It was worse than going to Hell. It was Hell on earth. At least get a high school education! Later on, we'd need a high school diploma to get even the lowest job, like digging ditches. Mother never let up on this line—never—as she sought to instill in us the motivation to pursue education. She taught us how to read and gave us books for presents on birthdays and other occasions.

One day, suddenly, a dark shadow fell across our home. Daddy took an axe and chopped up his piano. Then he broke everything in the house made of glass, starting with all the dishes. He smashed the glass covers on the pictures hanging on the walls. One corner of our living room was like a family shrine, whose focus was my parents' wedding photo on the wall. Hanging around this photo, and on little whatnot shelves on either side, were our treasured family photos and memorabilia. Daddy smashed everything. Something terrible was happening. What it was I didn't know. Helen, Wilhelmina, Mother and Daddy all seemed to understand. But James, Theophilus, and I were told to shut up, get out of the room, or slapped when we demanded to know what was going on. We were never told.

After that, the fighting started. Every Saturday night, without fail, Daddy started beating Mother. There was screaming and the thunder of our feet and bodies scuffling around as we all joined in the melee. It was everybody against Daddy, and we'd all hit him as hard as we could, trying to make him stop hurting our mother. The center of my frustration was that I was unable to hit Daddy hard enough. That was the beginning of my driving ambition to hurry and grow up tall and strong, like my daddy, but bigger and stronger than he, so that I could beat him down to the ground the way he beat my mother.

I remember the comment C. P. Snow made in *Variety of Men* about the childhood of Joseph Stalin, comparing it to other revolutionary leaders—

Nearly all the others came from professional families. Stalin alone was born in the depths of the poor. His father was not only an impoverished shoemaker, but an increasingly unsuccessful one. He took to vodka and to ill-treating his son. At a very early age Stalin had to reckon with savage brutality: he learned to be secretive, evasive, and enduring, and to keep his mouth shut. It was an awful home, and he learned his lessons well.

One day Daddy said he was going far away and wasn't coming back. He was going to find us another house, in Chicago, Arizona, or California. Mother was getting fat in the belly and we were going to have a new house and a new baby in the family. Meanwhile, we were going to go live on Grandpa Cleaver's farm. For my mother, moving onto the Cleaver farm in Wabbaseka was like going backwards, and my two sisters shared the same feeling. My two younger brothers were too young to know the difference, but for me it was a happy occasion. There were so many exciting things happening on the farm, so many worlds to explore.

Mother took a job teaching at the little school in the area, and she kept my two sisters with her all day. I had to go to school every afternoon, while one of the neighbor ladies kept James and Theophilus. I spent the rest of the time tagging behind Grandpa Cleaver as he did his daily chores. I'd help him feed the hogs and chickens, ride on the back of his horse-drawn wagon when he went to the company store. But my greatest pleasure was to take his dog, Shep, and go out hunting rabbits. When Shep spotted a rabbit, that rabbit was as good as in the pot. Shep would run it to the ground, grab it in his mouth, and shake it to death. Then he'd bring it back to me. Proudly, I'd run home with our catch. These were the days of kissing the earth, of touching and smelling wild things growing, of running barefoot through cotton fields, of fishing in rivers and dragging in crawdad holes, of watching Grandpa and his friends slaughter hogs, of later sneaking in the smokehouse and licking the salty smoked hams hanging there. Thus I spent the time waiting for my father to send for us.

An unfinished autobiography was among the papers Eldridge Cleaver left in his studio in Pomona, California, at his death in May 1998. Its pages were still in draft form, with question marks, blank lines, and indications in parenthesis of material he intended to add later. In order to publish excerpts in this collection, the material has been slightly edited and given the title The Autobiography of Eldridge Cleaver *based on his shorthand notations for his chapters, which were "ec1," "ec2" and so on.*

THE AUTOBIOGRAPHY OF ELDRIDGE CLEAVER

CHAPTER ONE

CHILDHOOD

"Eldridge, you are headed for the gas chamber," said my mother not once, but many times. Both of my grandfathers were ministers and the family was hoping that I would become one too. But I had different ideas.

My father was a pianist who started off playing in church but eventually switched to jazz. He came to hate all ministers. I think it had something to do with this relationship to his father, a Baptist minister. I was never given any details on why this change took place in my father. I just saw the results.

When I was a child my mother says I was a little angel. But life's experiences sometimes take us down perilous paths. When I was 12 my life took that turn. It was probably the result of the break-up of my family.

We lived in Arkansas at the time and when I was 12, we moved to California. That's when my life really began to change. Up until that time we had a good, close family life. My mother read a lot of books to her children, and was always encouraging us to read on our own. There were six children in the family, three girls and three boys. I was the third child and the oldest boy. I felt my older sisters were tyrants whenever they tried to tell me what to do.

Then my mother and father began to fight. It was very embarrassing to me because the other kids in the neighborhood would taunt me in a very cruel manner, and say things like "Who won last night?" The most embarrassing thing I remember was one day being out in the street playing marbles with my friends, when my mother ran by, my father chasing her. A real wipe for me.

I remember reaching the point where I wanted to be able to beat my father up. He was about as tall as I am now, about six feet two inches. I was so angry at him that even at 12 I used to go up against him.

It just devastated me to do this because deep in my heart I loved my father in so many ways. But that love seemed to reverse itself and turn into the most furious hatred. My primary ambition was to grow up and get big so I could punch him out.

I reached the point where I refused to cooperate with my father on anything. He would try to get me to perform tasks round the house, and I just wouldn't do it. For example, he had a curfew on his children, requiring us to be in the house by eight o'clock each night. Lots of times I didn't have anything to do, but still I would just sit outside and wait until it was long past eight o'clock before I would go inside, where there would be a tough spanking waiting for me. That's how I handled the bitter feelings I had for my father. Eventually my parents split up, and my father moved to Chicago.

I had a lot of energy, and a meanness in my heart, a deep hatred for the society in which I lived. I didn't know anyone more alienated than I was. The racial problems that were getting a lot of coverage in the news at that time focused my hatred and rebellious feelings toward America, the white man's society. I was part of an oppressed race, and I began to feel justified in doing anything I felt like to hurt white people and their so-called establishment. I was so angry that whenever I could do anything to upset white people it gave me a feeling of delight.

I was beginning to use guns and knew that sooner or later I was going to get into trouble so serious I would not be able to walk away from it. Sometimes I felt totally lost and out of control. I could see that if I continued on this path it would lead to the gas chamber, as my mother had warned me, or at least life imprisonment. My mother begged and pleaded with me to change my ways, but I would not listen. In my heart I knew where I was headed, but I was caught up in trying to beat the system, outsmart the law enforcement people, and avoid the inevitable as long as possible.

CHAPTER TWO

PRISON

I entered prison about the same time the United States Supreme Court outlawed segregation in the school system. I was caught up in the middle of the black-white controversy that was sweeping the country. I didn't understand the arguments that I was exposed to, and I couldn't decide for myself what was right and wrong. I felt the only way for me to go was to study a lot, and amass a lot of information, which I thought would allow me to get on top of things and decide what was really going on. Maybe even get control of my life.

Realizing my life was in shambles, I began to try to figure out what was going on. In prison, I had a lot of time to do that. I began to study at every opportunity. There was not much else to do in prison, so I had time on top of time to devote to my studies. It was a way of escaping. I had enough sense, however, to realize that prison is really a losing game. I was determined to turn a losing situation into a winning one by improving my mind. I was determined not to go out the same as when I came in. I figured that by gaining information and knowledge, I would get on top of the situation.

As I studied about society and subjects such as history, literature, and sociology, my resentment toward America just grew more intense. On the television news I watched black people being herded and corralled by white policemen with electric prods, which churned in my heart, as they did in the hearts of my fellow black prisoners. I became more and more inclined toward violence.

During my studying and talking to others who were studying the same things, I got to know a man named John Hall. He was considered the smartest man in prison, and we all looked up to him. Looking back now, I don't think he was that smart, because every time I went to prison, he was always there. I think the fact that he was there so long meant he was able to read more than the rest of us.

Whenever we argued over a subject, John was always the winner. Frequently I would challenge him to debates, but he always won.

"Eldridge," he said one day, "I know what you are looking for. Meet me tomorrow morning after breakfast and I will give you something that will do you a lot of good."

The next morning he gave me a copy of *The Communist Manifesto.* He said he personally was fascinated with the manifesto, and he took me aside and explained the language and words I would find that would be new to me.

I took the book back to my cell and stayed up all night reading it all the way to the end. When I finished, I felt I had received a great revelation about what was really going on. All those ideas I had been studying and groping with seemed to fall into a pattern. All my feelings of rebellion and hatred were justified by this document.

I had a very negative attitude toward police. It didn't matter if they were white or black. I hated all policemen. The manifesto identified them as the enemy of the people, and I could really relate to that. Businessmen were also presented as enemies of the people. The capitalist system was doomed, and it was open season on capitalists. Anything you could do to get rid of capitalism or hurry up its collapse was right and good.

What I was reading fit right in with my attitude and the things I had been doing. It gave me a political context, or justification, for what I was doing. I was no longer a criminal, but a revolutionary in support of a noble cause. I used the remainder of my time in prison to train myself for the day when I would get out, when I intended to apply the principles of the communist revolution.

I could see the times were ripe for revolution. The United States was involved in the unpopular Vietnam War. There was domestic turmoil over civil rights. The news was dominated with reports of local violence, and then it would switch to reports of the Vietnam War.

I saw problems in my own personality that I attributed to my early Christian upbringing. I felt I had been made into a softy, too much of a gentleman. It was hard for me to just go out and hurt people, to take the first swing. I would taunt and provoke people into attacking me first, then I would feel justified in taking them out. I soon learned this attitude would not help my chances of survival in prison. If someone got to me first, I might be killed and never get a chance to take them out.

I struggled to rid my heart of this softness. I wanted to become tougher, more disciplined. The atheistic part of the Marxist philosophy enabled me to do this. The Marxist doctrine taught me that religion was a hoax, pushed on the people to keep them blind, so they could be more easily exploited. I learned religion was the opium of the masses, that people were sedated by it. I began to look at churches as part of the system that was keeping black people subjugated to the white society. I viewed the American society as a modern form of black slavery, with the churches doing their part to keep this new form of slavery alive.

I began to focus on getting religion out of my system. All my childhood lessons about loving enemies and turning the other cheek had to go. As far as I was concerned, it was time to start fighting the enemy. I wanted to kill my enemies.

I was reading Bertrand Russell and his agnostic theories, as well as accepting the blatant atheism of Karl Marx. Reading Che Guevara was a major turning point for me. He said that in order to become a professional revolutionary, you had to be a cold, calculating, killing machine, able to slit a throat at the drop of a hat, and to walk away without looking back. That was the recommended attitude for a revolutionary. The destruction of a country is not child's play. It's bloodshed, bombs, terrorizing, and killing. I cultivated my heart and mind to become part of this.

While incarcerated in Soledad State Prison in 1966, Eldridge Cleaver wrote the following notes for an autobiography or novel based on his experiences while growing up in Los Angeles. It was first published in two installments in Ramparts *Magazine in 1969. By then, Cleaver had become a leading spokesman for the Black Panther Party. He had sought asylum in Algeria to avoid imprisonment in California, and was wanted by the FBI as a fugitive.* Ramparts *editor in chief Robert Scheer visited Cleaver in Algiers and returned with this manuscript. In his introductory note to* The Black Moochie, *Scheer wrote that it "provides an insight into an important part of Cleaver's early life and further evidence of his immense power as a writer. The names have been changed for legal reasons."*

Scheer also informed the readers in his introductory note of the intimidation he faced upon his return to San Francisco from Algiers. "I was promptly subpoenaed to appear before the Federal Grand Jury meeting in San Francisco," he wrote, "and ordered to turn over all records of activities performed on behalf of Eldridge Cleaver's legal defense. The State and Justice Departments have evoked a series of regulations making contact with Cleaver illegal; this subpoena is part of the general pattern of harassment. We regard these regulations as unconstitutional and intend to challenge them."

THE BLACK MOOCHIE

PART I

They called me "The Black Moochie," because I ran with the Mexicans. It started early; the word "Mexican" burned into my brain in Arkansas, where there were none. Mother told me that we would see Mexicans in Arizona. All the way on the train I kept asking her to show me a Mexican. I expected to see something beyond human, something beyond imagination. I don't remember the first Mexican I saw. It may have been a whole crowd of them. What I remember is pressing my face to the plate glass window of the Tortilletta in Phoenix, trying to see the Mexicans inside mixing masa with their feet, as it was said they did. I don't remember seeing them do that, but I remember being outraged at the idea of them doing it. It was unbelievable that people could put their dirty feet in food and still eat it. Worse, sell it to others to eat. Worse yet, others buying it knowing it was mixed by foot. My image of feet was of stinky feet, like my brother James's feet. James had real funky feet. What if a Mexican had feet like James and stuck them in the masa? It would be a violation of the Pure Food and Drug Act, for sure. Then we moved to Los Angeles, to Rose Hill, and I went to school with Mexicans. These were the first human Mexicans I knew. In Rose Hill, they detached themselves from shadows in my mind and became for real. Chicanos.

Arnaldo Martinez, Roberto Areaga, Nanny Goat, and me, we were natural buddies—perhaps because we were of the same pitch of insanity. We called Arnaldo "Junior," and Roberto we called "Jap," "Honorable Jap," and I don't even know Nanny's real name. They called me "Sapo." Negroes called me the "black moochie," with overtones of derision, because I put them down and ran with the Mexicans. Why did I dig the Mexicans more? I liked the way they did things. And then my family chose to move to Rose Hill instead of Watts or the East Side where all the Negroes lived, because there were some very phony Negro families in Rose Hill. The ones with boys my age had long since turned them into sissies by keeping them under the family thumb—like Charlie and Floyd Grant. Floyd was exactly my age, but he had no backbone. If his father told him to come home early and we wanted to stay out late, Floyd went home to his father and spoiled everything. Charlie was even more sissified than Floyd. The only other Negroes my age were Bobby Hooper and Donald, who was just a little younger. We ran together for a while, until the first time we went to Juvenile Hall. When we got out, Bobby became almost a saint. That left only the Mexicans. They were like me—wild, crazy, didn't give a damn. We were happy together.

I envied the way Junior's shoes would shine. Mine never would shine like that. I'd rub mine all night long, but they just wouldn't shine like Junior's. Junior used to come to school with his shiny shoes on and I'd get mad. Everybody dug the way his shoes held a shine. Junior would play the part, as if he didn't know what it was all about. But he knew, and he would stick his shoes out for everyone to see. Once I stepped on his shine on purpose, on the sly.

"Meet me after school, *mayate*," Junior said.

After school, everybody was there. Junior was overmatched, but what he taught me that day was that even though he was a little cat compared to me and even though he knew in advance that he would get whipped, there was a pride in fighting back when someone tried to bully you. We drew each other's blood, but in the years to come we never fought again and were the best of friends.

Mrs. Brick was my teacher and she looked like Betty Grable. All the cats were in love with her. We'd rub up against her and try to peep under her dress. We'd dream about her at night. She had a fine ass and big tits. She dressed sexy. I used to get a hard-on just looking at her. She knew that we wanted to fuck her, to suck her tits. One day when we were returning from the music room, Mrs. Brick marched the whole class up the stairs. I liked Michele Ortaga then. She was the most beautiful girl I'd ever seen. Her skin was white as milk and she had long black hair. She was very delicate, very feminine—even at that titless, shapeless age. What I liked about her was that whenever I looked at her she would blush, turn red from her neck up. Her ears would glow. I was the only boy who could make her change colors. While we were waiting at the top of the stairs that day, I found myself opposite Michele. I had been conscious of her beauty all afternoon. During music period I'd been staring at her, making her blush, and while we stood at the top of the stairs I was staring at her. I said to her: "I love you, Michele."

Her neck caught fire, the red flames lit up her ears. "I hate you!" Michele hissed at me. We traded words back and forth. For some forgotten reason, I wound up saying: "Your mother is fat as an elephant." Michele, hurt and embarrassed, burst out in tears. Mrs. Brick came to see what was happening. Michele told her I had called her mother an elephant. Mrs. Brick turned on me with flame in her eyes, and I could see a hatred that frightened me. "You black nigger!" she snarled, and slapped my face. It sounded like a shot going off in my ear—the words, I mean—I don't think I even felt the blow. Her words brought tears to my eyes.

From that day on, Mrs. Brick still looked like Betty Grable. She still had a fine ass and nice tits, she still dressed real sexy, and she still kept me with a hard-on. But my feeling for her was no longer the warm desire of the lover. What I felt for her was the lust/hatred of the rapist. I

felt about the same for Michele. I could still make her blush, but between us there was a deep abyss into which something of us that was
bathed in sunlight had fallen forever.

Years after graduating from the grammar school, me and Jap and
Junior were pushing Junior's car down North Huntington Drive, trying
to kick the motor over. Behind us a woman stopped her car to give us a
shove. I waved to the driver to guide her car's bumper into Junior's. Just
as I ran to jump into Junior's car, I saw that the driver of the other car
was Mrs. Brick. We recognized each other, smiled and waved. Junior,
Jap, and me had all been in her class together. "That's Mrs. Brick!" I
shouted as I jumped into Junior's car. She honked her horn and waved
and smiled as she passed us by and disappeared in front of us.

I remember Mrs. Brick. I remember Michele. Do they remember me?
Did we scar each other mutually? Can a girl you made both blush and
cry not remember you in some deep rhythm of her soul?

This land of blood. This soil groans under the weight of how we cut
each other to bits. The blood I have let. The blood I have bled. The
pain I have given. The pain I have felt. Michele Ortaga, girl of black
hair and white skin, girl with the flaming neck, I will carry your image
into eternity—graven into my soul, burnt forever into my skull, a part
of my life, real, significant, a memory of flesh and blood. This small
thing—that we chanced to attend the same school on this civilized
planet hurtling through space, that because we were of the same age we
were in the same class, that because we were in the same class I discovered the flutter of your heart. I knew how to make you feel anticipa-
tions of your budding womanhood by my way of looking budding
manhood into your eyes. Whatever hatred of you I carried for years
after that day on the stairs, I no longer have. I have for you now only
the pure love of the memory of your flaming neck, your bright eyes,
your smile at me, Michele.

Eagle Rock, Highland Park. Arroyo Seco Park. Freeway. The Los Angeles River. The Dam. The hills. The Midget Auto Races. Fishing. Hik-
ing. Model airplanes. The cops always somewhere, hovering, a vague
presence, reeking the stink of a bad dream. The sun. The dry dirt,
parched expanses. Birds—doves, killdees, sparrows, hawks, pigeons,
quail, robins. Snakes. Tarantulas. Gopher holes. Spiders. Rabbits.

The long twisting distances. The good feeling at the top of a steep hill
after the long climb up. The serenity of aloneness. A girl named Fay and
I on the hill at the tank. Fay sitting on the wall. Fay took everything ten-

der between us to the grave with her: beyond my power to pull her back from the clutch of death—death so cruel as to silence her laughter, still the beating of her passionate heart, make cold those hot lips of hers. She had such pleasure to give; she enjoyed life so. My heart pounding. How to protect Fay. Me standing on the edge of the cliff to frighten Fay. Going out farther on the lip of the cliff to make her ache for me. Fay in love with Cutie. My pain.

How I pursued her and won her love too late. Yes, I stalked her love as if it were a wild animal; I trapped it with an unobtrusive love. I was always there when she needed someone to fill the hours of her loneliness, to drive her around Los Angeles, to lend her money when her allotment check was late. I offered her companionship, protection, a helping hand that did not try to grasp her, though I ached to embrace her. This has to be rendered very delicately, very indirectly, because Fay was very delicate, very indirect, exquisite in the beauty of her existence. The earth flattered itself by decorating its face with Fay. Jail. Her death. The telegram: Fay passed away Tuesday morning at three A.M. Burial will be in Tulsa, Oklahoma. Signed Mother. The Valentine's Day card. Rickey. Her husband. Our hike. Selling dope. The rain. The narks wise to weather. Fay at my mother's. Her hair, her sweet scent, her body. The Wyamine tubes. Near wreck. Took her to the General Hospital. The fear, madness. The circles the brain goes round in. Burt's Store, the Projects. Fay waving at Frank, Cutie, Oldie, and me, as we rounded the bend in Frank's Chevy; she was sitting there on the stone stairs, reading a magazine, her legs held close together prettily, sexily.

Lulu Jean and Cassie side by side in the grass. I'm fucking first one, then the other. Lulu Jean has a thick patch of red hair. Cassie is bald and too small to enter, but in her mind she is big as a gate and she won't leave me alone long enough to enjoy Lulu Jean. Hot Lulu Jean, tight and moist and working toward you in search of a mutual moment of pleasure. But Cassie keeps threatening to "go tell" if I don't "do" her. We'd gone into the hills to pick wild mustard greens.

The most beautiful green grass of my life was in Arroyo Seco Park. It was like many green football fields placed side by side and end to end. The water sprinklers were always working. Somewhere someone was always mowing the lawn. We felt like aliens, expecting someone to run us away. We had no idea that we had a perfect right to use this city property, to be in the park, to stay as long as we liked. We had no sense of a "right" to use the park, or anything else—not even a right to life.

We'd stay mostly in the park, with our slingshots, trying to shoot birds. We were really good shots, as deadly accurate as rifles. We never got a killdee—not in years of trying. We thought them specially protected by God in person. We'd shoot straight at them and miss. Perfect shots, but never a dead killdee. Any other bird within range was in a heap of trouble. Our slingshot culture: a time existed when I couldn't hit the side of a barn with a marble: the time came when I could put out a match, hit the headlight of a moving car, knock a mourning dove off the telephone wire or out of a tree, brain a rabbit if it paused in its run to gauge its enemy. Our lives were given to finding car inner tubes that were of the right rubber. We favored red tubes, best for the stretch and snap-back. By stretching the rubber we knew if we had good stuff. We'd look for little cracks in the rubber when it was stretched to full tension. We'd haunt gas stations for old tubes of quality. We read the deterioration of the modern world through the decrease in the quality of the car inner tubes. Seeking tubes in El Sarreno, Alhambra, Pasadena. We went all the way to El Monte on foot once, but never again. Exploring the world. The madness of our foot treks! We might show up anywhere, we didn't care. It told of the quality of our lives, our needs.

Bobby Hooper was a dead-eye shot, could hit anything; Charlie and Floyd were good; Donald was good. The Mexicans were all good, and dreadful. They'd pass by at a distance with their vicious dogs. Sometimes we'd have our little wars, exchange vollies. I was deadly—the most accurate, the most daring shot. The others would be trying to creep up on a pair of doves: flap! I'd down a dove from way back. Incredible shot! Uncanny shot! Skill mixed with luck, that's all it was. The others thought maybe I had some dark secrets. I encouraged this superstition, but in truth I'd just take careful aim and let go (that was for long shots). Sometimes I'd hit; mostly I'd miss. But when we were within range, we were all deadly.

Hide-and-go-seek. Kick the can. Count to a hundred; count back down from a hundred to give everyone time to hide, then seek them out. Find them and beat them back to home to call them out. This was the moment of our heat—fondling the amazing bodies of girls in the seclusion of dark bushes, feeling their little hairs, their budding breasts, the warmth of their flesh, all caught up in the fever of our growth. Wild, implacable nights without care.

We moved in droves, sweeping over the earth like a plague of locusts, from Rose Hill of sweet youth to Ramona Gardens, past Lincoln Park, the next nearest cluster of niggers. To their dances on Thursday nights. Money for wine was a must. Two-fifths of Santa Fe to guzzle down as we walked the tracks of the Sierra Vista Local. Irene and Laura, Claudine and Elizabeth, Anne Bee—those hot-bodied black girls of our age, whose bodies we'd rub in the slow drag of the scrunch across the dance floor. Our knives open at the ready in our pockets in case the Mexicans wanted to get in, or in case the niggers wanted to get us, as they sometimes did, because of the girls. The sound of the blues thick in the dim room. Funk of our sweat mixed with wine-breath, cigarette smoke, stale air, cheap perfume, and hot snatch.

Filbert Duerte, me and Filbert hit it off. (What is this nostalgia reaching back into the dustbins of memory, dredging up old forgotten friendships with white people? Dusting them off and examining them?) They are all gone anyway, fled into the anonymity of the megalopolis, some of them like Houseman's lads and lassies, their mouths stopped with dust. Irma, I remember, and Katherine Bowlinda, and that little redheaded, green-eyed broad who used to talk with me all during Mr. Avakian's class. Virginia and her goofy brother Richard, who lived on Mercury Avenue but remained aloof from Rose Hill, from the world of the Projects and from the hills. But they are my life. Rex Wilkinson and Lloyd Collins spitting in each other's faces, laughing like idiots each time. And Mark, making his weird sounds like a barking dog. My mind drifts back through the years to the halls of the school once again. Mrs. Ritchard, Mrs. Collins, Lulu Bell, tall and high-yellow, sitting across the room from me in Mrs. Ritchard's room on the second floor, lascivious beyond her years with big tits and full ass, a woman's body in grammar school. Out each afternoon to sports: exercise, kickball, baseball, and dodgeball, my forte.

Mrs. Dwyer was my first teacher at Huntington Drive Street School. The class was in the garden my first day, I was shown the way to her. I remember her smiling, with greying hair, her dress blowing in the breeze—she remains essentially a blur. Veils of blue silk hang from her and flutter gently in the wind. There were days in the garden when she'd squat down to show someone how to turn the soil with a hand spade. We'd seize this chance to look under her dress at her dark parts, always hidden. Those strange parts of her, the contemplation of which caused a fever in one's blood. Mrs. Collins was mean. "Woe be unto you!" was her constant refrain. Lloyd's mother. High-yellow. Mean nigger bitch. Loved to slap you silly. Mrs. Readerman was beyond beautiful—she was unbelievable. How I used to wish that I was back in kindergarten again, back in Mrs. Readerman's room.

1946 or '47: the tunnel leading from the school gate under the Sierra Vista Local, the Pasadena Special, the Alhambra Line. This tunnel led to South Huntington Drive, from north to south. There was another one doing the same thing at the other end of the school yard. Each morning all classes lined up at eight A.M. sharp to pledge allegiance to the flag as it was run up the pole. "I hedge all-allegiance to the rag of the Disunited States of America and to the republic for which it falls, many nations, divisible, with liberty and justice for some." This was how we used to say it.

Saturdays and Sundays: Heaven was to take the street car downtown to one of the grand theaters. American movies in the golden age of my youth. Once we saw Danny, one of the Marijuanos, downtown with Beatrice, whom he later married. Beatrice used to go to Wilson with my sister, Helen. Most everybody else in Rose Hill went to Lincoln. Danny gave Jap a dollar to carry a little brown bag back to Rose Hill and keep it for him. The bag was full of brown cigarettes. "*Marijuana!*" Jap said excitedly to us. This was fantastic. We all felt as though we shared a great secret. We all wanted to be there when Jap returned the stuff to Danny. This was a big moment in our lives.

To the Catholic Church every Thursday at two P.M. for catechism, a way to beat the schoolroom. Always a chance to sneak out of church, away from the nuns. Jacqueline Coles in the Christmas pageant, singing in the choir. I could pick out her voice above all the others. She and I could have been in love. Her father probably talked against me, so that when I tried to hit on her she responded very maturely, as if what I proposed was kid stuff. Bitch. Married a professional football player. Had a baby. Got divorced. Became a cop.

Camp in the summer, up into the mountains. It may be that my first trip to jail was because I believed that I'd get a chance to go back to camp! That crazy show we put on at the Project. Me and Lloyd and Bobby doing The Cannibal King. The Movies. Federation Dances. The football we'd play on the vacant lots. Jimmy Jones was great. Broken field runner. Too short and not heavy enough to make varsity. Spark plug of the B team. Go, you Lincoln Tigers. Our team had spirit. Chauvinism. From Huntington Drive Street School, we would go on to Lincoln. Most of the patties went to Wilson in El Sarreno. We hated Wilson. They hardly ever beat us in anything. If they beat us in football, we'd just about die, hang our heads in shame. My soul was in Lincoln even when my body was still in Huntington Drive. I remember graduation day. A big deal. Festivities out on the blacktop in the blazing sun. It seemed like the day would never end.

The Judeos on Boundary. The Judeos in the little store across from the school. Tight mothers, selling penny candies for two cents. These were the type of Jews that made you antisemitic. But who knew whether or not they were really Jews? Except that they resembled my idea of what a Jew looked like. And they had accents. They were scurvy, weird. We'd only go to them when it was absolutely necessary. When we came into their store, they knew that we had no choice, so they did us in, openly hostile. There must be a billion grocery stores in America! Vegetables, bread, canned goods, bottles, meat in the display window, cookies, Cokes, goodies in cellophane bags.

How wonderful it was when mother got paid and came home with her shopping bags full. Sometimes we were such savages that we would not even go meet her, to help her bring home food for us to eat! I think I distinguished myself in that I was always trying to be helpful to her. I used to go help her clean up those schoolrooms, but I was so slow that I slowed her down.

I remember all of these things, these people. They deserve to live. I must make them live. Huntington Drive Street School, the core of our relationship, brought us all together. I feel that I knew and loved people then as I have never done since. There was more mutual love all the way around, more respect for natural ability. When someone picked me for their dodgeball team, they knew that they were picking a winner. It used to gas me all the way down to my toes to have a girl pick me as her first choice. Those were the beautiful days of my youth. Those are the days to which I flee for refuge. Those are the days that now have the power to restore my spirits. The beauty of our lives then—we were all fresh and could have been saved. But the death of our hope was being formed there without our knowing what or where. There is a love between the members of a school class. You come up through the ranks together and diverge in your separate ways, drifting further and further apart. How many of us made this scene of mine, this prison scene? In my years of confinement, I've run across few, if any. Did I, then, bring this virus with me from Arkansas? Do I have a rare blood type?

John, Howard, and George. Pretty George Johnson with the curly hair lived on the hill across the tracks. All those cats who used to seem

so much sharper than me, so much hipper, turned into weird cats—
duds. I mean this not disrespectfully but as an observation: Those cats
made weird trips in life. Howard, who used to beat up on me and John
for smoking pot, later on came to me to buy his joints. We'd get a kick
out of how he used to be so against weed. My life a tangent. I did a lot
of looking, a lot of lusting, because of this cross-cultural thing. The
Black Moochie. Incredible, me making all the scenes on the Chicano
circuit. We didn't comb the black circuit, so I was actually absorbing the
patterns of the Chicanos. The kick of cruising in the car interminably
with emphasis on digging the chicks. But all cats do it. It's just that our
circuit was East L.A. There was hardly ever a clash on the race thing, yet
I was excluded. When we went to weddings we ate outside, ostensibly
because we didn't want to go in, but really because of me. And my buddies, perhaps one at a time, would take a stroll inside. But I too used to
stroll inside sometimes. I was from Rose Hill.

Rose Hill Chinga. The memorable parties. The Zenda Ball Room.
Jam sessions at the Floral Drive-In Theater. The Angelus Ball Room.
The Narbo Grill—the one right there on Olympic and Central.
Hamms. Tubs. Armands. Madness! Tickler. Cutie. Frank. Me. Schem-
ing on the broads. Wasn't it my fault that they didn't score more often?
This is painful to admit, but it's the truth. I must have known this and
blinded myself to it. Trapped. Energy turning inward and not even
knowing it, not knowing what was happening. We made those scenes.
We were known on sight as regulars. Our ears were tuned to our circuit.
Vamps from Rose Hill, the guys with the bag. This was our license for
entry anywhere.

Gloria came to score one night with some cats. When she saw me at
Lincoln, she knew what I was up to. The word was out on me. My sharp
clothes told on me also. I was a fool seeking recognition. My '39 Chevy.
Seventy dollars. Got a ticket in it. Frank driving it with a broken leg.
Again the narks declined to take us in. What was the meaning of such
luck? We had been to the Apple Cider Mill on Mission Road. Bought a
case of beer. Cops spotted us. Followed our car. Frank, his leg broken,
tried to push me behind the wheel. Cops shook us down for dope but
found none. Let us go.

We were so stupid we couldn't even find any whores to buy pussy.
Walking around with hundreds of dollars in our pockets, walking
down the red light district and couldn't even find a whore. What was
happening? Frank wrecked my car. Flying up the street with the lights

out, right into a parked car. Cat in the parked car must have been fucking the broad; they were down out of sight. Frank flicked on the headlights just a second before hitting the car. The light enabled us to see the cat and the broad when they jumped up because of the crash. Frank paid for the damage to the other cat's car, but my car just sat there until the cops came and towed it away. I kept expecting to hear from the police, but never a word. Weird, some of the changes I used to go through.

My youth, the foundation years of my life.
Rose Hill Chinga
Neighborhood of fantastic people
People of my life
People who own my heart
People of Rose Hill
You I remember and love.
Those of you who shared mutual
Hate with me
I forgive you
I beg you to forgive me
We need each other;
We are all that we have
You live on in my memory
I've carried you with me all these years
I've carried you in love
To understand your lives
Back when our neighborhood was a prize-winning hamlet
Back when we wore the name Rose Hill with pride
Part of Los Angeles but whole unto ourselves.
When Peter Chavez was killed in war we all mourned
We all came to see his casket
To make the wake with his family.
Peter was of us
Peter was Rose Hill
Rose Hill Chinga.
When that car plunged over the hill
Going round the bend behind Burt's store
And crashed down on Mercury Avenue
The crash belonged to all of us
It burned into our souls equally.
When Lupe's father was found dead
A part of Rose Hill was found dead
A part of Rose Hill talked about itself.

Rose Hill Chinga
With shanty pads squatting on mud hills
People of this earth trudging up muddy paths
To their houses
Slipping and sliding in the mud
Walking on the grass to keep from falling, to keep one's footing
Sweet smells of the earth when the grass was green
No smog in Rose Hill
Far from the industrial heart of Los Angeles
A forgotten hamlet
A peaceful spot
Site of home
A jealous love of our sacred ground
We were bound to each other.
With what pride we owned the land
We knew Rose Hill as our own
We'd bow down on hands and knees to kiss our dirt
The birds in the sky were ours
The Housing Project was ours
The garbage collectors once each week were ours
The milk man making his rounds in the morning mist of dew was ours
The mail man delivering the mail was ours
The Good Humor Ice Cream man with his musical wagon was ours
The Helms Bakery Man with his musical wagon was ours
The bus that ran down Mercury Avenue was ours
The planes flying overhead were ours
The Catholic Church on Mercury Avenue was ours
The Protestant Church on Boundary Avenue was ours
The Negro Church on Junipero Street was ours
The corn the old men sowed in the hills was ours
The walnuts growing wild in the hills were ours
The peaches growing wild in the hills were ours
The apricot trees in our yards were ours
The fires that burned the dried grass each year were ours
The beauty of our women was ours
The strength of our men was ours
The squeals, laughter, and tears of the children were ours
We had a sense of ourselves.
We said Rose Hill and we meant all things in it.

Savage! Mean mongrel dog of my nightmares, tiger-colored hound of no understanding. You had a friend in me, you idiot, but you preferred me as an enemy. Tore my pants one day. Chased me every chance you got, barking and showing your murderous teeth. Why did you allow John,

Bobby, and even square-headed Lloyd to come around? Why did you focus your attack on me? Did you sense some evil force in me that was absent in the others? Mary and Joan—the only bitches in the whole neighborhood who were putting out ass to us and you had to be their dog! You foul mutt of a fuck! Savage. You well deserved your name, chewing tin cans, rags, and sticks of wood, car tires and old shoes. Did you resent the fact that I hung the name on you which stuck? Your name was Brownie, but you abused it with your scurvy sneak attacks, so I thought it was only fitting that you wear the name of your actions: Savage! Did you think you were a goat? You brought your death upon yourself. Your blood is not on my hands. I had no choice that night but to do you in, to sneak up on you as you so often had snuck up on others, and put a .22 slug in your crazy head. Did you see it coming, Savage, that night in the dark, from ambush, with your mad red eyes? You saw everything else. I anticipated that, true to your greed, as soon as you got wind of me, you'd come running, teeth bared, lips curled, head lowered. Splat! Boy, did you look surprised!

Fay, with Rickey on her lap, waited for me in the canary-yellow Dodge convertible with the black top. I entered the drugstore and copped five tubes of Wyamine. We downed a tube each and washed it down with black coffee at a Stan's Drive-In. Then we began our tour of the white man's wealthy city.

Lulu Jean and Maude danced naked for us. Mrs. Warren saw. One day from my yard I saw Mrs. Warren pee standing up like a man in her backyard.

Once I got Lulu Jean by a telephone pole at dusk. Caught her coming from the store with a loaf of bread. I had to hurry, she said, 'cause they were holding up dinner for the bread. I slipped it in her standing up. We both wiggled up on a good feeling.

Carolyn—felt her up in the swimming pool in El Sarreno. Little bitch thought she was hot shit. Did you think sticking my finger up your pussy was more dignified than my dick inside you would have been?

Polito's mother, sitting watching TV with her legs gaping open. She was my TV that night.

Henry Johnson was laughably stingy. His wife, Dorothy, never said anything—only had babies. Tee Tee was a punk. Henry's children hustled bottles and took the money home to him. It was strictly business with him. We swiped a box of bananas from Fontana's Market. Anne turned a trick with Don Trinni one Sunday. Mother saw her come out and hide the money under a bush and told me and Benny. Me and Benny got the money and told mother there was nothing there, then took Anne up on the hill and did it to her. Then we took her to the show with her money, treated her to popcorn, candy, and a soda pop.

The Vegetable Man. How he made a profit I don't know. We'd steal him blind. Here he comes with his truck. We'd run along behind and just take what we wanted. When he stopped for the housewives, we'd work one side while he was on the other. Watermelons, buckets of plums, apples, oranges, bunches of carrots—everything went. Once Mitch even picked his pocket with those bold fingers of his, just as there was a time when Mitch discovered a little hole in the counter at the hot dog stand at the Lincoln Park Speedway; through that hole we got dollars by the dozen. Then the Vegetable Man got a bus; instead of seats inside, he had racks of vegetables. Same story. In through the front door and out the back, pockets full.

Mary Goat needs a volume to herself. The only thing white left in those hills. Old as the hills themselves. Old and gnarled, she walked bent over with a stick. Had a herd of dogs, flocks of pigeons, cats, goats, rabbits—all living in the house with her. She was rich. We bought our house from her. There she comes. Everybody get out of her way! She'd crack your skull with that stick! From a safe distance, we'd taunt her with, "Mary Goat!"

I entered the Thrifty Drug Store on Daly Avenue, off Broadway near Five Points, and bought five tubes of Wyamine. Behind the nun's apartment house, across the street from the Catholic Church, I parked the Dodge one night—backed it in quietly and took care of business in the back seat with Jo Ann. Picked up Thelma at the bus stop and dropped her at the dentist's. Almost every day I picked the girls up at Lincoln High and drove them home. Narcotic agents stopped me once, Chester and me, in the Dodge. We were wasted on bennies and pot. "You made that U-turn like you owned the street," one said. "Are you guys high?" "No," I said. Although I didn't even have a driver's license, they told us to beat it, to be careful. We left in a hurry, amazed. I'd drive Nina to Enchandia Girls' School every morning; Irene to Lincoln. These were two of the choicest bitches ever created, and they guarded their Catholic cherries as though waiting for the Holy Ghost to rape them. Saving it, they said, for their husbands, some day. Crazy religious bitches, made my life miserable. I used to sit there trying to con them out of their box, rod hard as Chinese arithmetic, hard and throbbing, swollen big as a baseball bat between my legs. Agony. But they were unmoved. Amazing bitches. And I could tell that their pants were on fire too—only I was a fool, an idiot. I didn't know the game of peek-a-boo then, so I missed a lot of choice pussy. Sabu got Nina's cherry. Alley got Irene's.

We had a regular circuit, a territory we'd patrol. Frank had a natural genius for sniffing out choice broads whose parents kept them hidden away from the evils of the world—from horny cats like us. We'd drive down weird streets, spot the girls peeping out at us from behind huge bushes in their yards, through knotholes in tall fences, behind curtains drawn over dark windows. We'd wink at them, smile, waving at them, gesturing at them to be bold and defiant, to come on out. We'd stick out our tongues to let them know that we saw them as something good to eat. Sometimes they'd come running out. Sometimes they'd give us the nasty finger. Sometimes they'd turn their heads in distaste, disgust, contempt—obedient to Catholic virtues. Sometimes they'd tell us to come back after dark, and sometimes we'd have to beat it in a hurry, pursued by irate fathers, husbands, brothers, uncles, cousins, etc.

All the way to Tijuana, for those hundreds of miles from L.A., I was preoccupied with the dream of fucking a big Mexican whore. The miles blew by like wind, a steady flow of air through the wind visor of Frank's Chevy. Me, Frank, Cutie, Oldie. We dropped bennies and blew joints all the way. We didn't even see San Diego when we shot through it, down interminable strips of highway. My rod stayed hard all the way. We'd say of ourselves that we were young, dumb, and full of come, but only me and Oldie were young. Frank and Cutie were old and married, already made cynical by hatred of their wives. When we walked into the whorehouse, eight whores jumped up and rushed for me. My ego hit the ceiling. They argued over me in Spanish. I chose the one I thought offered the most convincing hints of erotic trips to come. She rushed me to a room. Three dollars for the room, seven for her. I thought her a cynical bitch. I couldn't understand why she wasn't madly in love with me by then, as hard as I was piling her. To shut her up, I gave her seven more dollars. Before I finally busted my nuts I had to shut her up two more times, seven dollars each time.

Frank and Oldie fucked. Cutie refused to touch a whore, stating weirdly that he didn't goof off like that on his wife. On the drive back, they laughed at me and said I was the biggest trick in the universe. I was bragging about how all the bitches rushed for me when we walked into the whorehouse. Frank laughed so hard he nearly wrecked the car, at 70 miles an hour. "You fucking fool!" he laughed. "Can't you see? Those whores know that you *mayates* are crazy for white skin! When you walked through that door, they didn't see you at all. They saw dollar signs all dressed up in rust-colored suede shoes, a rust beret, and a green slack suit!" I was despondent and bitter for weeks.

Alice struck me as being mature, trustworthy, and stable. So I asked her to keep my money for me. At first, I used to hide my money in the bushes, but I'd go crazy worrying about $1,000 out there in an old tin can or an old crumpled paper bag under a rock. So I asked Alice to keep it for me. $865. I was less worried. Alice smiled at me every day. I no longer worried about the narks catching me with all that money in my pocket, which I couldn't explain. Then one evening, Alice, walking with her son, got hit by a car. I went to General Hospital to see her. She was in traction, her leg broken, ribs busted, stitches in her skull, teeth knocked out. "Your money is in my closet, inside a Kotex box on the shelf." When I got there, the closet door was wide open and the Kotex box gone. I tore the whole closet up: nothing. $865! Francis was my number one suspect, then Alice's brother, Roger, His wife, Genevieve, starting making out with me, giving me the come on. A perfect crime; whoever did it got away clean. $865! I suspected everybody—except Alice. Months later, she got out of the hospital, but I stopped going around her pad. Couldn't stand the mystery. Months after that I came around. I was surprised to see all her new furniture. Redwood tables built on a Japanese kick. Overstuffed couch with matching chairs. Floor lamp that could be adjusted to three pitches of brightness. Twins. TV. That was Frank's money; I had to make it all up. Ran me in the red. Took me six months to balance the books.

Richard and Rudy used to taunt me: "At least I got a mother!" My most beautiful cap could be crumbled by that one all-purpose retort; that was the ace up their sleeve. Then one day their mother, Ruthie, ran off with Kinkie, the junk man. Richard and Rudy wore long faces then; I got my revenge for several years of torture.

The Savages. Someone put out that they were Communists. We gave them no peace: firecrackers through the mail slot in their front door, piss in their milk bottles, stolen milk, overturned garbage cans, rocks through windows, lights turned out at the central switch box, clothes stolen from their clothes line, insults hurled, air let out of their car tires at night to surprise them of a cold morning when they arose late for work.

There was something rigid in me, an inarticulate opposition, a dissent, that turned me away from the counsel of Dr. Smith.

Mona Phelps. Monica Laura. Rose Holquin. The beach. The crabs. Van Pelt. Embarrassed mother. No father.

PART II

What did I know? The sun hung bright in a hazy sky over Rose Hill. Nothing stirred during the day except the tortured housewives, salesmen, milkmen, mailmen, occasional policemen, little children, and the hustlers. I wasn't really hitting on anything. I was far from conquering the world, yet I didn't feel at its mercy. It was as though I had stepped outside the world, outside the system. I was not caught up in anybody's program or plan. In those days the world looked like a huge, swiftly spinning merry-go-round. And I was not on it; I was not running it. I didn't know who controlled it, how it worked, or what its mechanism was. This was the source of my humiliation—that I was failing, that I could not see my way to mastering this merry-go-round.

I was lying on my side, on the grass beneath a tree, watching the merry-go-round in its spin. I was drunk with a loathing for my own impotence. In my fantasy I saw, inside the City Hall, a huge room which I called, for whatever obscure, private reason, the "Map Room." In the Map Room, in the center of the Map Room, was a large table on which there was a big, ten-layer cake in the shape of Los Angeles County. Gathered round the table were 13 fat, greedy, white businessmen and politicians. The mayor, city councilmen, county supervisors, the police chief, the sheriff, the president of the Chamber of Commerce, and a cardinal. The president of the Chamber of Commerce wielded the knife. A Negro in a khaki uniform, well starched and tailor-made, stood beneath the table with a broom and dustpan, catching the crumbs and dumping them into a large stainless steel barrel. His job was to see to it that not a crumb hit the floor. His incentive was that all the crumbs he caught belonged to him; he could take them home to his wife and 69 children.

"Cut me a larger piece," the mayor said in a whining voice. He was hunched up to the table, an unctuous look on his face.

"If I give you a larger piece," said the president of the Chamber of Commerce, "there won't be enough to go around."

The president continued slicing up the cake, working swiftly, shoveling it out. He gave a huge slice to the chief of police and a smaller slice to the sheriff. The sheriff wore a sullen look, but he didn't speak out in protest as the mayor had; he drew up into a tight little knot and slinked off into a corner to gobble down his share. He looked around craftily, as if he had something up his sleeve, as if he didn't have anything to worry about and would get even in the end.

Superimposed upon this picture, but down in the lower lefthand corner, was a scene of six Negroes crowded around a pool table, shooting pool: All wore sullen scowls on their faces. The jukebox blared the blues in the background. A girl, naked except for a red ribbon through her hair, huge golden earrings, and another red ribbon worn lasciviously over her vagina at right angles to her cleft, and wearing red highheel slippers, twisted and turned to the music, sending undulating waves of erotic rhythm through the room. The pool player whose turn it was to shoot stepped forward into the circle of light. His face was a hideous composite: he resembled every black man I had ever known. In his face I could see myself, my father, my uncles, my brothers; I could see John, Bobby, Buster; I could see Joe Louis, General Banks. With a vicious succession of plunges with the cue, he sent the balls crashing into the pockets with thunderous cracks. Looking at the two pictures—of the Map Room in City Hall and the Pool Room in the City Dump—it seemed as if the movements of the people in each were synchronized. At the same time that the president of the Chamber of Commerce sliced off a piece of cake with the knife, the Big Mo plunged forward with his pool cue. And every time Stella made a movement with her body, the cardinal would sprinkle holy water over a guest, ring a little silver bell, or wave the heavy, golden, jewel-encrusted crucifix that hung around his neck.

The cardinal wandered perpetually through the Map Room, sprinkling holy water, smiling and waving his cross. When the president of the Chamber of Commerce offered him a piece of cake, he looked offended and refused vigorously, thrusting the proffered slice of cake aside. He went on sprinkling the guests with holy water and ringing the bell. Everyone smiled, including the chief of police. Instead of giving the slice of cake that the cardinal had refused to another guest, the president walked over into a dark corner to a little black table where a silver tray rested on an immaculate white silk napkin, and laid the slice of cake on this tray. It seemed like the natural thing to do, as if the table and silver tray had been placed there precisely for that purpose.

The Negro beneath the main table had his eyes on that juicy slice of cake. He felt that he had dibs on it. He resolved to wait until there was a lull at the main table, rush over, scoop up the slice of cake from the silver tray, and dump it into his stainless steel receptacle. Self-satisfied, he felt that he had a perfect plan. After waiting a bit, he decided that his chance had come. He laid down his dustpan and broom and was just preparing to dash over when he saw the cardinal stop at the table, gently set his holy water and bell down, reach beneath his red tunic, pull out a plastic bag, and with a few swift motions scoop up the slice of cake. In one continuous motion, he broke the slice of cake in half, wrapped one half in the plastic bag and concealed it under his tunic. Then he plunged the other half into his mouth and chewed vigorously. After a moment, he picked up the vessel of holy water and raised it to his lips. He washed the cake down with holy water, almost emptying the vessel. Then, mumbling in Latin, he began picking the crumbs off the silver tray, putting each crumb on the tip of his unusually long tongue. He didn't leave a single crumb on the tray.

Just as he picked up his silver bell, he noticed the Negro beneath the table, staring at him like a frozen statue, with open mouth and wide bug eyes. The cardinal, shaken by the intensity and surprise of the stare but quickly recovering, smiled at the Negro and, tossing a few drops of holy water his way, tinkled his bell in the Negro's direction and resumed his itinerary around the room. At the sound of the bell, the Negro snapped back to reality, shaking his head in bewildered disappointment as though he still did not believe what his eyes had seen. He concluded that he must have been dreaming. He picked up his dustpan and broom and, after carefully sweeping up a small pile of crumbs that had accumulated while he was preoccupied with the slice of cake on the silver tray, resumed catching the last of the crumbs as they fell. He worked with more enthusiasm than ever, glad that the party was about over so that he could be getting home to his wife and children.

On the wall, witty sayings:

God And I Are One—Cardinal Spareendtire.
Let Them Eat Cake—Marie Antoinette.
God Uses Cost Accounting in His Battle with Satan—Charlie Wilson.

We did what we had to in the ways that we knew. We took what we wanted whenever we could. The street light was a marvel. Sewers were out of sight. The cops cruised by with a case of hips. We'd see them, and even when we had committed no crime we shunned them, because just being who we were was a crime in their eyes. They had black and white cars—these L.A.P.D. boys—so we called them the Black and Whites to distinguish them from the narcotics officers and detectives, whose cars were unmarked. Somehow we feared the Black and Whites less. We watched them for traffic violations, but for the rough stuff, we looked out for the bulls in plain clothes.

We did not do these things; rather, they were done to us. But we felt guilty. Our terror was knee deep. We walked in a fog. Nowhere was there a way out. We grew up, grew older, and kept a keen eye out for a chance to move toward the future. We have played this cold role. Seldom in history has a people been called upon to perform these heroics. We made something out of nothing. We learned the wisdom in the sayings that "The shade of a toothpick beats the hot boiling sun," that "A drowning man would reach for a straw," and that "A nigger's freedom is in his mind." Even if we had expected or desired a pat on the back, there was none forthcoming. What we got was more hell. So we learned to boast of it. We owe these devils nothing, we would say. A white man has no rights that a black man is bound to respect, that is, the slave master has no rights that the slave is bound to respect. We had a unique problem, and a unique problem requires a unique solution. So we bored into the mud of North America and waited for something unique to come along.

Fruitie was unique. First of all, she was skinny, with bony legs that were always either ashy or shiny. Her teeth looked like they had been shaken up in the cup of two hands and then tossed into her mouth all at once, sticking out in whatever way they landed. Kissing her was like trying to kiss a cactus apple—which was her price. To fuck her, you had to suck her tongue first. Torture. This titless girl. The only thing good about her was her juicy, warm glove of a cunt. Once you got it in, you forgot all about her wild teeth and flat chest. She had a way of rolling her ass on your rod that made you close your eyes and just let go. It was then that she could really get you to suck her tongue or even kiss those faint rises of flesh on her chest that were her tits. Fruitie was unique.

On the train from Arkansas to Phoenix there were only me, Helen, Wilhelmina, and maybe James. We ran out of food. The porters were supposed to feed us according to a deal they had made with daddy, who was working on the railroad then, but on another line. A white lady sitting in a seat across from us gave us chicken. I no longer feel the pain of that day's hunger, but at the time I must have really been in pain, because I've learned how hateful hunger can be. And it was a five- or six-day ride from Little Rock to Phoenix. These people were taking care of business. The war was going on. Here we were, a few among thousands, in the great population shift of hundreds of thousands pouring out of the South heading West for jobs, for opportunities in California. Later, people would taunt each other that Kaiser had brought them out of the big foot country. All those wide-eyed people staring at each other, into those mute faces, seeking some hint of a future anticipated with a growing terror.

When I looked around, it seemed like there were orange trees lined up neatly along the sidewalk on both sides of the street, from horizon to horizon, each tree decorated with golden fruit like off-color Christmas trees. But this must have been the workings of my youthful mind. The Union Station is where we got off the train from Phoenix, Arizona. That our luggage got lost was only to be expected. As far as our family was concerned, all had been lost for some time now. Mother was pregnant in a black dress. She had red shoes on, garish like the country woman of her being. A high-yeller belle from Little Rock, Arkansas, by way of Phoenix. But she was game, pregnant or not. She found our bags, trunks, boxes, and got us all loaded in a cab, and there was daddy with a truck. Just like that: One minute we were lost in a chaos that seemed too far gone to reclaim, and then the next minute we were in a cab breezing down Central Avenue. Magic was possible in those days. The next minute we were carrying our things into a house. Then mother was taking me to school the first day, where the boys teased me about my bangs and because I said "over yonder" and "chunk me the ball." They said I was "countrified." I had to fight them to prove I was human. When they saw that I knew how to bloody their noses, they showed me their teeth in smiles and showed me how to get my bangs cut down to L.A. size.

It was in that house that music came alive for me. Before that, music may not even have existed. Songs like "I Wonder," by Cecil Gant, never stopped playing. These Negro blues swept into my soul and excited the very core of my being. I had found an anchor for one corner of my life. Since then, these sounds have never ended for me.

Gladys ran that house. She rented space by the room. Everybody who had a room to spare rented it to the thousands of Negroes pouring into the East Side each month. The devils would not let them live anywhere else. Negroes were channeled onto the South Los Angeles Reservation like oil being pumped into a dumping ground. Gladys was always arguing and cursing with somebody, threatening to kill somebody, screaming at somebody to cut down their radio or record player. Everyone was always running through the house screaming and cursing. The rooms were separated by curtains slung across the doors. You might be eating and a woman would run through naked and screaming, a man running behind her with a long knife in his hand. "We got to move out of here, Leroy." Mother told daddy time after time. "This place is driving me crazy!" Or sometimes you'd walk through someone's room and see them on the bed intertwined and grooving in the heat of their grinding. They'd pause long enough for you to pass through and as you secured the curtain behind you, you'd hear the bed start squeaking again as they tried to catch up to where they'd been before you interrupted them.

The Coca Cola Bottling Company on Central Avenue looked like a big battleship on the ground. There were portholes in the walls. We'd pass by and look in at the men working. The building was long and smooth and new. Everything else was ragged and falling down. On Sundays we'd go to the Rosebud Theater on Central Avenue, or to the Jinx Theater. Or, to splurge, we'd go to the Lincoln Theater. At night they played Keno, and silver dollars were to be won if you were lucky. The black people were all around you, making lots of beautiful black people's noise, raising hell. Fights broke out in the balcony. Girls screamed in the dark. Cigarette smoke curled up through the lights streaming from the movie projectors. People were constantly coming and going.

On Sundays, Negroes would dress up and walk up and down the street looking at each other. It was like a parade or carnival. Cars filled with black, brown, and yellow faces drove up and down the Stem, music blasting from their radios. Jukeboxes blasted different songs back to back. You could walk from one end of the Stem to the other and never be beyond the sound of music, black voices screaming out the blue funk of black lives. The Stem. Central Avenue. The different lives I've led on the Stem and the lives taken from me by the Stem. These lives lie upon one another like layers of skin, floors of a skyscraper, tiers of a cellblock, layers of a tall cake. These years and these days, changing hourly, are the icing between each layer, and my present self is spread over the top like blood trickling down an obsolete wall, soaking into the sod of me on the bottom.

Pat Moore's shop was upstairs, over the Club Alabam. I wanted my hair gassed, so Chester took me to Pat Moore's, complaining every step of the way that I was a fool. I wanted to please Lupe. I was 17, Lupe was 26—a woman over the flip little girls I'd been catching up till her. I wanted to impress her with how slick a cat I was. Pat Moore sat me in the barber's chair and draped a sheet over my shoulders, like a KKK man without his hood. Then he started greasing me down, spreading a thick gooey muck over my skin along the hairline, then rubbing it into my scalp to protect the flesh from the violent action of the hair-straightening chemicals he was about to apply. "If it gets too hot and burns more than you can stand, jus hollar," Pat said. Taking a rubber spatula, he began slapping the gas onto my head in big gooey lumps, like a woman slapping lard into a hot skillet. Taking a comb, he slowly worked the gas into my hair, inserting the comb at the front of my head and pulling it straight back along the curve of my skull to the end of my hair at the base of my neck.

Soon the comb was running through my hair without any opposition from the kinks. In a moment every last kink had been murdered outright, and each strand of my hair was stretched out on my head like an elongated corpse on a barroom floor. "You be looking like Rudolph Valentino in a minute," Pat said. The shit was beginning to burn my skull, but I didn't say anything. I wanted to leave it in as long as I could, because I had been schooled to the fact that, up to a certain crucial point, the longer you left the gas in, the straighter your hair became. If you left it in beyond that crucial point, then the acids and lye in the gas would eat all the hair off your head, would eat all the skin off, in fact theoretically it could eat your whole head off, bone and all. "O.K., Pat," I said, bolting from the chair at last. "Get this shit out quick, man." Pat led me to the sink and bent my head over it. Using a little green hose with a spray nozzle attached to it, he rinsed and washed and rinsed my head until every last trace of the gas was washed away, leaving a crop of weird-looking hair standing all over my head. (Looking back, these strands of hair impress me as the perfect metaphor for the anarchy existing among so-called Negroes in America. Each strand was a stranger to the other; each stood alone. They resembled a mob rather than an organized mass. Each strand seemed to be stumbling around blindly, seeking its true identity, seeing nothing of itself in the strands around it.) Pat said, "Now how do you want to wear it, my man? Want me to finger-wave it or set it in the pachuco style with a ducktail in the back?" "Stick

fingerwaves to me, baby," I said. And Pat went to work. When he finished, I had a do just like Nat King Cole. Had I chosen the pachuco, I'd
be looking like Sammy Davis, Jr.

I could hardly wait to get back to Rose Hill to see Lupe that night. I
went home and took a bath, careful not to wet my hair or move my head
too violently for fear of shaking out the waves. When I met Lupe that
night, under the clothesline next to Francis's pad at the end of the row of
apartments in the Projects, she said in her Mexican accent: "Eeeek! What
happened to your hair?" She led me out of the darkness into a patch of
light cast by the street light up at the top of the hill. "What did you do
to your hair?" she asked in a most horrified tone. "You've ruined it!" she
said, and tried to touch my hair. I knew that if she touched it she would
knock the waves out. Gasses are for looking at, not for touching. "No!"
I cautioned her, "don't touch it or you'll mess it up." "You're crazy,
Leroy!" she said. "I don't like your hair that way. I like it fuzzy like it was!"
Then, crying, she wrenched herself violently from my arms and ran into
her house.

Weaving back and forth, in and out of these other lives, a boy goes on
his way. Where his nose is headed he hardly has the sense to ask. He simply goes, following his own feet. And what a chase. The basic reality was
the marijuana. The yesca, the life stuff of the boy's existence. From the
moment when Chico cuts him into getting high, he rapidly develops as
a wise handler of the weed. More than his wisdom was his availability.
How he scampered about those hills with the bag.

Weighing out the pounds. Sacking up the cans. Rolling up the joints.
Conscientious businessmen getting ready for the evening's trade. People
coming from miles around to cop some of that good old Rose Hill marijuana, and we'd be there waiting for them with everything ready to go.
Joints all rolled, cans ready at $7 each—our specialty. Then the pounds.
The easy dollars. Easy money. Good name for a book. Easy come, easy
go. One must tell a great deal about reality in order to justify writing a
book, yet so many of these fools who tell nothing at all come off the
presses again and again. When I write, I want to drive a spear into the
heart of America.

ON BECOMING

Folsom Prison
June 25, 1965

Nineteen fifty-four, when I was eighteen years old, is held to be a crucial turning point in the history of the Afro-American—for the U.S.A. as a whole—the year segregation was outlawed by the U.S. Supreme Court. It was also a crucial year for me because on June 18, 1954, I began serving a sentence in state prison for possession of marijuana.

The Supreme Court decision was only one month old when I entered prison, and I do not believe that I had even the vaguest idea of its importance or historical significance. But later, the acrimonious controversy ignited by the end of the separate-but-equal doctrine was to have a profound effect on me. This controversy awakened me to my position in America and I began to form a concept of what it meant to be black in white America.

Of course I'd always known that I was black, but I'd never really stopped to take stock of what I was involved in. I met life as an individual and took my chances. Prior to 1954, we lived in an atmosphere of novocain. Negroes found it necessary, in order to maintain whatever sanity they could, to remain somewhat aloof and detached from "the problem." We accepted indignities and the mechanics of the apparatus of oppression without reacting by sitting-in or holding mass demonstrations. Nurtured by the fires of the controversy over segregation, I was soon aflame with indignation over my newly discovered social status, and inwardly I turned away from America with horror, disgust and outrage.

In Soledad state prison, I fell in with a group of young blacks who, like myself, were in vociferous rebellion against what we perceived as a continuation of slavery on a higher plane. We cursed everything American—including baseball and hot dogs. All respect we may have had for politicians, preachers, lawyers, governors, Presidents, senators, congressmen was utterly destroyed as we watched them temporizing and compromising over right and wrong, over legality and illegality, over constitutionality and unconstitutionality. We knew that in the end what they were clashing over was us, what to do with the blacks, and whether or not to start treating us as human beings. I despised all of them.

The segregationists were condemned out of hand, without even listening to their lofty, finely woven arguments. The others I despised for wasting time in debates with the segregationists: why not just crush them, put them in prison—they were defying the law, weren't they? I defied the law and they put me in prison. So why not put those dirty mothers in prison too? I had gotten caught with a shopping bag full of marijuana, a shopping bag full of love—I was in love with the weed and I did not for one minute think that anything was wrong with getting high. I had been getting high for four or five years and was convinced, with the zeal of a crusader, that marijuana was superior to lush—yet the rulers of the land seemed all to be lushes. I could not see how they were more justified in drinking than I was in blowing the gage. I was a grasshopper, and it was natural that I felt myself to be unjustly imprisoned.

While all this was going on, our group was espousing atheism. Unsophisticated and not based on any philosophical rationale, our atheism was pragmatic. I had come to believe that there is no God; if there is, men do not know anything about him. Therefore, all religions were phony—which made all preachers and priests, in our eyes, fakers, including the ones scurrying around the prison who curiously could put in a good word for you with the Almighty Creator of the universe but could not get anything down with the warden or parole board—they could usher you through the Pearly Gates *after you were dead,* but not through the prison gate *while you were still alive and kicking.* Besides, men of the cloth who work in prison have an ineradicable stigma attached to them in the eyes of convicts because they escort condemned men into the gas chamber. Such men of God are powerful arguments in favor of atheism. Our atheism was a source of enormous pride to me. Later on, I bolstered our arguments by reading Thomas Paine and his devastating critique of Christianity in particular and organized religion in general.

Through reading I was amazed to discover how confused people were. I had thought that, out there beyond the horizon of my own ignorance, unanimity existed, that even though I myself didn't know what was happening in the universe, other people certainly did. Yet here I was discovering that the whole U.S.A. was in chaos of disagreement over segregation/integration. In these circumstances I decided that the only safe thing for me to do was go for myself. It became clear that it was possible for me to take the initiative: instead of simply *reacting* I could *act.* I could unilaterally—whether anyone agreed with me or not—repudiate all allegiances, morals, values—even while continuing to exist within this society. My mind would be free and no power in the universe could force me to accept something if I didn't want to. But I would take my own sweet time. That, too, was a part of my new freedom. I would accept nothing until it was proved that it was good—for me. I became an extreme iconoclast. Any affirmative assertion made by anyone around me became a target for the tirades of criticism and denunciation.

This little game got good to me and I got good at it. I attacked all forms of piety, loyalty, and sentiment: marriage, love, God, patriotism, the Constitution, the founding fathers, law, concepts of right-wrong-good-evil, all forms of ritualized and conventional behavior. As I pranced about, club in hand, seeking new idols to smash, I encountered really for the fist time in my life, with any seriousness, The Ogre, rising up before me in a mist. I discovered, with alarm, that The Ogre possessed a tremendous and dreadful power over me, and I didn't understand this power or why I was at its mercy. I tried to repudiate The Ogre, root it out of my heart as I had done God, constitution, principles, morals, and values—but The Ogre had its claws buried in the core of my being and refused to let go. I fought the core of my being and refused to let go. I fought frantically to be free, but The Ogre only mocked me and sank its claws deeper into my soul. I knew then that I had found an important key, that if I conquered The Ogre and broke its power over me I would be free. But I also knew that it was a race against time and that if I did not win I would certainly be broken and destroyed. I, a black man, confronted The Ogre—the white woman.

In prison, these things withheld from and denied to the prisoner become precisely what he wants most of all, of course. Because we were locked up in our cells before darkness fell, I used to lie awake at night racked by painful craving to take a leisurely stroll under the stars, or to go to the beach, to drive a car on a freeway, to grow a beard, or to make love to a woman.

Since I was not married conjugal visits would not have solved my problem. I therefore denounced the idea of conjugal visits as inherently unfair; single prisoners needed and deserved *action* just as married prisoners did. I advocated establishing a system under Civil Service whereby salaried women would minister to the needs of those prisoners who maintained a record of good behavior. If a married prisoner preferred his own wife, that would be his right. Since California was not about to inaugurate either conjugal visits or the Civil Service, one could advocate either with equal enthusiasm and with the same result: nothing.

This may appear ridiculous to some people. But it was very real to me and as urgent as the need to breathe, because I was in my bull stage and lack of access to females was absolutely a form of torture. I suffered. My mistress at the time of my arrest, the beautiful and lonely wife of a serviceman stationed overseas, died unexpectedly three weeks after I entered prison; and the rigid dehumanized rules governing correspondence between prisoners and free people prevented me from corresponding with other young ladies I knew. It left me without any contact with females except those in my family.

In the process of enduring my confinement, I decided to get myself a pin-up girl to paste on the wall of my cell. I would fall in love with her and lavish my affections upon her. She, a symbolic representative of the forbidden tribe of women, would sustain me until I was free. Out of the center of *Esquire,* I married a voluptuous bride. Our marriage went along swell for a time: no quarrels, no complaints. And then, one evening when I came in from school, I was shocked and enraged to find that the guard had entered my cell, ripped my sugar from the wall, torn her into little pieces, and left the pieces floating in the commode: it was like seeing a dead body floating in a lake. Giving her a proper burial, I flushed the commode. As the saying goes, I sent her to Long Beach. But I was genuinely beside myself with anger: almost every cell, excepting those of the homosexuals, had a pin-up girl on the wall and the guards didn't bother them. Why, I asked the guard the next day, had he singled me out for a special treatment?

"Don't you know we have a rule against pasting up pictures on the walls?" he asked me.

"Later for the rules," I said. "You know as well as I do that that rule is not enforced."

"Tell you what," he said, smiling at me (the smile put me on my guard), "I'll compromise with you: get yourself a colored girl for a pinup—no white women—and I'll let it stay up. Is that a deal?"

I was more embarrassed than shocked. He was laughing in my face. I called him two or three dirty names and walked away. I can still recall his big moon-face, grinning at me over yellow teeth. The disturbing part about the whole incident was that a certain terrible feeling of guilt came over me as I realized that I had chosen the picture of the white girl over the available pictures of black girls. I tried to rationalize it away, but I was fascinated by the truth involved. Why hadn't I thought about it in this light before? So I took hold of the question and began to inquire into my feelings. Was it true, did I really prefer white girls over black? The conclusion was clear and inescapable: I did. I decided to check out my friends on this point and it was easy to determine, from listening to their general conversation, that the white woman occupied a peculiarly prominent place in all of our frames of reference. With what I have learned since then, this all seems terribly elementary now. But at the time, it was a tremendously intriguing adventure of discovery.

One afternoon, when a large group of Negroes was on the prison yard shooting the breeze, I grabbed the floor and posed the question: which did they prefer, white women or black? Some said Japanese women were their favorite, others said Chinese, some said European women, others said Mexican women—they all stated a preference and they generally freely admitted their dislike for black women.

"I don't want nothing black but a Cadillac," said one.

"If money was black I wouldn't want none of it," put in another.

A short little stud, who was a very good lightweight boxer with a little man's complex that made him love to box heavyweights, jumped to his feet. He had a yellowish complexion and we called him Butterfly.

"All you niggers are sick!" Butterfly spat out. "I don't like no stinking white woman. My grandma is a white woman and I don't even like her!"

But it just so happened that Butterfly's crime partner was in the crowd, and after Butterfly had his say, his crime partner said, "Aw, sit on down and quit that lying, lil o' chump. What about that gray girl in San

Jose who had your nose wide open? Did you like her, or were you just running after her with your tongue hanging out of your head and because you hated her?"

Partly because he was embarrassed and partly because his crime partner was a heavyweight, Butterfly flew into him. And before we could separate them and disperse, so the guard would not know who had been fighting, Butterfly bloodied his crime partner's nose. Butterfly got away but, because of the blood, his crime partner got caught. I ate dinner with Butterfly that evening and questioned him sharply about his attitude toward white women. And after an initial evasiveness he admitted that the white woman bugged him too. "It's a sickness," he said. "All our lives we've had the white woman dangled before our eyes like a carrot on a stick before a donkey: look but don't touch." (In 1958, after I had gone out on parole and was returned to San Quentin as a parole violator with a new charge, Butterfly was still there. He had become a Black Muslim and was chiefly responsible for teaching me the Black Muslim philosophy. Upon his release from San Quentin, Butterfly joined the Los Angeles Mosque, advanced rapidly through the ranks, and is now a full-fledged minister of one of Elijah Muhammad's mosques in another city. He successfully completed his parole, got married—to a very black girl—and is doing fine.)

From our discussion, which began that evening and has never yet ended, we went on to notice how thoroughly, as a matter of course, a black growing up in America is indoctrinated with the white race's standard of beauty. Not that the whites made a conscious, calculated effort to do this, we thought, but since they constituted the majority the whites brainwashed the blacks by the very processes the whites employed to indoctrinate themselves with their own group standards. It intensified my frustrations to know that I was indoctrinated to see the white woman as more beautiful and desirable than my own black woman. It drove me into books seeking light on the subject. In Richard Wright's *Native Son,* I found Bigger Thomas and a keen insight into the problem.

My interest in this area persisted undiminished and then, in 1955, an event took place in Mississippi which turned me inside out: Emmett Till, a young Negro down from Chicago on a visit, was murdered, allegedly for flirting with a white woman. He had been shot, his head crushed from repeated blows with a blunt instrument, and his badly decomposed body was recovered from the river with a heavy weight on it.

I was, of course, angry over the whole bit, but one day I saw in a magazine a picture of the white woman with whom Emmett Till was said to have flirted. While looking at the picture, I felt that little tension in the center of my chest I experience when a woman appeals to me. I was disgusted and angry with myself. Here was a woman who had caused the death of a black, possibly because, when he looked at her, he also felt the same tensions of lust and desire in his chest—and probably for the same general reasons that I felt them. It was all unacceptable to me. I looked at the picture again and again, and in spite of everything and against my will and the hate I felt for the woman and all that she represented, she appealed to me. I flew into a rage at myself, at America, at white women, at the history that had placed those tensions of lust and desire to my chest.

Two days later, I had a "nervous breakdown." For several days I ranted and raved against the white race, against white women in particular, against white America in general. When I came to myself, I was locked in a padded cell with not even the vaguest memory of how I got there. All I could recall was an eternity of pacing back and forth in the cell, preaching to the unhearing walls.

I had several sessions with a psychiatrist. His conclusion was that I hated my mother. How he arrived at this conclusion I'll never know, because he knew nothing about my mother; and when he'd ask me questions I would answer him with absurd lies. What revolted me about him was that he had heard me denouncing the whites, yet each time he interviewed me he deliberately guided the conversation back to my family life, to my childhood. That in itself was all right, but he deliberately blocked all my attempts to bring out the racial question, and he made it clear that he was not interested in my attitude toward whites. This was a Pandora's box he did not care to open. After I ceased my diatribes against the whites, I was let out of the hospital, back into the general inmate population just as if nothing had happened. I continued to brood over these events and over the dynamics of race relations in America.

During this period I was concentrating my reading in the field of economics. Having previously dabbled in the theories and writings of Rousseau, Thomas Paine, and Voltaire, I had added a little polish to my iconoclastic stance, without, however, bothering too much to understand their affirmative positions. In economics, because everybody seemed to find it necessary to attack and condemn Karl Marx in their writings, I sought out his books, and although he kept me with a headache, I took him for my authority. I was not prepared to understand him, but I was able to see in him a thoroughgoing critique and condemnation of capitalism. It was like taking medicine for me to find that, indeed, American capitalism deserved all the hatred and contempt that I felt for it in my heart. This had a positive, stabilizing effect upon me—to an extent because I was not about to become stable—and it diverted me from my previous preoccupation: morbid broodings on the black man and the white woman. Pursuing my readings into the history of socialism, I read, with very little understanding, some of the passionate, exhortatory writings of Lenin; and I fell in love with Bakunin and Nechayev's *Catechism of the Revolutionist*—the principles of which, along with some of Machiavelli's advice, I sought to incorporate into my own behavior. I took the *Catechism* for my bible and, standing on a one-man platform that had nothing to do with the reconstruction of society, I began consciously incorporating these principles into my daily life, to employ tactics of ruthlessness in my dealing with everyone with whom I came into contact. And I began to look at white America through these new eyes.

Somehow I arrived at the conclusion that, as a matter of principle, it was of paramount importance for me to have an antagonistic, ruthless attitude toward white women. The term *outlaw* appealed to me and at the time my parole date was drawing near, I considered myself to be mentally free—I was an "outlaw," I had stepped outside of the white man's law, which I repudiated with scorn and self-satisfaction. I became a law unto myself—my own legislature, my own supreme court, my own executive. At the moment I walked out of the prison gate, my feelings toward white women in general could be summed up in the following lines:

TO A WHITE GIRL

I love you
Because you're white,
Not because you're charming
Or bright.
Your Whiteness
Is a silky thread
Snaking through my thoughts
In redhot patterns

Of lust and desire.

I hate you
Because you're white.
Your white meat
Is nightmare food.
White is
The skin of Evil.
You're my Moby Dick,
White Witch,
Symbol of the rope and hanging tree,
Of the burning cross.
Loving you thus
And hating you so,
My heart is torn in two.
Crucified.

I became a rapist. To refine my technique and *modus operandi,* I started out by practicing on black girls in the ghetto—in the black ghetto where dark and vicious deeds appear not as aberrations or deviations from the norm, but as part of the sufficiency of the Evil of a day—and when I considered myself smooth enough, I crossed the tracks and sought out white prey. I did this consciously, deliberately, willfully, methodically—though looking back I see that I was in a frantic, wild and completely abandoned frame of mind.

Rape was an insurrectionary act. It delighted me that I was defying and trampling upon the white man's law, upon his system of values, and that I was defiling his women—and this point, I believe, was the most satisfying to me because I was very resentful over the historical fact of how the white man has used the black woman. I felt I was getting revenge. From the site of the act of rape, consternation spreads outwardly in concentric circles. I wanted to send waves of consternation throughout the white race. Recently, I came upon a quotation from one of LeRoi Jones' poems, taken from his book *The Dead Lecturer.*

A cult of death need of the simple striking arm under the street lamp. The cutters from under their rented earth. Come up, black dada nihilismus. Rape the white girls. Rape their fathers. Cut the mothers' throats.

I have lived those lines and I know that if I had not been apprehended I would have slit some white throats. There are, of course, many young blacks out there right now who are slitting white throats and raping the white girl. They are not doing this because they read LeRoi Jones' poetry, as some of his critics seem to believe. Rather LeRoi is expressing the funky facts of life.

After I returned to prison, I took a long look at myself and, for the first time in my life, admitted that I was wrong, that I had gone astray—astray not so much from the white man's law as from being human, civilized—for I could not approve my own motivations, I did not feel justified. I lost my self-respect. My pride as a man dissolved and my whole fragile moral structure seemed to collapse, completely shattered.

That is why I started to write. To save myself.

I realized that no one could save me but myself. The prison authorities were both uninterested and unable to help me. I had to seek out the truth and unravel the snarled web of my motivations. I had to find out who I am and what I want to be, what type of man I should be, and what I could do to become the best of which I was capable. I understood that what had happened to me had also happened to countless other blacks and it would happen to many, many more.

I learned that I had been taking the easy way out, running away from problems. I also learned that it is easier to do evil than it is to do good. And I have been terribly impressed by the youth of America, black and white. I am proud of them because they have reaffirmed my faith in humanity. I have come to feel what must be love for the young people of America and I want to be part of the good and greatness that they want for all people. From my prison cell, I have watched America slowly coming awake. It is not fully awake yet, but there is soul in the air and everywhere I see beauty. I have watched the sit-ins, the freedom rides, the Mississippi Blood Summers, demonstrations all over the country, the FSM movement, the teach-ins, and the mounting protest over Lyndon Strangelove's foreign policy—all of this, the thousands of little details, show me it is time to straighten up and fly right. That is why I decided to concentrate on my writings and efforts in this area. We are a very sick country—I, perhaps, am sicker than most. But I accept that. I told you in the beginning that I am extremist by nature—so it is only right that I should be extremely sick.

I was very familiar with the Eldridge who came to prison, but that Eldridge no longer exists. And the one I am now is in some ways a stranger to me. You may find this difficult to understand but it is very easy for one in prison to lose his sense of self. And if he has been undergoing all kinds of extreme, involved, and unregulated changes, then he ends up not knowing who he is. Take the point of being attractive to women. You can easily see how a man can lose his arrogance or certainty on that point while in prison! When he's in the free world, he gets constant feedback on how he looks from the number of female heads he turns when he walks down the street. In prison he gets only hate-stares and sour frowns. Years and years of bitter looks. Individuality is not nourished in prison, neither by the officials nor by the convicts. It is a deep hole out of which to climb.

What must be done, I believe, is that all these problems—particularly the sickness between the white woman and the black man—must be brought out into the open, dealt with and resolved. I know that the black man's sick attitude toward the white woman is a revolutionary sickness: it keeps him perpetually out of harmony with the system that is oppressing him. Many whites flatter themselves with the idea that the Negro male's lust and desire for the white dream girl is purely an esthetic attraction, but nothing could be farther from the truth. His motivation is often of such a bloody, hateful, bitter, and malignant nature that whites would really be hard pressed to find it flattering. I have discussed these points with prisoners who were convicted of rape, and their motivations are very plain. But they are very reluctant to discuss these things with white men who, by and large, make up the prison staffs; I believe that in the experience of these men lies the knowledge and wisdom that must be utilized to help other youngsters who are heading in the same direction. I think all of us, the entire nation, will be better off if we bring it all out front. A lot of people's feelings will be hurt, but that is the price that must be paid.

It may be that I can harm myself by speaking frankly and directly, but I do not care about that at all. Of course I want to get out of prison, badly, but I shall get out some day. I am more concerned with what I am going to be after I get out. I know that by following the course which I have charted I will find my salvation. If I had followed the path laid down for me by the officials, I'd undoubtedly have long since been out of prison—but I'd be less of a man. I'd be weaker and less certain of where I want to go, what I want to do, and how to go about it.

The price of hating other human beings is loving oneself less.

Barred by prison authorities from mailing the manuscript of a book he'd written out to publishers, Cleaver smuggled it out in the form of letters to his attorney, Beverly Axelrod. Ramparts's publisher, Edward Keating, a liberal Catholic sympathetic to Cleaver's plight and impressed by his talent, decided to publish a few as "Letters from Prison," which ultimately led to the publication of Soul on Ice *in 1968.*

In his introduction, Maxwell Geismar called Soul on Ice *one of the literary discoveries of the 1960s, in which he heard echoes of Richard Wright's* Native Son, *and saw a moral affinity with* The Autobiography of Malcolm X. *In American terms, Geismar wrote, it represented "the only comparable approach to the writings of Franz Fanon."*

A DAY IN FOLSOM PRISON

Folsom Prison,
September 19, 1965

My day begins officially at 7:00, when all inmates are required to get out of bed and stand before their cell doors to be counted by guards who walk along the tier saying, "1, 2, 3 . . ." However, I never remain in bed until 7. I'm usually up by 5:30. The first thing I do is make up my bed. Then I pick up all my books, newspapers, etc., off the floor of my cell and spread them over my bed to clear the floor for calisthenics. In my cell, I have a little stool on which I lay a large plywood board, about 2½ by 3 feet, which I use as a typing and writing table. At night, I load this makeshift table down with books and papers, and when I read at night I spill things all over the floor. When I leave my cell, I set this board, loaded down, on my bed, so that if a guard comes into my cell to search it, he will not knock the board off the stool, as has happened before. Still in the nude, the way I sleep, I go through my routine: knee bends, butterflies, touching my toes, squats, windmills. I continue for about half an hour.

Sometimes, if I have something I want to write or type so that I can mail it that morning, I forgo my calisthenics. But this is unusual. (We are required, if we want our mail to go out on a certain day, to have it in the mailbox by about 8:00. When we leave our cells at 7:30 to go to breakfast, we pass right by the mailbox and drop in our mail on the way to the mess hall.)

Usually, by the time I finish my calisthenics, the trustee (we call him tiertender, or keyman) comes by and fills my little bucket with hot water. We don't have hot running water ourselves. Each cell has a small sink with a cold-water tap, a bed, a locker, a shelf or two along the wall, and a commode. The trustee has a big bucket, with a long spout like the ones people use to water their flowers, only without the sprinkler. He pokes the spout through the bars and pours you about a gallon of hot water. My cell door doesn't have bars on it; it is a solid slab of steel with fifty-eight holes in it about the size of a half dollar, and a slot in the center, at eye level, about an inch wide and five inches long. The trustee sticks the spout through one of the little holes and pours my hot water, and in the evenings the guard slides my mail in to me through the slot. Through the same slot the convicts pass newspapers, books, candy, and cigarettes to one another.

When the guard has mail for me he stops at the cell door and calls my name, and I recite my number—A-29498—to verify that I am the right Cleaver. When I get mail I avert my eyes so I can't see who it's from. Then I sit down on my bed and peep at it real slowly, like a poker player peeping at his cards. I can feel when I've got a letter from you, and when I peep up on your name on the envelope I let out a big yell. It's like having four aces. But if the letter is not from you, it's like having two deuces, a three, a four, and a five, all in scrambled suits. A bum kick. Nothing. What is worse is when the guard passes my door without pausing. I can hear his keys jingling. If he stops at my door the keys sound like Christmas bells ringing, but if he keeps going they just sound like—keys.

I live in the honor block. In the other block, the fronts of the cells consist of nothing but bars. When I first moved into the honor block, I didn't like it at all. The cells seemed made for a dungeon. The heavy steel doors slammed shut with a clang of finality that chilled my soul. The first time that door closed on me, I had the same wild, hysterical sensation I'd felt years ago at San Quentin when they first locked me in solitary. For the briefest moment I felt like yelling out for help, and it seemed that in no circumstances would I be able to endure that cell. All in that split second I felt like calling out to the guards, pleading with them to let me out of my cell, begging them to let me go, promising them that I would be a good boy in the future.

But just as quickly as the feeling came, it went, dissolved, and I felt at peace with myself. I felt that I could endure anything, everything, even the test of being broken on the rack. I've been in every type of cell they have in the prisons of California, and the door to my present cell seems like the most cruel and ugly of all. However, I have grown to like this door. When I go out of my cell, I can hardly wait to get back in, to slam that cumbersome door, and hear the sharp click as the trustee snaps the lock behind me. The trustees keep the keys to the cell of the honor block all day, relinquishing them at night, and to get into your cell, all you have to do is round up the trustee in charge of your tier. Once inside my cell, I feel safe: I don't have to watch the other convicts any more or the guards in the gun towers. If you live in a cell with nothing but bars on the front, you cannot afford to relax; someone can walk along the tier and throw a Molotov cocktail in on you before you know it, something I've seen happen in San Quentin. Whenever I live in one of those barred cells, I keep a blanket within easy reach in case of emergency, to smother a fire if need be. Paranoia? Yes, but it's the least one can do for oneself. In my present cell, with its impregnable door, I don't worry about sabotage—although if someone wanted to badly enough, they could figure something out.

Well . . . after I've finished my calisthenics and the hot water has arrived, I take me a bird (jailbird) bath in the little sink. It's usually about 6:00 by then. From then until 7:30, when we are let out for breakfast, I clean up my cell and try to catch a little news over the radio. Radio?— each cell has a pair of earphones!—with only two channels on it. The programs are monitored from the radio room. The radio schedule is made up by the radio committee, of which I am a member.

At 7:30, breakfast. From the mess hall, every day except Saturday, my day off, I go straight to the bakery, change into my white working clothes, and that's me until about noon. From noon, I am "free" until 3:20, the evening mandatory lockup, when we are required, again, to stand before our cell doors and be counted. There is another count at 6:30 P.M.—three times every day without fail.

When I'm through working in the bakery, I have the choice of (1) going to my cell; (2) staying in the dining room to watch TV; (3) going down to the library; or (4) going out to the yard to walk around, sit in the sun, lift weights, play some funny game—like checkers, chess, marbles, horseshoes, handball, baseball, shuffleboard, beating on the punching bag, basket ball, talk, TV, paddle-tennis, watching the other convicts who are watching other convicts. When I first came to Folsom, I was astonished to see the old grizzled cons playing marbles. The marble players of Folsom are legendary throughout the prison system: I first heard about them years ago. There is a sense of ultimate defeat about them. Some guy might boast about how he is going to get out next time and stay out, and someone will put him down by saying he'll soon be back, playing marbles like a hasbeen, neverwas, blasted back into childhood by a crushing defeat to his final dream. The marble players have the game down to an art and they play all day long, fanatically absorbed in what they are doing.

If I have a cell partner who knows the game, I play him chess now and then, maybe a game each night. I have a chess set of my own and sometimes when I feel like doing nothing else, I take out a little envelope in which I keep a collection of chess problems clipped from newspapers, and run off one or two. But I have never been able to give all my time to one of these games. I am seldom able to play a game of chess out on the yard. Whenever I go out on the yard these days, I'm usually on my way to the library.

On the yard there is a little shack off to one corner that is the office of the Inmates Advisory Council (IAC). Sometimes I visit the shack to shoot the bull and get the latest drawings (news). And sometimes I go out to the weight-lifting area, strip down to a pair of trunks, and push a little iron for a while and soak up the sun.

At 3:20, lockup. Stand for count. After count, off to the evening meal. Back to the cell. Stand for count at 6:30. After the 6:30 count, we are all let out of our cells, one tier at a time, for showers, to exchange dirty socks and towels for clean ones, a haircut, then back to the cell. I duck this crush by taking my showers in the bakery. At night I only go to exchange my linen. In the honor block, we are allowed to come out after the 6:30 count every Saturday, Sunday, and Wednesday night to watch TV until 10:00, before we are locked up for the night. The only time I went out for TV was to dig the broads on Shindig and Hollywood-A-Go-Go, but those programs don't come on anymore. We recently got the rule changed so that, on TV nights, those in the honor block can type until 10:00. It used to be that no typing was allowed after

8:00. I am very pleased to be able to get in that extra typing time: I can write you more letters.

On Thursday I go out of my cell after the 6:30 count to attend the weekly IAC meetings. These meetings adjourn promptly at 9:00. On Saturday mornings, my day off, I usually attend the meetings of the Gavel Club, but this past Saturday I was in the middle of my last letter to you and I stole away to my cell. I enjoyed it so much that I am tempted to put the Gavel Club down, but I hope that I don't because that's where I'm gaining some valuable experience and technique in public speaking.

On the average I spend approximately seventeen hours a day in my cell. I enjoy the solitude. The only drawback is that I am unable to get the type of reading material I want, and there is hardly anyone with a level head to talk to.

There are quite a few guys here who write. Seems that every convict wants to. Some of them have managed to sell a piece here and there. They have a writers' workshop which meets in the library under the wing of our librarian. I've never had a desire to belong to this workshop, partly because of my dislike for the attitude of the librarian and partly because of the phony, funny-style convicts. Mostly, I suppose, it's because the members of the workshop are all white and all sick when it comes to color. They're not all sick, but they're not for real. They're fair-weather types, not even as lukewarm as good white liberals, and they conform to the Mississippi atmosphere prevalent here in Folsom. Blacks and whites do not fraternize together in comfort here. Harry Golden's concept of vertical integration and horizontal segregation about covers it. The whites want to talk with you out on the yard or at work, standing up, but they shun you when it comes to sitting down. For instance, when we line up for chow, the lines leading into the mess halls are integrated. But once inside the mess hall, blacks sit at tables by themselves and whites sit with themselves or with the Mexicans.

There's this one Jewish stud out of New York who fell out of Frisco. He thinks he is another Lenny Bruce. In point of fact he is funny and very glib, and I dig rapping (talking) with him. He's a hype but is very down with the current scene. Says that he lived in North Beach and all that, and that he has this chick who writes him who is a member of the DuBois Club in Frisco. Well, this cat is well read and we exchange reading material. He says that at home he has every copy of

The Realist published up to the time of his fall. *The Evergreen Review* kills him. We communicate pretty well and I know that stud is not a racist, but he is a conformist—which in my book is worse, more dangerous, than an out-and-out foe. The other day we were talking about the Free Speech Movement. He was reading a book by Paul Goodman, *Growing up Absurd,* which he had with him. We were very hung up talking and then it was time for lunch. We got in line and continued our conversation. He was trying to convince me that the whole FSM was predicated on the writings of Paul Goodman, and that he had heard, with his own ears, Mario Savio say as much. Then all of a sudden I noticed this cat grow leery and start looking all around. He made me nervous. I thought maybe someone was trying to sneak up on us with a knife or something. When he kept doing this, I asked him what the fuck was the matter with him. He turned real red and said that he "just remembered" that he had to talk to another fellow. I dug right away what the kick was, so I said, "later," and he split. I'm used to such scenes, having a 400-year heritage of learning to roll with that type of punch. I saw him in the mess hall looking very pushed out of shape. I had to laugh at him. I felt that he was probably thinking that if the whites put the blacks in the gas chambers they might grab him too if he was with me. That thought tickled me a little as I watched him peeping around like a ferret. One of his points of indignation is that, he says, he will never forgive Israel for kidnapping and killing Eichmann, and he gets mad at me because I take Israel's side, just to keep the conversation alive. Too much agreement kills a chat. What really bugs him is when I say that there are many blacks who, if they were in the position, would do a little rounding up of the Eichmann types in America. A few days later he told me, "You saw through me the other day, didn't you?"

"I see through you every day," I told him. He looked as if he expected or wanted me to hit him or something. I told him that he was good for nothing but to be somebody's jailhouse wife and he laughed, then launched into a Lenny Bruce-type monologue.

My own reaction is to have as little as possible to do with the whites. I have no respect for a duck who runs up to me in the yard all buddy-buddy, and then feels obliged not to sit down with me. It's not that I'm dying to sit with him either, but there is a principle involved which cuts me deeply.

Talk about hypocrisy: you should see the library. We are allowed to order, from the state library, only non-fiction and law books. Of the law books, we can only order books containing court opinions. We can get any decision of the California District Court of Appeals, the California Supreme Court, the U.S. District Courts, the Circuit Courts, and the U.S. Supreme Court. But books of an explanatory nature are prohibited. Many convicts who do not have lawyers are forced to act *in propria persona*. They do all right. But it would be much easier if they could get books that showed them how properly to plead their cause, how to prepare their petitions and briefs. This is a perpetual sore point with the Folsom Prison Bar Association, as we call ourselves.

All of the novels one *needs* to read are unavailable, and the librarian won't let you send for them. I asked him once if he had read a certain book.

"Oh, yes!" he exclaimed.

"What did you think of it?" I asked.

"Absolutely marvelous!" he said.

"How about letting me send to the state library for it?" I asked.

"No."

Books that one wants to read—so bad that it is a taste in the mouth, like Calvin C. Hernton's *Sex and Racism in America*—he won't let you have.

"The warden says 'no sex,'" is his perpetual squelch.

There is a book written by a New York judge which gives case histories of prostitutes. The authors explore why white prostitutes, some of them from the deepest South, had Negroes for pimps, and I wanted to reread it.

"No Sex," said the librarian. He is indifferent to the fact that it is a matter of life and death to me! I don't know how he justifies this because you can go over to the inmate canteen and buy all the prurient potboiling anti-literature that has ever been written. But everything that "is happening" today is verboten. I've been dying to read Norman Mailer's *An American Dream,* but that too is prohibited. You can have *Reader's Digest,* but *Playboy?*—not a chance. I have long wanted to file suit in Federal Court for the right to receive *Playboy* magazine. Do you think Hugh Hefner would finance such an action? I think some very nice ideas would be liberated.

The library does have a selection of very solid material, things done from ten years ago all the way back to the Bible. But it is unsatisfactory to a stud who is trying to function in the last half of the twentieth century. Go down there and try to find Hemingway, Mailer, Camus, Sartre, Baldwin, Henry Miller, Terry Southern, Julian Mayfield, Bellow, William Burroughs, Allen Ginsberg, Herbert Gold, Robert Gover, J. O. Killens, etc.—no action. They also have this sick thing going when it comes to books by and about Negroes. Robert F. Williams' book, *Negroes with Guns,* is not allowed any more; I ordered it from the state library before it was too popular around here. I devoured it and let a few friends read it, before the librarian dug it and put it on the blacklist. Once I ordered two books from the inmate canteen with my own money. When they arrived here from the company, the librarian impounded them, placing them on my "property" the same as they did my notebooks.

I want to devote my time to reading and writing, with everything else secondary, but I can't do that in prison. I have to keep my eyes open at all times or I won't make it. There is always some madness going on, and whether you like it or not you're involved. There is no choice in the matter: you cannot sit and wait for things to come to you. So I engage in all kinds of petty intrigue which I've found necessary to survival. It consumes a lot of time and energy. But it is necessary.

Eldridge Cleaver continued to work as a writer in the midst of the tumultuous political commitment, extensive travel, and personal setbacks that marked his years in exile. Granted political asylum in France between 1972 and 1975, he worked on the book that includes this chapter. Cleaver experimented with different titles, including at one time calling the book Over My Shoulder *and later it became* Promises to Keep, *taken from a Robert Frost poem that ends with the lines, "The woods are lovely, dark and deep, But I have promises to keep, And miles to go before I sleep." For this initial publication, the book's title has been shortened to* Promises.

PROMISES

CHAPTER TWO

When talking about prisoners, lawyers, and the courts in the state of California, the case of Caryl Chessman has to be the point of departure. In 1948 Chessman, the Red Light Bandit, was convicted of rape, kidnapping, and a host of other charges flowing from what he allegedly did to his victims. The state said that Chessman's modus operandi was to impersonate a police officer and vamp on unwary couples making out in parked cars in Los Angeles' lovers' lanes. He would drive up in his car with a red spotlight flashing away, imitating the LAPD. He'd tell the couple that they were under arrest, handcuff the man, and then take gross liberties with the girl. The seeming inability of the police to capture the Red Light Bandit set off a righteous clamor in the press. Each week he'd strike again. Each time he struck, the clamor grew louder. There were calls for the resignation of the chief of police. Finally they caught him. Chessman's arrest was a great day for the LAPD. After a circus trial, which captured headlines for weeks, the death sentence was imposed and Chessman was taken to San Quentin's death row to await execution.

Before the date of his execution rolled around, Chessman discovered that the stenographic reporter who recorded the proceedings at his trial had died before transcribing his notes and preparing the transcript as required by law. On top of that, this particular stenographic reporter, an expert in his field with several decades of experience, had developed a very personal style, a unique shorthand that was impossible for the other experts to decipher. So Chessman found himself in the happy position of being on death row with no valid record as to why he was there. He claimed, of course, that he was innocent, that he had arrived on death row by mistake, and that he should be released, forthwith. It was up to the state to prove that he was rightfully on death row. Without the stenographic reporter's transcript to point at for proof, the state was in a ridiculous position.

Instead of remedying the situation by taking Chessman back to court, retrying him, and then resentencing him to death, the state attorney general took a dogmatic position and tried with all his force to execute Chessman without going to the expense of a new trial. As a result, the case got tangled up in the red tape of the judicial system, and Chessman, seeing his opportunity to stay alive, began filing writs and petitions to every court in the land. In the process, Chessman became an acknowledged expert in the law. He won many favorable decisions from the courts, including several in the U.S. Supreme Court, which forced the state of California to adhere a little closer to the Constitution of the United States. It became a test whether or not the state of California was going to lose face, which would have happened had Chessman been released, by being forced to admit that their system of justice was not perfect.

In the end, the state gassed Chessman. But by the time they actually killed him, it was an act of ritual murder performed by the state in naked defiance of world public opinion. It took the state of California, finally, 12 years to get Chessman into the little green room and drop the pill on him. By the time they killed Chessman, they hated him more for the example he had set for other prisoners than for the crimes of which he had been convicted. For he had spawned, by his successful example, a contingent of jailhouse lawyers throughout the prison system, opening up the law books and bringing them down to earth in a convict's eyes. He drove home the point that even though a person was in prison, convicted and forgotten, it was never too late or too hopeless for him to take his case back to court. Since that time, the jailhouse lawyers have kept the attorney general's office jumping in a neverending struggle to cover up and patch up a leaky judicial system.

My focus on Chessman was that he had used a book more or less about himself, which he wrote while on death row, for money. *The Kid Was a Killer* was the title of Chessman's book and it sold like hotcakes all over the world. From his earnings, Chessman, hired one of the best lawyers in the country, who almost sprung him, not just down from death row, but into the outside world. He had taken his own despised life as a criminal and written about it, thus transforming a negative experience into a positive tool for action. Even though Chessman was executed in the end, to convicts he became a powerful symbol of resourcefulness, defiance, and the will to fight for one's life and freedom.

Although I myself was not on Death Row, I was walking among the living dead, those who had not been sentenced to death by the courts, but who knew very clearly that the prison officials would prefer them dead, and were perfectly capable of engineering their deaths. Ultimately, the stakes were the same. To get out, then, my game also would have to be strong.

I had accumulated a stack of manuscripts in my cell, writings at which I had been scratching away for the last couple of years. Judging from the flood of shallow, knuckle-headed books being published at the time—the first half of the sixties—I thought that I might be able to put something down. At the very least, I should be able to strike up a conversation with someone outside. I thought that through the process of submitting my manuscript to prospective publishers, I might establish contact with somebody. And that contact, somehow, would have to be turned into money, which in turn would be transformed into a lawyer.

I made a selection of pieces from my manuscripts, retyped it all very neatly to give it at least that much uniformity, and then gave it the provocative title "White Woman, Black Man." The procedure laid down by the rules of the director of the Department of Corrections was that all manuscripts written by prisoners must be censored by the prison librarian before being allowed to leave the prison. The librarian at Folsom was a fat, redheaded faggot with eyeglasses a quarter inch thick, a flabby neck, and a round, rosy face. We called him the Dean of Women, which seemed like the natural thing to do, because his name was Dean Gregory.

I placed my manuscript in a nice new envelope, filled out the proper forms authorizing payment of the postage from my meager prison account, took it all down to the library, and laid it on the Dean. The Dean accepted my manuscript, with his impatient, bothered airs, and told me that he would read it and let me know in one week whether or not he'd allow it to go out. Two weeks passed with no word from the Dean. Finally, I went down to the library and hung around until I had a chance to speak with the Dean. He told me that he had turned my manuscript over to Associate Warden Walter Craven, whose job it was to supervise all of the guards, enforce discipline, and ensure the orderly functioning of prison routine. That my manuscript was now in Craven's hands was definitely bad news.

There was no such thing as a pleasant encounter with Associate Warden Walter Craven, and I had already encountered him several times. Once, for speaking at a meeting with other black prisoners, Craven sent me to the Hole, on a charge of "agitating a situation likely to lead to racial violence." All we were doing was discussing a clash that had taken place in San Francisco between civil rights demonstrators and the police. Another time, Craven sent me to the Adjustment Center for 90 days' observation after finding me guilty of eating unauthorized food, a grave infraction, in his eyes. I had traded some pastry, which I ripped off from the bakery, where I worked, for some chicken diverted from the employee's dining room, where Craven and his friends ate their meals. Essentially, Craven had sent me to the AC for eating up some of his food.

About a week later, the Dean of Women summoned me to the library, called me into his office, pulled my manuscript out of a drawer in his desk, tossed it on top, and said:

"This will not be allowed out of the prison because it contains a racist interpretation of history."

I was shocked—and pissed off. I told Dean that was absurd. He told me it was Craven's opinion, and the decision was out of his hands. I believed that Associate Warden Craven's reasons for blocking my manuscript had nothing at all to do with his literary standards. He was more concerned with the practical problems of nipping opposition in the bud, of controlling prisoners, and not allowing anything to get started that might get out of hand. His key intention was keeping the prisoners cut off as far as possible from contact with the outside world. Chessman had already taught them all they wanted to know about books written in prison.

However outraged I was by Craven and Dean Gregory's action in blocking my manuscript, I was also happy, because their administrative censorship gave me a weapon with which to fight them. They were wrong, as prison officials, for imposing censorship in the absolute sense of not even allowing my manuscript to leave the prison. If what I had written was useless, then nobody would be forced to read it. I had heard enough about censorship in general to know how often the censor tries to block something good. I thought that censorship was one of the worse crimes that the state is capable of committing, a violation of the most fundamental right—the right to speak, the right to give one's opinion, which boils down to the right to think. There is no valid distinction between thinking and expressing one's thoughts, because expression is vital to the process that we call thought. And I knew enough about America to know that censorship is a bad word and that prison officials who go to court to justify suppressing literary manuscripts are in an untenable position. I was as elated as a forty-niner who had just struck gold. I decided to file a suit in the federal court against the California Department of Corrections in general and against Gregory and Craven in particular for suppressing my manuscript.

My only purpose was to get out of prison. To do that I had to build up my case and get myself a lawyer. My plan had been to sell my manuscript and get enough money to hire a lawyer. Now that was blocked, I had to achieve the same results by other means. I gloated as I poured over court decisions and legal texts, whipping my case into shape. At last, it was finished. I filed a suit claiming that the prison officials violated my constitutional rights by refusing to allow me to send my manuscript to prospective publishers. About a week later when I received notification from the federal district court that my suit had been placed on the calendar, routinely but officially, it was all I could do to contain my happiness. Now it was time to enter into phase two.

I got hold of a book, published by the California Bar Association, which listed the addresses and phone numbers of all its members. I began writing letters to lawyers, mentioning my conviction to them, but placing heaviest emphasis on my current suit over my suppressed manuscript. To each lawyer, I offered to give my manuscript as payment in return for legal assistance. I basically ran down the same story to each lawyer—it had practically turned into a form letter. The letter was designed to appeal to them financially, politically, and in the case of black lawyers, racially. I made it my business to write at least one letter each day, to a different lawyer, and sometimes I managed to fire off a couple.

None of the black lawyers ever answered my letters. Probably, they would argue, because they were poor oppressed blacks and couldn't afford to pay a secretary the way white lawyers could. But in my opinion they were just a sorry bunch of unconscionable scoundrels, interested only in the bird in hand, and not giving a good goddamn about what might be in the bush. Many of the white scoundrelly lawyers didn't answer my letters either, and those that did were not helpful.

But I was determined to keep the letters flying. I stepped up my campaign, averaging at least two letters a day, and sometimes three. I kept this up for several months. Every day I would drop something in the mailbox. I was reaching out from behind those walls in the only way available to me, and I would keep reaching until I got hold of something. I was as serious as arsenic, sustained by the faith that if I persevered I could unlock that strong front gate. Meanwhile, I kept filing documents in the federal district court in order to keep my suit alive.

PART TWO REVOLUTION

Black Panther Party National Headquarters window shattered by the bullets of two Oakland policemen, September 10, 1968. © Pirkle Jones, 1968.

"Babylon," the term Eldridge Cleaver adopted from the biblical Book of Revelations was his favorite epithet for America because it was synonymous with decadence and corruption. At the top righthand corner of his typewritten manuscript is the date June 14, 1971. That indicates he was in Algiers, rocked by the Black Panthers' startling series of purges which in February had culminated with his expulsion as well as that of the International Section of the Black Panther Party, of which he was the leader.

In the brief outline attached to the manuscript, he wrote that this "book seeks to put in a meaningful context . . . the consequences of the assassinations of President Kennedy, Malcolm X, Martin Luther King, and Robert Kennedy . . . in terms of how these events completely changed the course and direction of the Afro-American people's struggle." He wrote further that he would "deal with the true, inner history of the Black Panther Party . . . and the development of the violent encounters with the police," acknowledging that what he intended to say would "multiply my enemies and make my existence even more precarious, which is not exactly what I need at this time!"

Writing about his ideas for the book's structure, Cleaver said, "I'm trying something deliberate. It fits the contours of my skull. I think it is possible in this way to say what I want to say for the first time. I do not want to argue too much with editors, this time." Although Uptight in Babylon *was never finished, the excerpt published here sizzles with an irreverent, passionate, and powerful voice rarely heard in America.*

UPTIGHT IN BABYLON

1

By the time I got out of prison, December 12, 1966, both President Kennedy and Malcolm X were already dead. The Black Panther Party was two months old, and the arteries of the second Johnson administration had already publicly hardened. Martin Luther King had less than 16 more months to live, and two days following his death I myself would be shot. In less than two years from that day I walked out of prison, I would have to flee the country.

The nation, struck dumb by events and the deluge of blood unleashed under Johnson, was wondering what had happened, what had gone wrong. The people had risen up in anger to beat back Barry Goldwater, hoping against hope that Johnson would save them. Instead, Johnson had given them all, and even more, that they had voted against. The mood of the cheated people was that they had been cheated. They had gotten burned twice in a row. First, they had warded off Nixon, only to have their choice, Kennedy, killed. The brain that they voted for had gotten shattered with lead. Instead, they ended up with Johnson. But Johnson had played it halfway cool that first year in office. He was not to really show his hand until after the '64 election, when he was safely in office again. Second, they had rejected the madness offered up by Goldwater, voted for peace and an end to the violence and injustice at home. I will not bother even to argue with anyone who says this is not true. The greatest public debate since the Civil War had taken place in Babylon, and the American people had voted for justice and peace, both at home and abroad. The record was clear then and it is still clear now—to my mind, even clearer.

When I left prison, I knew perfectly well that I was going to war. I was merely being transferred to another front. The battle raging outside those walls was exactly the same one raging within. I knew that racist pigs and their black lackeys who controlled the prison, the racist convicts, and the revolutionary convicts, both black and white, were a microcosm of what awaited me outside those walls. What I was walking away from was what I was walking into. Nothing was left behind. But I was glad to get out, because there were guns outside and I knew that I would have a chance to get my hands on one. In fact, I had already insured that my guns would be waiting.

I had reached certain conclusions by the time I left prison: that secret, conspiratorial machinery existed in America involving some of the most powerful and best-known men in the land, and that this machinery had killed President Kennedy and Malcolm X; that the goal of this machinery was the fascisization of the American social order; that black people faced the alternatives of genocide or war for liberation; that many more people, myself included, were going to be killed, but that we had to do all that we could because time was short, and that it was possible, if we fought hard, to defeat this conspiracy and rebuild America along the lines of our dreams.

And this dream had not grown dim. In spite of the pigs, in spite of all that had happened, faith in the ability of men to deal with the present and build a human future had not been lost. It had not even been staggered. But I was uptight. I was uptight because I was convinced that a coup d'etat had gone down, and that, far from seeing through the plot, the people seemed all to have been taken in. The unfolding of Johnson's maneuvering the nation deeper into the war in Vietnam, and the fore-runner moves that he was making for repression at home, principally against blacks, but also against whites who opposed him and his belli-cose policies, in any significant way, indicated to me that one had to move fast.

I have never believed that it was too late to get something done, or to stop something from happening. This may be the assassin's perspective. I say that, because when I left prison, I was already prepared to kill. In-deed, I had reached the conclusion that there was no other way. There was time to try to mobilize the people, but in the final analysis the shit would have to be arbitrated with the gun. You might say, that when I left prison, I was totally preoccupied with the technical aspects of launching the assault against a fortress of fascism that was beginning to take shape out of the ruins of the Kennedy administration. Targets were becoming visible. It was a fair time to shoot. I felt myself to be in an ex-treme minority—what was necessary was to widen that base. The only other people whom I knew firsthand who were ready for war were the convicts I was leaving behind in prison.

According to my thinking, millions of Americans across the land were also ready, but I had not seen them face to face. As far as their existence was concerned, my proof came from observations I'd made from the doubtful perspective of a prison cell, based on the media and the inde-pendent impact of events. I had to see for myself. After hitting the streets, I found that my analysis had not been that much lacking. There was indeed a quorum for revolution in Babylon. I saw the heroic resis-tance put up by the people against the pigs. My only criticism was that the people still clung to the symbols of good, while the enemy had al-ready crossed over to total evil.

It was time for war, a people's war against the fascist pigs, but the people were still calling for peace. The deepest desire of the people—for peace at home and abroad—had been turned around into an argument against violence against pigs. The slogans for peace had never meant that, but this was the pig interpretation. I traveled throughout Babylon, rejecting the Lou Harris–Gallup Polls while taking one of my own: The people were ready to resort to the appropriate method for stopping the pigs, but they were not ready for war, simply because they did not realize, yet, that only war was appropriate.

The accent on youth that had been key to the Kennedy administration helped to define youth as a relevant political condition that was not to be despised—and that could be used. Kennedy had moved to co-opt youth, and succeeded in pulling quite a few. Many white radicals that I met in my travels had been die-hard Kennedyites, not the Peace Corps variety, but of those millions who, out of the religious fervor and morbid honesty of youth, had laid awake at night all bothered and worked up, asking themselves in all seriousness, What Can I Do For My Country? Throughout the land, the answer to their question was being delivered via the pigs' billy clubs. Those who were not directly brutalized by the pigs themselves may as well have been. They all knew someone who had, or television provided them with saturation doses of the vicarious experience.

I set my hopes on the youth. I was convinced that they would make the revolution, and I was not interested in the details. There was a host of Jewish writers who would elucidate that. I, for one, did not believe that all the Jews had become liars. Neither did I believe that all whites were racists dedicated to maintaining a racist set of affairs. I knew that the struggle of black people for national liberation was the foundation of the American Revolution. The antiwar movement, and the support that the antiwar whites gave to the black liberation struggle, was the other key. These were the revolutionary roots buried deeply in the history of America. If the American people were going to rise up and overthrow the fascists, they would do so on the wings of these two dark eagles. It didn't matter if the two dark eagles didn't already realize their vast potential—the Jewish writers would explain it to them. But before that could happen, blacks would have to stir up a white heat. Blacks, who had everything to lose, would—if they moved correctly—have everything to gain.

2

As President John Fitzgerald Kennedy's funeral procession moved slowly down the street, I was watching it all on television in the exercise yard of Folsom Prison. Martin Luther King, his hands thrust stiffly into the pockets of his dark topcoat, stepped from the curb of the sidewalk into the street, staring, as though transfixed, at the horses and the bier as they passed in front of him. King looked thunderstruck, uptight. I wondered what he was thinking. The TV camera studied King's face. Some of the convicts were crying, others were rejoicing.

"He looks like he just lost his best friend," a convict said as he watched King's face on the television screen.

King's reaction to the death of Kennedy posed a sharp contrast to that of Malcolm X, who, a few days later, was suspended from the Black Muslim movement by Elijah Muhammad for observing that Kennedy's assassination was "a case of the chickens coming home to roost."

It is easy to say that the assassination of a president changes the course of history. That the death of Kennedy destroyed Martin Luther King is easy to assert, but difficult to prove. Martin Luther King was not simply a nonviolent fool who thought he was the black reincarnation of Mahatma Ghandi. He had something other than self-delusions up his sleeve. He had a long-range plan, and whatever it was, Kennedy was the key. That look of dread on King's face when Kennedy's coffin passed in front of him, his ambivalent, hesitant gesture of stepping with one foot off the curb, yet keeping the other one there, had an aspect of total confusion about it. He may have known that not only were the remains of JFK passing before him in that box, but also the corpse of his own master plan. With that murderous cracker, Lyndon Johnson, already sworn in as commander in chief, King may even have known then that his own days were numbered. One thing he clearly understood: there were sharpshooters in the land from whom no target could purchase sanctuary. Malcolm knew this too, and he began to call for the black sharpshooters to come forth. It may be that when the history of our times is set into perspective, the assassination of Kennedy will mark the point where politics in America were transformed into war. That may have been what King sensed as he stood there in the street.

It has often been claimed that Afro-Americans turned to violence when nonviolence died. The question becomes, then, when did nonviolence die? Something may be dead long before its corpse begins to stink. If we focus on the assassination of Martin Luther King as marking the death of nonviolence, we may be dealing more with the stink than with the dirty deed. Pursuing this line of thought leads to the flip conclusion that King was Kennedy's puppet. Kennedy did co-opt the nonviolent civil rights movement, that is true, but he did it by harnessing it as one of the vehicles of his own power. And not just because he dug the "Negro Vote," which he did—but because he had neocolonialist designs upon the world, including Afro-America. It was for this reason that Malcolm liked to refer to Kennedy as "The Fox." Malcolm never really looked upon Martin Luther King as an Uncle Tom, although he probably did call him that at various times—but who didn't?

What Kennedy needed inside Babylon was relative peace and stability, and the key to achieving that was a nonviolent civil rights movement, because Kennedy knew that there was and always would be a movement as long as Afro-Americans were oppressed inside Babylon. The fact that Afro-Americans were oppressed was not Kennedy's major concern; there was nothing about his life to indicate that. But since he was stuck with a movement, Kennedy wanted to keep it under control, and since he was at the helm of an empire of violence, the president of a country that was built on and sustained by violence, anything that was nonviolent would seem to be under control—or, at least not dangerous.

On the other hand, Martin Luther King's goal in life was not to be controlled, by Kennedy or anybody else. What he wanted was progress, for his people, and Kennedy could relate to that, as long as the progress was slow, because to him, a movement that moved slowly could be fronted off as peace. Nonviolence is the key. A Noble Prize for peace and a telephone call to Coretta once when King got arrested was a price any fox in Kennedy's position would have been willing to pay. The nightriders of America's ruling circle may not have dug it, but Kennedy knew that he already had them blocked. What he was trying to do was make the block stick.

Kennedy's vision of the world was that every man was equal—the Declaration of Independence–U.S. Constitution–Bill of Rights view—and being the first Irish Catholic President of the United States, he probably believed it in his heart. If some men were rich and others poor, Kennedy could relate to a war on poverty. To his way of thinking, that was better than a war on the rich. And the only possible type of war on poverty that was not also a war on the rich would be a nonviolent war. So rather than call King a puppet, it's better to say that he just fitted neatly into Kennedy's scheme of things, not withstanding the fact that King's vision of the world, of humanity, of the future, was far deeper, greater, and more universal than that held by Kennedy. King's vision, in fact, was noble. But that's not why he was given the Nobel Peace Prize.

Kennedy represented a cross between an Irish cop and an Irish priest. Naturally, cops and priests prefer to deal with a black preacher than, say, a Malcolm X. So Kennedy backed King. That's all King needed, he had Jesus and his Father working for him in Heaven. All he required down here on Earth was someone from on high who would always go his bail. With that in hand, blinded by prayer and brooding over the human suffering that he saw all around him, all over the world, King would have been content to stand outside the gates of Eden a thousand years to convince St. Michael to lay down his flaming sword, to beat it into a plowshare to feed the poor. So, when Kennedy's head was blown away, King's light went out. However, King did not turn and flee the flaming sword. He stood there like David facing Goliath, but without a slingshot. King was still out to save his people, but instead of extinguishing the flame and laying aside his sword, he had to deal with the fact that the guardian at the gate suddenly donned a suit of armor, and Jesus, once again, was nailed to the cross.

3

We were dancing with death, and we knew it. But we did not call for the music to stop. Instead, we called for the band to play louder, stronger, and longer, because the essential objective was to speed up time. The pigs had a head start on us. In one sense, they had been running since time began, but in the sense that mattered, they had been into their game since the day they murdered Kennedy. Memories of the Boston Tea Party and the slave revolts sustained us in our faith. That hard core of beauty at the heart of the American dream was real, but buried. We had to bring it up for air, to blow away the lies and the bloodstained history that had hidden it. I had witnessed in Tennessee, that same Tennessee that later killed King, the white youth of the South take a stand on the side of that better tomorrow straining to be born inside Babylon.

I traveled with Stokely Carmichael to Vanderbilt University, in Nashville, where he was to speak. Martin Luther King was on the same program, to offer nonviolence again. Senator Strom Thurmond, then one of the most dangerous racists in the land, was there to reiterate what he had been repeating for years. Stokely threw the entire state into an uproar. All of the organized forces in the political machinery of Nashville demanded that Stokely not be allowed to speak. They predicted a riot. The state Legislature passed a resolution ordering Vanderbilt to rescind Stokely's invitation. Someone pointed out that the Legislature did not have that power because Vanderbilt was a private school. If it lacked that power, the members of the Legislature didn't seem to know. Nashville's black bourgeoisie, through the mouth of the president of the local branch of the NAACP, invited Stokely to leave town. But the meeting would go on, Stokely would speak, and there would be a riot.

When we walked into the auditorium, King was waiting to speak. Seated in the front row with his legs crossed, King looked tired but still ready to deal with anything. We did not know, and if he did, King did not show it, that just one year after that night, something in that very same state would find him with which he could not deal: a bullet in his head. When King spoke that night, I had a moment of panic. The way he spoke about it, nonviolence seemed not to be dead. The audience received him well, this same audience that the day before had booed Senator Strom Thurmond. Even though someone hung out a Confederate flag from the balcony to greet Stokely, backing up the gesture with a savage rebel yell, the reception of the audience was thunderous. If the crowd was not signaling its approval, at least it was shouting "right on." But one thing was certain: the students were applauding their own victory by defending their right to hear the speakers of their choice. I had sat in on a meeting that the SNCC people had with the Vanderbilt students the day before. Mostly they just looked at each other, struck dumb by the cruel history they shared. They had united against the combination of men and forces that were determined to make it even crueler. For that moment, they defeated the men and the forces, within the limits of that framework of action. That for me confirmed the truth that the people will win when they rise up firmly to defend their rights.

Something else was made clear: the pigs can neither understand nor accept such defeats. The defeat of the pigs has got to be final. They have to be put down so they can't rise up again, even if they will it—and they will. That same night, after Stokely had spoken, Nashville exploded with violence and the signal had been a gunshot, fired, of course, by a pig. The storm troopers of the Nashville Police Department vamped on the black students of Fisk University and Tennessee A&I University. The first night they shot up Fisk, running in rampage throughout the campus. The next night they shot up A&I, but when they tried to storm that campus, the students, barricaded inside their dorms, cut loose at them with guns, and they held the campus for about two days, during which the entire black community became a war zone under siege. The power of the people—this time armed—was again revealed. And the more massive, more brutal power of the state was also seen.

The spirit and the reality of rebellion was everywhere. The common denominator was the pigs. Pigs had invaded the campuses, pigs had attacked the hippies, pigs had vamped on the antiwar movement, and pigs were still all-out on the black man's back, going now, it seemed, for the black man's head. The rebellion in the black community was manifested by the Black Panther Party or local versions of the same thing. In the white community, it was a writhing mass of rebellious humanity that took on sharp outlines around the war in Vietnam and the content of higher education. People were becoming more serious in seeking answers to the pressing questions of the day. James Bond novels disappeared from the best sellers list, and panty raids gave way to raids on secret files in the college president's office to reveal the link between laboratory research and the slaughter in Vietnam. Crowding into phone booths gave way to taking over the dean's office. A rhythm of ups and downs in the American Revolution was defining itself. After the first explosions on the college campuses, it was claimed that the movement was dead. Nothing now seemed further from the truth. A faith was rising that the American Revolution had become self-perpetuating, sustained by its own inner strength. The upsurge of the counter culture, rooted in the beatniks of the fifties, crazy in its politics of dope and love, was a powerful part of the rebellion because its break with Babylon was for keeps. The beatniks had died only a dialectical death and were back now in greater numbers, with longer hair and more relevant politics. They wanted the pigs off their backs so that they could smoke dope, fuck, and listen to music. The black movement, after sinking to a low ebb, was back—and the niggers had guns.

In 1967, after the Black Panther Party first started calling pigs by their real name—pigs—it was interesting to watch that definition catch on and spread. It struck some tortured nerve in the American psyche and relieved it of its pain. It entered the mind like a knife, and stuck. The Pigtorials that appeared in our party newspaper, graphically depicting the true nature of the beast, accelerated the drawing of the line between the people and the pigs. The alacrity with which this image of the guardians of the law was snatched up and employed by the people spoke of alienation deeper than the sea. The sea that we needed, which would allow the American guerrillas to swim around the nation like fish, was there. The chill in those waters was the ice of death, but now death was everywhere, and spreading swiftly.

The coffins were coming back home from the Nam in a rising tide. Those soon to be killed or transfigured in some other ghastly form were being dispatched to the Nam in ever-rising numbers. Millions of American people were turning to the streets to demonstrate their opposition to the war. As it grew clearer to them that Johnson didn't give a fuck what they said or did, I watched their anger mount. Many people just couldn't believe that the government, which they had been taught was theirs, could spit in their faces and mock the blood of their sons with such callous disregard for their opinion. That their sons were dying to save Democracy from Godless Communism began to smell like horseshit straight from LBJ's ranch.

Since the Democrats were in power, the shit could not be blamed on the Republicans, except to say that they were guilty too. Talk started about forming a third party. Many people were saying that electoral politics were dead and if the twitches in that carcass truly were a sign of life, then the coming presidential election, in 1968, would surely end it. In Dearborn, Michigan, the people, through their own initiative, placed the issue of the war on the ballot and voted again for peace. In California, over 200,000 people signed enough petitions to qualify a Third Party under California's fucked-up laws. This party was called the Peace and Freedom Party, speaking explicitly to the issue of war in Vietnam and war in Babylon. Branches of this party, notably in New York, sprang up, and many of the people who could not relate to the calls for violence in the streets found this an acceptable way to strike their blows against the system.

The number one target of the public wrath was Lyndon Johnson. Everyone was squaring off, seeking a vantage point, so that they could be sure to get a piece of his ass. The secret connection between Johnson and Nixon had not yet been revealed, and everybody took it for granted that the old dog, running all his life, would surely run again. The connection between Johnson and Nixon, at least to my mind, was not to become clear until Johnson announced that he would retire. Bursting like a clap of thunder over a movement that had hitched its kite to Johnson's coattails, his announcement showed once again that the fascist conspirators were playing for keeps. Everybody thought that Johnson, out of a love of Humphrey, was stepping aside to make way for him. It wasn't until Robert Kennedy got offed that Johnson's real reason for getting out of sight became clear. If he had looked at all like he was still a candidate, another dead Kennedy out of his way would have been too tall a tale. Later, the plot was to become transparent, sharp enough for the blind to see. With Johnson, Kennedy, and Humphrey all out of the way—the Hump shot down with the Democratic Convention, with a little help from Nixon's friends, the pigs—Nixon was a shoo-in.

4

October 28, 1967

As I hurried up the stairs to my apartment, I could hear the phone inside ringing. I hit the lock with my key and rushed to the phone.

"Where have you been?" It was Barbara Easley. Something, some shrill hint of panic in her voice, made me perk up.

"What's happening," I said, noncommittally, trying to dig where she was coming from.

"Haven't you heard?" she asked in disbelief.

"Tell me," I said.

"Hold onto your hat." Then a long pause. She asked, "You mean you haven't heard anything?"

"No," I said, "I've been out of town, just walked through the door. What's up?"

"Huey is in the hospital, shot pretty bad in the stomach, but alive. One pig is dead and another one is almost dead, shot several times. It happened last night in Oakland. Everybody's trying to find you! Where you been?"

This was the beginning, the unleashing of that rage. My skin was crawling while I tried to sort it out. One pig dead. Good. Another wounded. Good. Huey wounded, bad. But still alive, good.

It had happened. We all knew that it was coming. When, where, how—all had now been answered. The Black Panther Party had at last drawn blood, spilled its own and shed that of the pigs! We counted history from Huey's night of truth.

> *On the night of October 27, 1967, in the wee hours of that darkness, guns blazed in the heart of black Oakland, on 7th and Willow Street. The quiet of the night was shattered by the minor thunder of the guns. Death stalking a circle around warring men and the shadow of death created from the blaze leaping from the barrel of a gun. A pig white lay dead, deep-fried in the fat of his own bullshit, and another pig white lay there, similar to the dead one in every respect except that he did not die. This was a rare moment of death for the oppressor and triumph for the oppressed. This beautiful spark of glory on the streets, in the dark, in Babylon, lights the way for Lil Bobby to find room in which to die a warrior's death and light to show the others who remain and fight how to finish the job of offing the pigs.*

October 27, 1967–April 6, 1968, two dates connected on the grid of time, two events unbilically linked, by blood, by necessity, in that aspiration of the vanguard heart. We measured ourselves by Huey. When he moved, we followed. What he did became our goal. On Huey's night of truth, the Black Panther Party was one year old. As political parties go, still an infant bursting into being. Huey did not make us want to kill. The desire to shed pig blood was already there, burning in our hearts, latent in our genes, inherited from slave ancestors who dreamed of shedding blood for hundreds of years. But Huey sent our spirits soaring when he laid Officer John Frey out, sprawling on the ground in his own blood, and gave new content to our daydreams. He took those dreams down from the clouds and shaped them into bullets. Our fierce, searing hatred of oppression and of our oppressors became focused in a deed, and a winding road disappearing in the haze of a blazing sky stretched out before us.

OFF THE PIGS! This cry burst forth from the innermost recesses of our pain. It was neat and to the point. We meant exactly what it said. Theory and practice rolled up into one. The abstract possibility became concrete in the deed. We wore broad grins on our faces, for we shared a secret. A circle had been closed. The last link in a chain had clicked shut: it was the click of a trigger, metal kissing metal, and Huey was alive, in triumph, and the pig was dead, defeated. We stood before the Deed, transfixed by its truth, transported by the easy calculation of its frequent repetition. It was a pinhead's worth of victory lost in the clutter of the vast reaches of the empire of Babylon, but not lost on us.

Something deep had happened by offing pig Frey—Huey made a profound political statement. The great fear was that we would die, or be killed, before we, too, took our quota of heads. To guarantee against this calamity, one had to move fast, before time ran out. There is no way to accurately access the qualitative leap in consciousness wrought in the Afro-American psyche by Huey's deed. The tidal wave that was to sweep the nation spread out from our midst.

After that phone call from Barbara Easley, I sat by the window of my apartment, watching the cars go by below on Castro street. I sat there for a long time. I remember a black and white patrol car driving past, and I remember thinking of how sweet it would be to snipe those pigs from my window. I felt a sense of power, of tactical advantage, because those pigs didn't even know that I was there and, more than that, they had no idea that I was thinking about how to kill them.

I ran downstairs into the basement under my apartment building, where I kept my guns hidden. I took them out and weighed them in my hands. An M–1 carbine, a 12-gauge shotgun, and a 357 magnum Python.

Later on, I drove over to Oakland to meet with the other Panthers, in a park. There were eight of us. We only had two topics of conversation: how to bust Huey out of jail, how to off some more pigs. Clearly, we knew everything else was irrelevant.

The Black Panther Party then was only one year old. Having founded the party, Huey, through his deed, had given it a soul and launched it on its course, hurling us, at the speed of light, into the unknown future. Lil Bobby was there, grinning from ear to ear, hating all this talk, anxious instead to move against the pigs, impatient for blood.

5

After Huey offed pig officer Frey, I slowly began to hold myself in contempt. With each passing day the situation became more acute. I was lagging. I felt out of it. There are 161 days between October 28, 1967 and April 6, 1968. Each and every one of those days I savored the prospect. I never spoke directly of it with anybody. Yet, a storm was raging inside. Sometimes, I wondered if I was afraid. When I imagined that I myself might be killed, I'd stare dumbly at the image of me dead. I wondered if I was lying when I concluded that I didn't care. I needed to be clear on this point. Was I or was I not willing to die? On some days, the thought refused to settle down and come into focus.

One hundred and fifty-nine days later, Martin Luther King was killed. When I heard the news, I confronted myself again for the briefest moment. The question that had been bugging me vanished, or else was answered. I only knew that it no longer mattered. I loved Martin Luther King—and yet I hated him. I could have killed him myself—yet I could have worked with him. During my lifetime, he was the only man actually to have in his hands the power to liberate our people, and he wouldn't use it. Perhaps he didn't know he had it. Maybe he dreaded all this bloodshed. I think he hoped for a miracle. Dreaming, tarrying, he was blocking Malcolm. Malcolm had him up against the wall, and would have taken that power out of his hands, but he was prevented. If Martin Luther King had been killed before Malcolm. . . .

I had resolved to follow the course that was charted by Malcolm X. When I encountered the Black Panther Party, I knew that this was the thing of gold. For the first ten months—December 12, 1966 to October 27, 1967—it had all been a question of talking. Until then, our shootings were secrets that held. But when Huey killed pig Officer John Frey, our deeds became public. Our work was cut out for us. Huey P. Newton overnight became a symbol containing the potential of epic proportions that would lead us in war. What remained to be done was to put the symbol to work. I took for myself the task of building this symbol. Huey P. Newton had to be born again. Before October would come round again, Huey's conviction for killing pig Frey would be a month old, I would have one month left before I had to leave, but the Black Panther Party would be a national organization that had rallied a revolutionary quorum amongst the American people around Huey Newton.

6

We, the people, forget things too easily, because all we wanted was a decent life. We tend to forget that there are those among us who seek power and glory and will stop at nothing, including destroying themselves, us, and the world, to get it. But I was in prison during the Kennedy years, I watched them come and I watched them go. The Kennedy years came, first of all, because Kennedy was rich. But so was Nixon. The millions behind them were simply what it took to seriously run for president in the United States. After that, it was the promise of what Kennedy would do for people that got him elected. All that shit about Kennedy coming across better on television than Nixon is just that, shit. Nixon comes across as a turd no matter what the media, including face to face. It was what came out of his mouth, what he projected as his vision, that made the people reject him at the polls. His vision was too dim.

The misery that eats away at the hearts of the oppressed derives precisely from how we feel about the past. By their actions in the present, men have the power to maintain a system of oppression, which makes the history of that oppression even colder for its victims. The interpretation of the past that had to be dealt with when John Fitzgerald Kennedy was president was offered by Malcolm X, who uttered naked truth. Such truth needs to put on clothes. Otherwise, it calls for blood. When it is shown that the injustices of our time were rooted in the crimes of the past, and this is clearly seen by enough people, then immediate redress is in order. That comes only through revolution. Kennedy was moving to take the sting out of the past, by dealing with the present, in order to protect the future. Kennedy believed this was the only way to forestall revolution. It was either that or fascist repression. President Kennedy was not a fascist, and that was fatal. America had reached the choice between revolution and fascism. Kennedy hoped to turn both of these aside. Kennedy was killed for opening up the door that had locked out the past, because when Martin Luther King walked in, he brought the past with him.

To the whites who hated him, Kennedy was a fool to even listen to King. But Kennedy wasn't really listening to King. He was listening to Malcolm, to Fidel Castro, to Ho Chi Minh, to Mao Tse-Tung, Patrice Lumumba, and Che Guevara. These revolutionaries convinced Kennedy that it was better to deal with King. He also knew that this change had to come. This is where he united with King. They both knew that the change had to come. What they didn't want, both of them, was for that change to be violent.

On the other hand, there were those who thought that the revolution swirling across the world could be blocked. For the opportunistic majority of America's white racists, the crucial question was: is it possible, by any means, for the blacks to be stopped. All those who say no become fair game for these white hunters, whether they actually get killed or not. But those who say no, and also exercise power, must go. Kennedy knew that there were white men in the land prepared to kill to block that. Kennedy had said no during his campaign for election, and he won. Nixon, telling them yes, the blacks could be stopped with law and order, had been rejected at the polls.

But—Nixon almost won. Some men seem to shrug it off after they lose a race for the presidency. Nixon appeared shattered. He must have really wanted it. He did. He continued to pursue it. He campaigned for eight more years! He got it, and he is going to keep it. You will have to take it away from him. His tactics have become more ruthless.

After the defeat of 1960, Richard Milhous Nixon picked up the gun. And he has never put it down. If Richard Nixon actually didn't have anything to do with all the blood that paved his way to power, it can still be argued that the blood helped him on his way. It can also be argued that if Nixon didn't actually have a hand in the planning, it did not hurt his chances of becoming president if the rightwing forces controlling the army and the police created a situation that destroyed the National Convention of the Democratic Party and absolutely damned their candidate, Humpty Humphrey, to defeat.

To an old man who really wanted to be president, John Fitzgerald Kennedy was bad news. Not only that, there were all those younger brothers. Robert, Teddy, and then John-John. Any old man who really wanted to be president could not deal with that, except with the gun. And Richard Nixon was already old. Not as old as Hoover, but old. And if Ramsey Clark really hated Hoover, then the Kennedys could not have loved him. Nixon was into Hoover, and had been for years, and into every other spy in the land. Not only that, Nixon is from California, where I was in prison. His hometown is Whittier, California, which is the city that hosts the first reform school that I ever went to in my life. Any man from Whittier who became president would have to be a killer. The sun never shines in Whittier, and everything there is white, including politics and history. I'm not saying that Nixon actually killed Kennedy, I'm just raising the question, what if he did?

If there actually were a well-organized, high-level conspiracy behind the assassination of President Kennedy, then what was its goal? To remove him from office. To make way for someone else. Not Johnson, but his clique. Johnson was the key. No matter what happened, Johnson would in fact have the power in his hands. A rightwing coup d'e-tat in Babylon wouldn't necessarily have to be made public. Conceivably, if it went off according to plan, the evidence could be locked up in a vault for a thousand years. And killers sworn to secrecy could be trusted not to tell.

I do not know whether Nixon killed Kennedy, but I do know that he's trying to murder all of our dreams. There was less death in the world under Kennedy. See how the blood has mounted since then! Both Malcolm and King were killed under Johnson, and Nixon has turned us into a nation of pallbearers and gravediggers. In the almost ten years since the killing of Kennedy, the official solution to the racial problem has shifted from integration to a policy that approaches apartheid. The federal government, which was more or less willy-nilly allied with the just aspirations of the blacks under Kennedy, has gone over to the side of the fiends. This titanic turnabout was engineered slowly, by stages, while Johnson and then Nixon talked out of both sides of their mouths. Leave it to them, and they will have you believe that it is all just a question of luck, that no one planned it, and that it all just happened that way.

The Black Panther Party was born under Johnson. Even Malcolm didn't call for the gun until after Kennedy was killed, which shows how reactionary violence begets revolutionary violence, and why we have an internal war on our hands today. The black man has never asked America for miracles, he reserved that to God. Four hundred years of oppression inside Babylon has made him wiser than that. Neither did we ask for Nixon, or Johnson, or the rise of the South. We asked for our civil and human rights. Instead of getting our rights, we have been killed, jailed, and driven underground, en masse. Now we ask for nothing. Instead, we are moving to take what we want.

7

The press gave heavy play to the fact that King was in Memphis to support a strike by that city's garbage men, all of whom were black. Also, he was beating the drums for his Poor People's March on Washington. But his main man, JFK, was no longer in the White House. King didn't fit at all into the cracker strategy plotted by Lyndon Johnson. Besides that, LBJ had made it crystal clear that he took a dim view of poor people marching, except off to war. King, looking for leverage, had finally made a major speech in Atlanta, attacking Johnson's escalations in Vietnam. Also, he had committed the indiscretion of publicly criticizing J. Edgar Hoover, who retaliated, on the public level, by calling King a liar.

King made a tactical retreat from that battle. (Not that King was afraid of Hoover or any other crowned head: He was at his best when clearly overmatched. Kneeling down upon his knees in public, King knew how to turn the power of the mighty into a kind of boomerang.) But King, like many who were vastly better placed and more secure, declined to fuck with Hoover. Rumor had it that King could not deal with the keyhole information that Hoover had amassed on his private life, after years of listening to taps on King's phones and bedrooms, snooping through walls and peeping through misplaced window shades.

King, and his whole philosophy of nonviolent action, was under serious siege from the very bowels of Afro-America. Malcolm X was dead, but the shooting that he had predicted had already started. The torch had been lit, and major cities throughout the land had been set aflame by blacks, who, in total disregard of King's advice, had begun to fight back. Huey P. Newton had already killed pig officer Frey. King knew that blacks were coming for blood. King knew that his fantastic, self-abnegating dictum, "If there must be bloodshed, let it be our blood!" was dead, drowned in the gallons of black blood that had already been let. King died, it is said, still clinging to his belief in nonviolence. There may never be a single clue unearthed to contradict that. But history is replete with examples of aberrations among the clergy, in all directions, to the right and to the left. The examples of men of the cloth who had lain down the Bible and picked up the gun may have begun to nibble away at the outer fringes of his nightmares. Certainly, the center of the Afro-American struggle had shifted several notches to the left, and King knew that he no longer stood on that spot. When he kneeled down to pray now, he knew his was like a voice crying in the wilderness. His speeches became even more filled with dire warnings and lamentations. He might have included in his prayers, during those last days at least, the doubting lines that Jesus was said to have uttered, "My God, why hast Thou forsaken me?"

8

The arrogance of white racist America could no longer be tolerated. Not just our criminals, but even our children were being murdered. What we needed was a way out of that bag. What if there really was a way, for black people through their own initiative, to break the power white America held over them and liberate themselves? What if it really was possible for black people to be safe and secure from the whites, their destiny in their own hands, and that there was nothing, try as they might, that the whites could do to block them? What if there was a foolproof way for black-assed niggers, inside Babylon, to move, successfully, for our freedom? That would mean all niggers who could relate to that would embark, in one way or another, upon that road, and any nigger who could not relate to that could go fuck himself. It took longer than four hundred years, but the Afro-American people, as a whole, have got it into their heads that it is possible for them to be free—free of the tyranny, exploitation, oppression, terror, and sheer racist inhumanity of white America.

"Free at last! Free at last! Thank God Almighty, we are free at last!" In his speech to the more than 250,000 people who marched on Washington in 1963, King quoted those words above, projecting them, after hundreds of years of reiteration by generations of blacks, as still being the guiding goal of our people. This cry from the soul, this mournful, verbal bleeding, was uttered when the first slave catcher put his white hand on the first black flesh. It was set to music and rhyme on the plantations of the South by a people who were blocked and knew themselves to be trapped under the heel. Other peoples were vamped on after us, and, although enslaved, they have taken back their freedom—but we are still uptight.

Many blacks among us *believe* in freedom, but there are some who don't. Many blacks actually believe, in their hearts, that it is impossible for blacks to be liberated from whites, unless whites want it that way. They throw up both hands when blacks talk of liberating themselves. Churches are full of them, but so are the streets. That's why Martin Luther King cannot be accused of being a coward. In fact, he was very brave. What was wrong with him was that he was Christian, and actually believed in God. That's why we called Malcolm X "The Sword."

From the murkiest depths and dungeons of Babylon, an army of black hands reached out to Malcolm. Millions of others reached out to King. But we had become convinced that what was needed to turn the trick was a Black Army, and with that Black Army, we believed, the prize of our freedom could be won. Malcolm brought this realization to the fore. No wonder, then, he began to speak of blood and revolution, saying, "Revolution is bloody, revolution is hostile, revolution knows no compromise, revolution overturns and destroys everything that gets in its way."

The bloods who flocked to join the Black Panther Party did so on the explicit belief that they were joining that army, and that they were going to war. We were going to fight the war to liberate our people, against all who came. We would start with those who were already there, the cops, who occupied our communities and rained down terror upon the heads of our people, without a doubt. That's why we were exasperated with those who looked upon Huey's deed as just a shootout between a black brother and some cops and were glad that Huey had won. To us, that was just the opening round of fire. There would be more. In fact, we began to plan them. The fever was upon us. We wanted to move. We had learned the only language that America understood, violence, and we were determined to speak, and be heard, and have the last word, because we knew that we were right, and that justice was on our side.

But a race of oppressors who have weathered every stormy attempt by the people they oppress to throw off that oppression will never give up their belief that they can still hang on until their power is actually broken. Armed struggle in Babylon, Malcolm taught, was the only way to break those chains. As far back as when Malcolm first said it there were those who believed. Indeed, the belief itself was nothing new. Toussaint L'Ouverture had done it, in Haiti, with guns. And though it happened long ago, perhaps it was a proof that we still needed. Everything else between then and now had gotten crushed, though there had been bold and brave attempts. The defeat of every fallen generation of blacks in Babylon has been a challenge hurled in the face of each succeeding one. And to a freedom fighter, the cruelest fate, the bitterest destiny is to die before the people are free.

This is where King floundered. His strategy of nonviolent resistance was in direct contradiction to the deepest aspirations of the heart. This didn't stop King from being a fine man and an eloquent speaker. But what he was saying began to sound insane. Kennedy was dead. Malcolm was dead. The shooting had already started. Huey P. Newton had already been charged with murder, and was going through the changes of being tried for killing Frey. The Black Panther Party was spreading like a wild prairie fire across Babylon. Black hearts from coast to coast demanded not a fair trial for Huey but that he be set free. We were not fools. There were those of us who had broken with the wolf tickets of the past and we really meant it. We knew exactly what we were doing.

In fact, Malcolm's death had been a signal to move, but the hands that pulled those triggers were black. Those black hands shot us back into two years of shock and forfeit, it took us two years to bounce back. Stokely Carmichael brought the shit halfway back in line. When Huey offed pig Frey, it put us back on target. If we were ultimately mistaken, then we were lost. Even if we were right, we were in trouble. The actual fighting, though it had already started, still had to be done, and carried out to the last shot.

9

April 6, 1968

Suddenly, what I was doing loomed before me as absurd, futile. I switched off the tape recorder, tossed the microphone down, and stood up, staring at my cluttered desk. I was in my cubbyhole in the San Francisco office of *Ramparts* magazine. It was about five P.M. Usually, I would straighten out the things on my desk, lock up in the drawer whatever I didn't want to lose before leaving the office in the evening. But now such gestures seemed meaningless. I looked at my watch. I still had about half an hour to kill. Then, I was to drive to a friend's house, pick up an AR–15 rifle, and transport it across the Bay Bridge, to Oakland, where it was to be used, that very night, against whatever member of the Oakland Police Department happened to appear.

Martin Luther King was dead. He had got it in the neck, shot, by a sniper, while standing on the balcony of his motel room in Memphis, Tennessee. I felt naked and exposed. Later, that night, I was to stand naked again, wounded in the foot, arms raised in surrender to what looked like all the guns in the world thrust in my face by a force of the combined police departments of the San Francisco Bay Area. And while I stood there, Lil Bobby Hutton was blown away by a barrage from those guns, shattering once again the silence of the night that we ourselves had first interrupted with the thunder of our guns, as we moved, with intent to kill, against members of Oakland's thin blue line.

With the same motion that you move away from something old you move into something new. It could be a frantic break away from an old hang-up, or it may be that no thought has been given at all to what lies ahead. One can be fed up with a certain way of doing something, and remaining in that same posture becomes a form of doom. When you're in a situation that you know is killing you, the thrust is toward another scene, toward another set of circumstances, to alter in some fundamental way the prevailing crisis, to shift, if possible, the odds in one's favor.

Stranded in a universe without a God, racing blindly through time and space, without a compass, a map, or even a clear sightline on what it's all about inside our cosmic puzzle, I was in no mood to be fucked with. Since by "fucking with me" I meant things like genocide and slavery, I was prepared to be serious. If I had died a rogue, a rapist, or some other sort of thug, I would not know what to tell my mother, let alone any other human being.

10

Part of my reason for being in hate with the pigs was purely subjective, too close to my heart to be objectified, rationalized, or smuggled into ideology. I say "in hate with the pigs" because I refer to an emotion as enduring as love. If I just hated these pigs, it might pass away, being as transient as only loving somebody. But if I'm in hate with them, just as when one is truly in love, it goes deeper, lasts much longer. Indeed, it has even been said, that when you are in love it shall never die. And I had a true hatred for these pigs. There was nothing in life that I hated more than a prison, recognizing it to be no more and no less than the ultimate restraint in life, this side of the final restraint of execution, legally or illegally imposed. Let me explain.

I have never gone to prison for things I did not do, and I have gone five times. When I found out that the pigs of Babylon were guilty of crimes against humanity surpassing all criteria that can be used to judge social behavior and must be condemned, I was appalled, not because I learned this while I was in prison, but precisely because the same men responsible for imprisoning me and keeping me confined there until they decided I could leave were themselves active participants in criminal practices that had gone on for hundreds of years.

Since they talked so much to the people about justice, "moral values," human rights, and the duty of all citizens to respect and obey by the law, I wanted to see justice done, to them—yes, because they had done it to me. Although I call this being subjective, I distinguish it from being selfish, or egocentric, because without resorting to ideology I knew that I was standing on my rights, rights that existed before men had defined them or gave them any ideological framework.

I saw no reason why these criminals should not be stopped, and then, if we capture them alive, held to answer before a revolutionary tribunal of the people. My vision of myself was that I had gotten into that, and I didn't want, or feel the need, for any other life. I became part of an army that had been marching down through history. My people had been enslaved inside Babylon. Enslaved—if you can dig it. Enslaved! (I still sit and marvel at that state: *Slavery.* It's eerie to even think about what it really means.) And even if there is no God, and my mother's prayers were blind, if a black man in Babylon can hear anything he should hear all the prayers of all the black mothers who have kneeled and prayed on that soil.

I believed that it was the central duty of every Afro-American to fight for the freedom and the liberation of our people. I believed that it was the duty of every American to fight to establish in reality a government of the people, by and for them. I believed in the rights enshrined in the Bill of Rights and in all the other documents that spoke in such clear measure about human rights. I believed that all of this was interconnected, that the struggle of my people was part of the struggle of the American people, that the struggle of the American people was part of the struggle of the people of the world, and that the struggle of the people of the world was part of the struggle that had been the history of the world—the struggle of the people for a better life, against systems that oppress us and suffocate our hearts, against all existing status quos from their inception, against the usurpation of the machinery of the state and it's use as an instrument of repression, against everything that in anyway contributes to the existence of a world in which people can be enslaved. There can be no higher duty for a man than to destroy or control all the forces that threaten the very existence of his people. If that meant that I had to change my own life then my life would just have to change. The same held true for everybody else.

I could dig men throughout history who have picked up the gun, or the rock, or the stick, or the arrow, and all those who had faced fire to get at the enemy, I could dig most of all. Maybe I felt I the need to purge myself of some secret guilt, maybe I knew that I had debts to society that society didn't even know that I owed, or maybe what I felt that I owed could not be collected, or even measured by the commercial terms used in Babylon. Maybe what I owed had nothing to do with trade or goods, maybe because all that I really believed in, lost as I am in space, was that my death will be the price I pay to live. I reached this conclusion through a process of inversion, since I did not know what lay beyond the moment of death, but I am bombarded by voices from the past that are speaking to me now because they spoke out during their time. So, to compensate for that possible nothing, I saw no reason for not dealing with it all, here and now.

After his parole from a nine-year stay in prison, Eldridge Cleaver became a writer for Ramparts *magazine, whose efforts had been crucial to his release.* Ramparts *was a unique radical monthly then, a slick magazine with extraordinary cover art, about the size of* Time *magazine. It published the works of a constellation of artists, writers, and scholars critical of the Vietnam War and social policies of the government and it enjoyed a national circulation. One of Cleaver's first assignments was to cover the controversial Black Power spokesman Stokely Carmichael. At the time this article was written, Carmichael was the Chairman of the Student Nonviolent Coordinating Committee (SNCC) and Cleaver was identified as the chair of the San Francisco Bay Area's Malcolm X Afro-American Society.*

MY FATHER AND
STOKELY CARMICHAEL

My father, at whose house I had spent the night after arriving in Chicago, accompanied me to the SNCC office. "Jesus," he said, "this is really rock bottom. This is the poorest section of the Negro part of town. Why would anyone want to set up an office down here?" My father is not too hip to the action these days. He's like many old Negroes: They woke up on the white man late in their lives and are very bitter to learn that they have been tricked. The building was an old wooden apartment house about five stories high with a faded brownstone exterior. You had second thoughts about opening the door to go in. SNCC was on the third floor. We made our way up the dark stairs and knocked on the door.

"Who is it?" A girl's voice filtered through the door. It must have been only a ritual you go through before opening your door to anyone, because when I answered "Eldridge," the door was opened. She'd never seen me, but she stepped back to let us come in. Inside, a record player was booming out John Coltrane. A chubby little baby was romping about on the floor, and an intense young black man was hunched over a typewriter painfully pecking at the keys. I explained who I was, and said I had arranged to meet Stokely Carmichael.

The girl regarded me narrowly for a moment, her intelligent brown eyes emitting a very soft twinkle. Softness was her central quality. She looked soft and warm, soft and brown, and her hair was worn in the natural style of blacks who are no longer ashamed of the hair with which their race is endowed. We took off our coats and the girl got on the phone and started calling people to find out where Stokely was. "I know he's supposed to be here at twelve-thirty," she said.

The youth at the typewriter turned out to be the son of Sarah Wright, the noted black poet. He was busy working on an essay attacking American imperialism both abroad and in the black ghettos. He kept picking up books from his desk and asking me if I had read them: *Das Kaptial,* Nkrumah's *Neo-Colonialism, The Wretched of the Earth.*

"I want to go to Africa to study," he kept saying, "I got to get ready, I got to get my stuff together."

The girl hung up the phone and turned to me. "Stokely will be available about one o'clock."

I didn't want to hang around that office with my father until one o'clock, mainly because he had begun asking a barrage of questions: Who's Nkrumah? Who wrote that book? So I told them that I would go pick up my luggage and hustle right back. Pa and I had lunch together. Then he ran and got his camera and started snapping pictures of me. I explained to him that this was a very important assignment for me and I had better get back alone because these people might not like it if I brought anyone else along.

When I got back to the SNCC office there was another cat there. He turned out to be David Llorens, a black writer whose works I knew. He had been sent over to take me to Stokely.

We sped through the icy Chicago streets towards the house where we were to meet Carmichael. He was sitting on the couch with a telephone in his hand. In the days to come I was to be with Carmichael almost constantly, and when he was not moving, making speeches, or eating, he was on the telephone. He simply could not sit down for ten minutes

without being called to the phone or feeling the urge to call someone
up himself.

We ate, ran red lights to get downtown as fast as possible. Stokely was
an hour late for a TV taping with Irv Kupcinet, Chicago's leading TV
personality. A white lady got on the up elevator. She was reading a sheaf
of papers and didn't notice us until the elevator doors closed. Then she
looked to her left and flinched when she saw Cleveland Sellers, immediately averting her eyes. Then she looked to her right and there was
Carmichael in his ubiquitous dark glasses. Finally, she looked back over
her shoulder into my face. She suddenly grew very rigid and seemed to
shrivel up. When she reached her floor she rushed from the elevator as
though from some evil presence. After the doors had closed we all had
a big laugh. "They can't do with us and they can't do without us,"
Carmichael said.

When the elevator reached Kupcinet's studio, a throng, Kupcinet in
the center, was waiting. Carmichael was rushed to his seat. Center stage
was set up with a coffee table surrounded on three sides by comfortable
couches facing the TV cameras. Seated on one of the couches was Congressman Roman Pucinski, a member of Adam Clayton Powell's House
Education and Labor Committee and a leader in the fight to strip Powell of his chairmanship. Also present were Archibald Carey, a Negro
judge and the preacher of a large Negro Christian church; Rich C.
Kriegel, a representative of the U.S. State Department; and Studs Terkel,
a liberal Chicago radio commentator.

The show started out amiably enough with a few mild questions
about Adam Clayton Powell and the then fresh news of the action
against him in Congress. Congressman Pucinski rambled off all the
clichés against Powell, and endorsed every one of them. Then
Carmichael got to talk. He wanted to know why Pucinski and his fellow
congressmen were so willing to strip Powell of his position but wouldn't
raise a finger to oust congressmen from Mississippi and Alabama who
held their seats because Negroes had been intimidated, murdered, and
kept from voting.

Carmichael then talked about Vietnam. He had brought with him a
briefcase filled with authoritative material because he wanted to be able
to back up every remark with quotes from respectable types. Congressman Pucinski, the man from the State Department, and Judge Carey
carried the ball for the Johnson administration, while Carmichael and

Terkel emerged united against them. "I'm not being political!" Carmichael would scream. "We're discussing the lives of human beings. Men, women and children are being butchered in Vietnam every day. I'm talking about murder.

Murder! Do you hear? I'm talking about the fact that if I kill a man with slanted eyes on the street, I go to jail, but if I do it in Vietnam, I get a medal. I'm talking about who has the right to tell me to go commit murder. Who has the right to define for me who my enemies are? Killing another person is the most serious step that a man can take. If I ever reach the point where I want to kill someone, I'm going to be the one who makes that decision."

Pucinski, Carey, and Kriegel couldn't understand why Carmichael said that he would not fight in that war, or why Terkel was so concerned about America becoming a nation of moral monsters. After it became clear that it was hopeless to try to communicate on those issues, Carmichael said, "Hey, Bobby Dylan has the perfect line for you cats: 'You know something is happening but you don't know what it is, do you Mr. Jones.'" Just before the show broke up, Carey sighed heavily, admitted that he was confused and that most of what had been said that day had gone over his head. The State Department's man made an announcement that he was opening a recruiting office in the area and he gave a long list of the various skills in which he was interested. When he had finished, David Llorens said, "He didn't say poets; he doesn't want any poets!" It was out luck to get into the same elevator with the man from the State Department. All the way down David Llorens kept asking him, "Why don't you ask for poets?" And the State Department man kept answering, "I didn't read all the list, I didn't read all the list."

As we drove away from the studio, the radio was blowing black music. It was during this drive that I began to form my picture of Carmichael. The record "Tell it Like It Is" began playing. This is a soulful song, the blues, of the people. When it first came on, Carmichael gave a loud whoop, clapped his hands and began singing along with the radio. I wondered how Martin Luther King or Whitney Young or Roy Wilkins would have reacted to the same music.

We headed down to the ghetto to talk to the black nationalists at the headquarters of a group called ACT for Freedom. There were about 200 black radicals inside waiting for Stokely. The first question took us all by surprise. "Stokely," a cat with a Jomo Kenyatta skull cap asked, "What're you doing downtown talking to white folks? Why don't you have time for your own people?"

"I don't know what you mean when you say I don't have any time for my own people. For the past six years my entire life has gone to my people."

"Then why is it that every time you come to Chicago," another cat asked, "you always come to talk to white folks?"

This was followed by a barrage of similar statements. They knew Stokely was going to speak that evening at the University of Chicago. At least ten people voiced similar points of view, and they became increasingly bitter. I was surprised to see that Stokely was sitting in front of the throng with his legs crossed, listening very calmly to criticism that had become very personal. He broke his silence at one point to say, "My record speaks for itself," but mostly he just heard them out. One of them quoted LeRoi Jones on the futility of talking to white folks. Then they quieted down to hear Stokely defend himself.

"I came to Chicago to speak at the University because some people there got together, set up a meeting, sold tickets, and asked me to come. That was a paid engagement. We need money to operate, brothers and sisters. Those are the hard facts of life. You cats sit here and talk all this shit, but what are you doing? If you want me to come here and speak to you, why don't you organize a meeting and then ask me to come? Are you willing to finance my activity? Are you? This is one of the major pitfalls of black people. We want to control our organizations, but we are not willing to support them. Then when we see someone else trying to do the job the best he can instead of lending a hand, we lay back and take pot shots at him.

"I'm going to tell you cats just like it is. My base is in the South. I have support in the South. But you cats are not really with me. The police could grab me and beat my head in, and you cats won't do a goddamn thing about it. But when the police messed with me in Atlanta, niggers got together and tore the town up—and they let me go. The police let me go because they knew that the black people weren't going to just stand around and let them fuck over me. We've got to understand that. We've got to make the white man understand that there are 20,000,000 black people. That's why I'm supporting Adam Clayton Powell. I'm not supporting Powell because I think he is such a shining example to black people. I'm supporting Powell because he's the most powerful black politician this country has ever had. So when they stripped him of his power they were castrating a black man who was in a position to help us.

"We have just started our drive to organize black people in the Northern ghettos. We have to proceed the best way we know how. And you cats shouldn't be waiting around for us to come in. Get up and start organizing the people. *Organize!* That is the only thing that counts."

"Stokely," one man asked, "why don't you move to Chicago and help us get rid of Martin Luther King?"

Stokely broke into a smile. The mood of the meeting had shifted, and from that moment on there was no more criticism of Stokely. It became clear that the earlier criticism was something of a ritual. The full love which they all felt for him began to flow through the room, and you could feel it in the air. "We can't be everywhere at once," Stokely answered. "And we don't want to get into a fight with King. We have enough on our hands fighting the Man. Daley would like nothing better than for SNCC to get into a fight with King. That way he could get rid of us both. If you want to get rid of King—or anybody else—it's up to you to get together right here in Chicago. There are enough black people in Chicago to take over—if you get together and get rid of the Uncle Toms. Once you start organizing you'll find that things start happening and you'll be able to do anything. And don't worry about ideology. I always say that my work is my ideology. You'll find that after you get going, your ideology will develop out of your struggle."

At that point Cleveland Sellers, program coordinator for SNCC, stepped in. "I'm sorry folks, but he has to go. We're already late. We were supposed to be at the University at eight o'clock."

"Let the white folks wait!" somebody shouted from the back of the room. "We waited 400 years for them, so let the bastards wait on us now!"

From backstage at the University hall, we could see that the ACT cats had done a very peculiar thing. They had stationed themselves around the hall at strategic points, similar to the way in which the Fruit of Islam elite guards stand at Black Muslim meetings. They were guarding Stokely. They appeared to be unarmed.

During the question period following Stokely's enthusiastically received speech, a white girl asked him who the guys standing guard were, and if he thought he needed protection from the white students.

"Do you want me to introduce you to them?" Stokely asked her. "They are a beautiful bunch of black brothers. They are looking out for me."

There has always been the drama in the black psyche in America that a generation of men would arise and go back to the South to strike the chains from the slavemaster's minds. Stokely Carmichael belongs to the first generation of Negroes who had the courage to return. The generations of Negroes who kicked off the sit-ins among black college students is different from anything that has gone before. Now it is six years later and these youngsters have grown into tough, battle-tested veterans. They have become conscious revolutionaries. Having started out trying to change the world by forcing America to re-examine its conscience, these revolutionaries have been frustrated in that approach, and they now look with scorn upon doctrines that ask them to love their enemy. Carmichael says: "I'm not in the Movement out of love. I'm in the Movement because I hate. I hate racism and I'm out to smash it or it's going to smash me. When we first went down South, the papers tried to make it look like we wanted to sit next to Bull Conner and Ross Barnett and eat hot dogs. That's a lie. We went down South to render those crackers impotent over our lives."

They went South. In this fact is contained a revolution. There is a vast difference between Negroes who are willing to go South and all those generations whose ambition was to flee the South. A cycle has been completed. The real work for the liberation of black people has begun.

A new cycle has begun in another way, too: the great popular black nationalist leaders like Marcus Garvey, Elijah Muhammad, and Malcolm X all never finished high school. Stokely Carmichael is the first of his stature to receive a college degree.

The history of the national liberation struggles in Africa and in the world in general hints that the success of the struggle for liberation awaits the arrival of intellectuals who have thrown off the shackles of the slave and are willing to put their talents and genius selflessly to work for the masses. Up until now, one of the traditional complaints of the black masses has been of the treachery of black intellectuals. Most of the first rate black writers America has produced have been men with little or no formal education, such as Richard Wright and James Baldwin. And of the first rate black writers, like W. E. B. DuBois and Ralph Ellison, who have had a formal education, none until now have been able to communicate with the black masses of his time. But today the college-educated LeRoi Jones is part of a new generation of black writers, just as Stokely Carmichael is part of a new generation of radical black leaders.

Among Stokely's important future plans is a trip to Africa. This trip will be a key move in SNCC's drive to internationalize black America's struggle for human rights. But contrary to a lot of doctrinaire black nationalists, Stokely believes that the most important area outside the USA, as far as forging working alliances is concerned, is Latin America. Within the next ten years, the struggle for liberation from American domination throughout Latin America will provide black America with some very important and strong allies. By turning such a hopeful eye toward Latin America, Carmichael gives a hint of a quality that is forever breaking through and which distinguishes him from a lot of black nationalists who have been overtly influenced by the racist philosophy of the Black Muslims. "We've got to learn who to coalition with and who not to coalition with. We've got to make specific alliances on specific issues. My enemy's enemy is my friend. I may not love him; I may even hate him. But if he can help me get the hooks and claws of the eagle out of my throat, I want to talk to him."

The Student Nonviolent Coordinating Committee has already formed an official, public alliance with the independence movement in Puerto Rico. SNCC has agreed to throw its influence behind Puerto Rican nationalists in their struggle for U.N. membership and recognition as a sovereign nation. In turn, the Puerto Rican nationalists have committed themselves to an all-out effort to raise the problem of black America before the U.N. and to lobby unceasingly for support in this effort from the Afro-Asian bloc.

Carmichael is very bitter against people who refuse to take a principled stand on the issue. He says, "When Muhammad Ali took a stand against the war in Vietnam, I was very happy, because now I had someone else to back me up. But when white America screamed on the cat and he folded up, that did not make me too happy."

The essence of what Carmichael is doing is calling for a showdown with racism. He says, "the civil rights movement was good because it demanded that blacks be admitted into the system. Now we must move beyond the state of demanding entry to the new stage of changing the system itself." He is calling for a showdown. In this context, he, along with other activists I talked with during the tour, was very resentful of the passive role the Black Muslims have been playing. "They talk strong, but they won't do anything but kill another black man," one man told me.

Each time he gave a talk, Stokely would quote *Alice in Wonderland*. "'When I use a word,' Humpty Dumpty said in a rather scornful tone, 'it means just what I choose it to mean, neither more nor less.'

'The question is,' said Alice, 'whether you *can* make words means so many different things.'

'The question is,' said Humpty Dumpty, 'who is to be master, that's all.'"

Stokely told his audiences that one of the most important aspects of the struggle for Black Power was the right to define. Black people have been the victims of white America's definitions. White people defined black people as inferior, as Negroes and niggers, as second-class citizens. By reacting to white America's definitions, the blacks allowed themselves to be put in a bag which white America controlled. But now black people must demand the right to define themselves. White America has defined black as evil, Carmichael explains. "I have a little syllogism for that. According to America, everything black is evil; I am black, therefore, I am evil.

"There is something wrong with that," he goes on to explain, "because I am black and I am good." He never fails to score heavily with his audience when he says that.

His favorite example of this always elicited a hysterical response, from both black and white audiences. "Here's a perfect example of the power to define in action. During the civil rights movement, black leaders would say: 'We want to integrate.' And then white people would come along and define what integration means. They'd say: 'You want to integrate? That means that you want to marry my daughter.' What the Negro leaders had actually meant was that they wanted more jobs, better schools, housing, and an end to police brutality, and things like that. But when the whites defined integration as meaning blacks wanted to marry their daughters, these leaders lost out by reacting to the white definition. 'We don't want to be your brother-in-law, we want to be your brother. We don't want to live in your bedroom, we just want to live next door.'

"The point is that when these Negroes started reacting to these white definitions, they were backed against the wall before they knew what was happening. They had come in with an indictment that put white America on the defensive. But by allowing white America to define what integration meant, these Negroes allowed themselves and the people for whom they spoke to be placed on the defensive. That is a bunch of crap.

What we must do is define our own terms. When whites come to me with that crap, I just tell them, look, 'Your daughter, your wife, your sister, your mama—the white woman is not the queen of the earth, she's not the Virgin Mary. The white woman can be made just like any other woman. Now let's move on.' We must not react to white definitions.

"When I say Black Power, I know exactly what I'm talking about. But the white man runs up to me and says, 'Black Power: that means violence, doesn't it?' I refuse to react to that. I know what I'm talking about. If the white man doesn't know what I'm talking about, that's his problem, because black people understand me and that is who I'm talking to anyway."

On this same point, Carmichael points out how forces hostile to the black liberation struggle can steal the fire of the movement by co-opting its slogans. He says that LBJ killed the civil rights movement the moment he stood before nationwide TV and said, "We shall overcome." "But he will never," Carmichael says, stand before the nation and say, 'We want Black Power.'"

While confined in California's Vacaville Prison after his arrest on April 6, 1968, for his role in a shoot-out between the Oakland police and Black Panthers, Cleaver managed to smuggle out the following letter, which was originally published in Ramparts magazine.

THE COURAGE TO KILL:
MEETING THE PANTHERS

I fell in love with the Black Panther Party immediately upon my first encounter with it; it was literally love at first sight. It happened one night at a meeting in a dingy little storefront on Scott Street in the Fillmore district, the heart of San Francisco's black ghetto. It was February 1967. The meeting was the latest in a series of weekly meetings held by a loose coalition functioning under the name of the Bay Area Grassroots Organizations Planning Committee. The purpose of the coalition was to coordinate three days of activities with the worthy ambition of involving the total black community in mass action commemorating the fourth anniversary of the assassination of Malcolm X. The highlight and culmination of the memorial was to be the appearance of Sister Betty Shabazz, Malcolm X's widow, who was to deliver the keynote speech at a mass meeting at the Bayview Community Center in Hunter's Point.

Among the topics on the agenda for this fortuitous meeting was the question of providing security for Sister Betty during the twenty-four hours she was to be our guest in the Bay Area. There was a paranoia around—which I did not share—that assassins by the dozens were lurking everywhere for the chance to shoot Sister Betty down. This fear, real or imagined, kept everybody uptight.

I had arrived at the meeting late, changing at the last minute a previous decision not to attend at all. I was pissed off at everyone in the room. Taking a seat with my back to the door I sat there with, I'm sure, a scornful frown of disdain upon my face. Roy Ballard (if the normal brain had three cylinders his would have one) sat opposite me, across the circle formed by the placement of the chairs. He, above all, understood the expression on my face, for he had done the most to put it there; this accounted, I thought, for the idiot grin on his own.

On Roy's left sat Ken Freeman, chairman of the now defunct Black Panther Party of Northern California, who always looked to me like Dagwood, with his huge round bifocals and the bald spot in the front of his natural. On Roy's right sat a frightened-looking little mulatto who seemed to live by the adage, "It's better to remain silent and be thought a fool than to open one's mouth and remove all doubt." He probably adopted that rule from observing his big fat yellow wife, who was seated on his right and who had said when I walked in, just loud enough for me to hear, "Shit! I thought we agreed after last week's meeting that *he* wouldn't be allowed to attend any more meetings!"

Next to her sat Jack Trueblood, a handsome, earnest youth in a black Russian cap who represented San Francisco State College's Black Students Union and who always accepted whatever tasks were piled upon him, insuring that he would leave each weekly meeting with a heavy load. On his right sat a girl named Lucky. I could never tell why they called her that—not, I'm sure, because she happened to be Roy Ballard's old lady; maybe because she had such a beautiful smile.

Between Lucky and myself sat Marvin Jackmon, who was known as a poet, because after Watts went up in flames he had composed a catchy ditty entitled "Burn, Baby, Burn!" and a play entitled *Flowers for the Trashman*. (It is hard for me to write objectively about Marvin. My association with him, dating from the third week of December 1966, ended in mutual bitterness with the closing of the Black House. After getting out of prison that month, he was the first person I hooked up with. Along with Ed Bullins, a young playwright who now has a few things going for himself off-Broadway, and Willie Dale, who had been in San Quentin with me and was trying to make it as a singer, we had founded the Black House in January 1967. Within the next two months the Black House, located in San Francisco, became the center of non-Establishment black culture throughout the Bay Area.)

On my right sat Bill Sherman, an ex-member of the Communist Party and at that time a member of the Central Committee of the Black Panther Party of Northern California. Next to Bill was Victoria Durant, who dressed with what the black bourgeoisie would call "style" or, better yet, "class." She seemed so out of place at those meetings. We were supposed to be representing the common people—grassroots—and here was Victoria ready to write out a $50 check at the drop of a hat. She represented, as everyone knew, the local clique of black Democrats who wanted inside info on everything even hinting of "organizing" in their stomping grounds—even if the price of such info was a steady flow of $50 checks.

Then there was Marianne Waddy, who kept everybody guessing because no one was ever sure of where or what she really was. One day she'd be dressed in flowing African gowns with her hair wrapped up in a pretty *skashok,* the perfect picture of the young Afro-American lady who had established a certain identity and relationship to traditional African culture. The next day she would be dressed like a man and acting like a man who would cut the first throat that got in his way.

Next to Marianne sat a sneaky-looking fellow called Nasser Shabazz. Sitting between Nasser and Ken Freeman, completing the circle, was Vincent Lynch, as smooth and black as the ebony statues he had brought back from his trip to Nigeria and the only member of the Black Panther Party of Northern California I ever liked or thought was sincere. Somewhere in the room, too, was Ann Lynch, Vincent's wife, with their bright-eyed little son, Patrice Lumumba Lynch. Ann was the head of Black Care, the women's auxiliary to this Panther Party. These sisters spent all of their time talking about the impending violent stage of the black revolution, which was inevitable, and how they, the women, must be prepared to care for the men who would be wounded in battle.

I had come out of prison with plans to revive the Organization of Afro-American Unity, the vehicle finally settled upon by Malcolm X to spearhead the black revolution. The OAAU had never really got off the ground, for it was stopped by the assassin's bullets that felled Malcolm on the stage of the Audubon Ballroom in New York City. I was amazed that no one else had moved to continue Malcolm's work in the name of the organization he had chosen, which seemed perfect to me and also logically necessary in terms of historical continuity. The three-day memorial, which was but part of the overall plan to revive the OAAU, was to be used as a forum for launching the revival. In January, I had put the plan on paper and circulated it throughout the Bay Area, then issued a general call for a meeting to establish a temporary steering committee that would see after things until the start of the memorial. At this time we would have a convention, found the Bay Area branch of the Organization of Afro-American Unity, and elect officers whom Sister Betty Shabazz would install, giving the whole effort her blessings in a keynote address on the final day of the memorial.

By February the plan had been torn to shreds. If the plan was a pearl, then I had certainly cast it before swine, and the biggest swine of all, Roy Ballard, had hijacked the plan and turned it into a circus. It soon became clear that if the OAAU was to be reborn, it would not be with the help of this crew, because all they could see was the pageantry of the memorial. Beyond that, their eyes blotted out all vision. Far from wanting to see an organization develop that would put an end to the archipelago of one-man showcase groups that plagued the black community with division, they had each made it their sacred cause to insure the survival of their own splinter group.

From the beginning, when the plan was first put before them, they took up each separate aspect and chewed it until they were sure it was either maimed for life or dead. Often after an idea had gone around the circle, if it still showed signs of life they would pounce upon it and rend it some more. When they finished, all that was left of the original plan was a pilgrimage to the site where a sixteen-year-old black youth, Matthew Johnson, had been murdered by a white cop; putting some pictures of Malcolm X on the walls of the Bayview Community Center; a hysterical speech by Ken Freeman; and twenty-four hours of Sister Betty Shabazz's time.

In all fairness, however, I must confess that the whole plan was impossible to achieve, mostly because it did not take into account certain negative aspects of the black man's psychological heritage from four hundred years of oppression here in Babylon. Then, too, I was an outsider. Having gone to prison from Los Angeles, I had been paroled to San Francisco. I was an interloper unfolding a program to organize *their* community. Fatal. It didn't matter to them that we were dealing with the concept of the Black Nation, of colonized Afro-America, and that all the boundaries separating our people were the stupid impositions of the white oppressors and had to be obliterated. Well, no matter; I had failed. Proof of my failure was Roy Ballard, sitting there before me like a gaunt buzzard, presiding over the carcass of a dream.

Suddenly the room fell silent. The crackling undercurrent that for weeks had made it impossible to get one's point across when one had the floor was gone; there was only the sound of the lock clicking as the front door opened, and then the soft shuffle of feet moving quietly toward the circle. Shadows danced on the walls. From the tension showing on the faces of the people before me, I thought the cops were invading the meeting, but there was a deep female gleam leaping out of one of the women's eyes that no cop who ever lived could elicit. I recognized that gleam out of the recesses of my soul, even though I had never seen it before in my life: the total admiration of a black woman for a black man. I spun round in my seat and saw the most beautiful sight I had ever seen: four black men wearing black berets, powder blue shirts, black leather jackets, black trousers, shiny black shoes—and each with a gun! In front was Huey P. Newton with a riot pump shotgun in his right hand, barrel pointed down to the floor. Beside him was Bobby Seale, the handle of a .45 caliber automatic showing from its holster on his right hip, just below the hem of his jacket. A few steps behind Seale was Bobby Hutton, the barrel of his shotgun at his feet. Next to him was Sherwin Forte, an M–1 carbine with a banana clip cradled in his arms.

Roy Ballard jumped to his feet. Licking his lips, he said, "For those of you who've never met the brothers, these are the Oakland Panthers."

"You're wrong," said Huey P. Newton. "We're not the Oakland Panthers. We happen to live in Oakland. Our name is the Black Panther Party."

With that the Panthers seated themselves in chairs along the wall, outside the circle. Every eye in the room was riveted upon them. What amazed me was that Roy Ballard did not utter one word in contradiction, nor was there any other yakkity-yak around the room. There was absolute silence. Even little Patrice Lumumba Lynch seemed to sit up and take notice.

Where was my mind at? Blown! Racing through time, racing through the fog of a perspective that had just been shattered into a thousand fragments. Who are these cats? I wondered at them, checking them out carefully. They were so cool and it seemed to me not unconscious of the electrifying effect they were having on everybody in the room. Then I recalled a chance remark that Marvin Jackmon had once made. We were discussing the need for security at the Black House because the crowds were getting larger and larger and we had had to bodily throw out a cat who was high and acting like he owned the place. I said that Marvin, Ed, Dale and I had better each get ourself a gun. As I elaborated on the necessity as I saw it, Marvin said: "You need to forget about the Black House and go across the bay and get with Bobby Seale." And then he laughed.

"Who is Bobby Seale?" I asked him.

At first he gave no answer, he seemed to be carefully considering what to say. Finally he said, "He's arming some brothers across the bay." Though I pressed him, he refused to go into it any further, and at the time it didn't seem important to me, so I forgot about it. Now, sitting there looking at those Panthers, I recalled the incident with Marvin. I looked at him. He seemed to have retreated inside himself, sitting there looking like a skinny black Buddha with something distasteful and menacing on his mind.

"Do you brothers want to make a speech at the memorial?" Roy Ballard asked the Panthers.

"Yes," Bobby Seale said.

"O.K.," said Ballard. "We have the program broken down into subjects: Politics, Economics, Self-Defense and Black Culture. Now which section do you brothers want to speak under?" This was the sort of question which in my experience had always signaled the beginning of a two-hour debate with this group.

"It doesn't matter what section we speak under," Huey said. "Our message is one and the same. We're going to talk about black people arming themselves in a political fashion to exert organized force in the political arena to see to it that their desires and needs are met. Otherwise there will be a political consequence. And the only culture worth talking about is a revolutionary culture. So it doesn't matter what heading you put on it, we're going to talk about political power growing out of the barrel of a gun."

"O.K.," Roy Ballard said. He paused, then added, "Let's put it under Politics." Then he went on to start the specific discussion of security for Sister Betty, who would pick her up at the airport, etc. Bobby Seale was jotting down notes in a little black book. The other Panthers sat quietly, watchfully.

Three days before the start of the memorial, I received a phone call from Los Angeles. The man on the other end identified himself as Hakim Jamal, Malcolm X's cousin by marriage. He would be arriving with Sister Betty, he said, and both of them wanted to talk with me. They had liked, it turned out, an article on Malcolm that I had written and that was published in *Ramparts*. We agreed that when they got in from the airport I would meet them at the *Ramparts* office in San Francisco.

On the day that Sister Betty and Hakim Jamal were to arrive in San Francisco, I was sitting in my office tinkering with some notes for an article. One of the secretaries burst through the door. Her face was white with fear and she was shouting, "We're being invaded! We're being invaded!"

I couldn't tell just who her invaders were. Were the Chinese coming? Had the CIA finally decided to do *Ramparts* in? Then she said, "There are about twenty men outside with guns!"

I knew that Hakim Jamal and Sister Betty had arrived with their escort of armed Black Panthers.

"Don't worry," I said, "they're friends."

"Friends?" she gasped. I left her there with her eyes bugging out of her head and rushed to the front of the building.

I waded through *Ramparts* staff jammed into the narrow hallway, fending off the frightened inquiries by repeating, "It's all right, it's all right." The lobby resembled certain photographs coming out of Cuba the day Castro took Havana. There were guns everywhere, pointed toward the ceiling like metallic blades of grass growing up out of the sea of black faces beneath the black berets of the Panthers. I found Hakim Jamal and Sister Betty surrounded by a knot of Panthers, who looked calm and self-possessed in sharp contrast to the chaotic reactions their appearance had set off. Outside where Broadway ran in four lanes to feed the freeway on-ramp and to receive the heavy traffic from the off-ramp, a massive traffic jam was developing and sirens could be heard screaming in the distance as cops sped our way.

I took Jamal and Sister Betty to an office down the hall. We talked for about fifteen minutes about Malcolm. Sister Betty, her eyes concealed behind dark glasses, said nothing after we were introduced. She looked cool enough on the surface, but it was clear that she felt hard-pressed. Huey P. Newton was standing at the window, shotgun in hand, looking down into the upturned faces of a horde of police. I left the room to get Sister Betty a glass of water, squeezing past Bobby Seale and what seemed like a battalion of Panthers in the hall guarding the door. Seale's face was a chiseled mask of determination.

A few yards down the hall, Warren Hinckle III, editor of *Ramparts,* was talking to a police lieutenant.

"What's the trouble?" the lieutenant asked, pointing at the Black Panthers with their guns.

"No trouble," Hinckle said. "Everything is under control."

The policeman seemed infuriated by this answer. He stared at Bobby Seale for a moment and then stalked outside. While I was in the lobby a TV cameraman, camera on his shoulder, forced his way through the front door and started taking pictures. Two white boys who worked at *Ramparts* stopped the TV man and informed him that he was trespassing on private property. When he refused to leave they picked him up and threw him out the door, camera and all.

When it was agreed that it was time to leave, Huey Newton took control. Mincing no words, he sent five of his men out first to clear a path through the throng of spectators clustered outside the door, most of whom were cops. He dispatched a phalanx of ten Panthers fast on their heels, with Hakim Jamal and Sister Betty concealed in their midst. Newton himself, along with Bobby Seale and three other Panthers, brought up the rear.

I went outside and stood on the steps of *Ramparts* to observe the departure. When Huey left the building, the TV cameraman who had been tossed out was grinding away with his camera. Huey took an envelope from his pocket and held it up in front of the camera, blocking the lens.

"Get out of the way!" the TV man shouted. When Huey continued to hold the envelope in front of the lens, the TV man started cursing, and reached out and knocked Huey's hand away with his fist. Huey coolly turned to one of the score of cops watching and said:

"Officer, I want you to arrest this man for assault."

An incredulous look came into the cop's face, then he blurted out: "If I arrest anybody it'll be you!"

Huey turned on the cameraman, again placing the envelope in front of the lens. Again the cameraman reached out and knocked Huey's hand away. Huey reached out, snatched the cameraman by the collar and slammed him up against the wall, sending him spinning and staggering down the sidewalk, trying to catch his breath and balance the camera on his shoulder at the same time.

Bobby Seale tugged at Huey's shirt sleeve. "C'mon, Huey, let's get out of here."

Huey and Bobby started up the sidewalk toward their car. The cops stood there on the point, poised as though ready to start shooting at a given signal.

"Don't turn your backs on these back-shooting dogs!" Huey called out to Bobby and the other three Panthers. By this time the other Panthers with Sister Betty and Jamal had gotten into cars and melted into the traffic jam. Only these five were still at the scene.

At that moment a big, beefy cop stepped forward. He undid the little strap holding his pistol in his holster and started shouting at Huey, "Don't point that gun at me! Stop pointing that gun at me!" He kept making gestures as though he was going for his gun.

This was the most tense of moments. Huey stopped in his tracks and stared at the cop.

"Let's split, Huey! Let's split!" Bobby Seale was saying.

Ignoring him, Huey walked to within a few feet of the cop and said, "What's the matter, you got an itchy finger?"

The cop made no reply.

"You want to draw your gun?" Huey asked him.

The other cops were calling out for this cop to cool it, to take it easy, but he didn't seem to be able to hear them. He was staring into Huey's eyes, measuring him.

"O.K.," Huey said. "You big fat racist pig, draw your gun!"

The cop made no move.

"Draw it, you cowardly dog!" Huey pumped a round into the chamber of the shotgun. "I'm waiting," he said, and stood there waiting for the cop to draw.

All the other cops moved back out of the line of fire. I moved back, too, onto the top step of *Ramparts*. I was thinking, staring at Huey surrounded by all those cops and daring one of them to draw, "Goddam, that nigger is c-r-a-z-y!"

Then the cop facing Huey gave it up. He heaved a heavy sigh and lowered his head. Huey literally laughed in his face and then went off up the street at a jaunty pace, disappearing in a blaze of dazzling sunlight.

"Work out, soul brother!" I was shouting to myself. "You're the baddest motherfucker I've ever seen!" I went back into *Ramparts* and we all stood around chattering excitedly, discussing what we had witnessed with disbelief.

"Who was that?" asked Vampira, Warren Hinckle's little sister.

"That was Huey P. Newton," I said, "Minister of Defense of the Black Panther Party."

"Boy, is he gutsy!" she said dreamily.

"Yeah," I agreed. "He's out of sight!"

The quality in Huey P. Newton's character that I had seen that morning in front of *Ramparts* and that I was to see demonstrated over and over again after I joined the Black Panther Party was *courage.* I had called it "crazy," as people often do to explain away things they do not understand. I don't mean the courage "to stand up and be counted," or even the courage it takes to face certain death. I speak of that revolutionary courage it takes to pick up a gun with which to oppose the oppressor of one's people. That's a different kind of courage.

Oppressed people, Fanon points out, kill each other all the time. A glance through any black newspaper will prove that black people in America kill each other with regularity. This is the internalized violence of oppressed people. Angered by the misery of their lives but cowed by the overt superior might of the oppressor, the oppressed people shrink from striking out at the true objects of their hostility and strike instead at their more defenseless brothers and sisters near at hand. Somehow this seems safer, less fraught with dire consequences, as though one is less dead when shot down by one's brother than when shot down by the oppressor. It is merely criminal to take up arms against one's brother, but to step outside the vicious circle of the internalized violence of the oppressed and take up arms against the oppressor is to step outside of life itself, to step outside of the structure of this world, to enter, almost alone, the no-man's-land of revolution.

Huey P. Newton took that step. For the motto of the Black Panther Party he chose a quotation from Mao Tse-tung's *Little Red Book:* "We are advocates of the abolition of war; we do not want war; but war can only be abolished through war; and in order to get rid of the gun it is necessary to pick up the gun."

When I decided to join the Black Panther Party the only hang-up I had was with its name. I was still clinging to my conviction that we owed it to Malcolm to pick up where he left off. To me, this meant building the organization that he had started. Picking up where Malcolm left off, however, had different meanings for different people. For cats like Marvin Jackmon, for instance, it meant returning to the ranks of Elijah Muhammad's Nation of Islam, denouncing Malcolm as a heretic and pledging loyalty to Elijah, all in Malcolm's name. For Huey, it meant implementing the program that Malcolm advocated. When that became clear to me, I knew what Huey P. Newton was all about.

For the revolutionary black youth of today, time starts moving with the coming of Malcolm X. Before Malcolm, time stands still, going down in frozen steps into the depths of the stagnation of slavery. Malcolm talked shit, and talking shit is the iron in a young nigger's blood. Malcolm mastered language and used it as a sword to slash his way through the veil of lies that for four hundred years gave the white man the power of the word. Through the breach in the veil, Malcolm saw all the way to national liberation, and he showed us the rainbow and the golden pot at its end. Inside the golden pot, Malcolm told us, was the tool of liberation. Huey P. Newton, one of the millions of black people who listened to Malcolm, lifted the golden lid off the pot and blindly, trusting Malcolm, stuck his hand inside and grasped the tool. When he withdrew his hand and looked to see what he held, he saw the gun, cold in its metal and implacable in its message: Death-Life, Liberty or Death, mastered by a black hand at last! Huey P. Newton is the ideological descendant, heir and successor of Malcolm X. Malcolm prophesied the coming of the gun to the black liberation struggle. Huey P. Newton picked up the gun and pulled the trigger, freeing the genie of black revolutionary violence in Babylon.

The genie of black revolutionary violence is here, and it says that the oppressor has no rights which the oppressed are bound to respect. The genie also has a question for white Americans: which side do you choose? Do you side with the oppressor or with the oppressed? The time for decision is upon you. The cities of America have tested the first flames of revolution. But a hotter fire rages in the hearts of black people today: total liberty for black people or total destruction for America.

The prospects, I confess, do not look promising. Besides being a dumb nation, America is mad with white racism. Whom the gods would destroy, they first make mad. Perhaps America has been mad far too long to make any talk of sanity relevant now. But there is a choice and it will be made, by decision or indecision, by action or inaction, by commission or omission. Black people have made their choice; a revolutionary generation that has the temerity to say to America that Huey P. Newton must be set free, also invested with the courage to kill, pins its hopes on the revolutionary's faith and says, with Che: "Wherever death may surprise us, it will be welcome, provided that this, our battle cry, reach some receptive ear, that another hand reach out to pick up weapons, and that other fighting men come forward to intone our funeral dirge with the staccato of machine guns and new cries of battle and victory."

June 15, 1968

This piece is named for Alprentice "Bunchy" Carter, whom Eldridge first met in the mid-1960s in Soledad Prison. Eldridge wrote these pages after the devastating loss of his closest friend, whom he had persuaded to become a Black Panther leader in Los Angeles.

Bunchy, along with another Los Angeles Panther, Jon Huggins, was killed on January 17, 1969, in a shoot-out that erupted on the UCLA campus with members of Us, a black nationalist organization led by Maulana Karenga. The killing was later revealed to have been instigated by a secret FBI counterintelligence operation known as COINTELPRO.

"Bunchy" was found among a trove of Eldridge Cleaver's manuscripts that the Bancroft Library of the University of California at Berkeley located and acquired after his death. It was probably part of the draft of an unfinished book entitled Uptight in Babylon *that Eldridge began writing during 1971. He said that the book was "an interpretation of life and events in the United States during the 1960s," in which he would present "the true inner history of the Black Panther Party, but in a context larger than the Black Panther Party itself" and include profiles of key people.*

BUNCHY

I tried again to use this opportunity during our conversation to convince Huey that Malcolm X was the symbol of our unity, and that we should treat Malcolm the way that he was proposing that we treat him.

Huey said that he saw the relationship between himself and me and others who spoke for the party, as the same as the relationship between Jesus and John the Baptist and the Disciples, or the same as that between Elijah and Malcolm and the other ministers of the Nation of Islam. He said that it was necessary to elevate him, to build him up, to get people to respect him, and acknowledge his authority. I told him that it was very difficult to do this since he was still alive and running around where people could see him. When both John the Baptist and later the Disciples were speaking, the great one that they talked about was not on the scene. And in the case of Elijah, he was old and sick and not on the set, so that Malcolm was able to talk about him like that, give all praises and credit to him in the name of Allah.

Huey said that I either had to do it his way or I couldn't be in the party. Then, before leaving my pad, he said: "Don't tell any of the other brothers about what we discussed because I don't think that they can understand it."

I decided then to join the Black Panther Party. I thought that, in time, it would be possible to influence Bobby and Huey to deal with Malcolm X, because what Malcolm had to offer was exactly what Huey and Bobby did not have. There was no problem in this regard with the rank and file of the party. Talking to them was just like talking to the brothers in prison. I continued to talk the way that I did naturally, to salvage some of the cadre that seemed interested in moving with the struggle to a higher level.

Bobby, also, began to accept the new point of view. I could see him working the prison ideology into his rap. But Huey, I discovered, was a different story. So I gave up, at an early stage, in trying to explain anything to him. What I did was talk around him and over his head. Once he came to my pad, angry, and told me that he had heard me on the radio and that what I had said was good, except for one point: I had not mentioned the name of the Black Panther Party. I had talked a lot about Malcolm X. It was then that I fully understood where Huey was coming from on the point of Malcolm X.

"Malcolm X is not the leader of the Black Panther Party," Huey said. There was ice in his voice, and when I looked at him he was embarrassed, and blushed.

I had a long talk with Huey that day, because we had to reach an agreement or it was not going to be possible for us to work together. I was not about to stop talking about Malcolm X, and he knew that from our previous conversation. Huey told me that he felt funny trying to correct me because I was older than he was and partly because I seemed to know more about what was going on than he did. He asked me if I wanted to be the leader of the Party. If so, he said, he would turn it over. I assured him that I accepted his leadership and would carry out his orders.

After we started putting out the newspaper, Huey used to dictate his regular column to me, then I would "edit" it for him. In fact, I would listen to him talk for awhile, about a current problem that we were immediately confronted with and which was on everybody's mind, then I would write an essay on the subject, salting it with phrases that he coined. Later, Huey would say: "I didn't say that," or, "did I say that?" or, "I didn't say that that way, did I?" It was weird, but it passed. And that was how we functioned.

The work that had to be done was so intense that many things were overlooked as little things that, later, in fact turned out to be big things. We were moving openly and publicly against the police, with guns, and I was on parole. There was no room for jiving and no room for pettiness, so many bones were left unpicked. But when Bunchy got out of prison, he refused to join the Black Panther Party, and that brought everything to a halt.

The day Bunchy was released from Soledad Prison, he came up to San Francisco to my pad and spent the night.

"What's wrong with you, Eldridge?" Bunchy asked me, "Have you gone out of your motherfucking mind? Don't you know a poo-but when you see one? Let's not get hung up with these college boys!"

I had been in touch with Bunchy while he was still in prison. The information that I conveyed to him was necessarily limited, but adequate enough to give him a general idea about what was going on. After I filled him in on the details, Bunchy said that he could not relate to the structure of the Black Panther Party, which was bullshit because there was no structure at that time. What it was, though, was that Bunchy could not relate to Huey as his leader. We agreed that, since he had just got out of prison, the best thing for him to do was just cool it and check things out for a month or two. Anyway, he had been gone for four years, and now was the time to fulfill a convict's dream: to get his hot hands on some soft, female flesh. The next day he left for Los Angeles.

Baby Dee, another nigger who was in Soledad with us—in Soledad, it was me, Bunchy, and Baby Dee. Bunchy brought us all together, but at first I was Bunchy's friend and Baby Dee was Bunchy's friend—and he got out of prison just a little ahead of Bunchy. For about the first three weeks, Bunchy disappeared, at the bottom of a bed of roses, then he reappeared, first by telephone, then by plane. It reached the point where we would see each other almost each week. Either he'd come up to the Bay Area, or I'd go down to L.A.

When Bunchy came to the Bay Area, he'd get together with Baby Dee and they'd go party, for the whole weekend. I would see Bunchy when he first arrived in the Bay Area. We'd get high together and argue about the struggle. Baby Dee lived in Marin City, a suburb outside of San Francisco, and I was trying to get Baby Dee to start a branch of the party in Marin City and Bunchy to do the same thing in Los Angeles. "This is what we agreed to do in Soledad! Except that it's called the Black Panther Party instead of the Organization of Afro-American Unity!" I'd condemn and denounce both him and Baby Dee for partying while the whole world was on fire.

It reached ridiculous proportions. Baby Dee's sister, Joyce, belonged to a women's club, whose reason for existence was that it provided a cover for married women. Each week they'd have a party that rotated from pad to pad. Since the sisters were all foxes, these parties were always well attended. They all freaked out over Bunchy. According to Bunchy, he was so pretty that it brought tears of envy from other men's eyes when they saw him. Bunchy had a gigantic Afro haircut, maybe the baddest natural on the set, back in the days when naturals had power and manifested a conviction. During those days, very few pigs wore their hair natural, and if such things could be legislated, it would have been against the law—Illegal Hair. It reached the point where these weekly parties became a personal showcase for Bunchy and Baby Dee.

At the time, I told Baby Dee and Bunchy that I was going to write an article about them so that the brothers in Soledad would know what they were doing, and I guess I'm doing that now. I knew what Baby Dee and Bunchy were doing, and I dug it. In fact, every nigger in Babylon was doing the same thing, except that Bunchy and Baby Dee took it out of sight.

In 1967, one year after Stokely Carmichael, Black Power, Black Is Beautiful, I'm Black and I'm Proud!, niggers had already put on their blackness. It was the day of resurrection. We were climbing out of the grave of whiteness. It was the universal homecoming of self. We were back into our thing. It blew our minds just to look at each other. Brothers tripped out looking at sisters and sisters tripped out looking at brothers. Soul was running wild and that's how we wanted it. It had not yet become cultural nationalism. LeRoi Jones himself was still off into a white bag, and he was not yet Amiri Baraka. Ron Karenga had already started playing Batman in Los Angeles, and Rap Brown was just coming onto the set.

Babylon had begun to burn at an ever-higher pitch. There was very little talk left about the Long Hot Summer because there was fire year round.

Blackness started to well up and spread, not from the top of society down, but from the bottom up. The Black Muslims had unleashed something among the people, let loose something that had been dormant and hidden. It spiraled up, turning around everything that it touched. It turned social classes around, and it turned culture and politics around, and in the guise of black capitalism it has even turned the American economy around. In a certain sense, the year 1967 marks the date that blackness turned the black bourgeoisie around. People had already forgotten about the fact that Roy Wilkins and Whitney Young had gone on television to denounce Stokely Carmichael for saying dangerous things like "We want Black Power!" Brothers and sisters had Black Power parties, and there was a dance called Black Power, and the Impressions, singing about "We're a winner!" fit right in.

This group of women, of which Joyce was a member, started staging fashion shows. I heard that Bunchy and Baby Dee were going to model some clothes at one of these fashion shows. They came by my pad that day. After discussing it, they assured me that it was true.

This was after the party had gone to Sacramento, into the state capitol building, with guns, and I had gotten busted. The situation was absolutely serious. I had gotten out of jail by the skin of my teeth and the pigs were openly looking for the right excuse to rip me off—and here these niggers were modeling clothes! I ran them out of my pad that day, and told them that I never wanted to see them again until they were ready to join the party. They still continued to drop by my pad, but I would just curse them out and then shine them on. I wasn't as mad at them as I acted, because I loved the niggers and couldn't really get mad at them. But I acted like I hated them, told them so, and we traded insults.

One night they came by my pad, both of them drunk. We were trying to get together an issue of the Black Panther newspaper. As usual, I vamped on them and talked about them like they were low-down, dirty, scurvy dogs. I called them cowards for not joining the party. What did I want to say that for! Baby Dee leaped on me and knocked me over backward. I fell on something and almost broke my back. I mean I was righteously hurt. I looked at the nigger, then I looked at Bunchy. Both of the niggers were standing there blinking, drunk out of their skulls. If

I was going to do anything about it, I'd have to shoot the nigger. I had a gun handy, but that was out of the question. Shoot Baby Dee or Bunchy? Not possible! So I just analyzed the shit to them and said that the fact that they had attacked me physically proved that they knew that they were doing wrong and were mad at me for denouncing them. They looked at me with confused expressions on their faces, helped me off the floor, and split out of the pad.

The next time I saw them they were members of the Black Panther Party. But between those two times, Huey got shot, arrested, and charged with killing an Oakland pig, and it was a brand new world.

In August 1967, the Black Panther Party became totally immobilized. At that time, Bobby Seale, Emory Douglas, and about ten other Panthers were locked up in jail on sentences growing out of our actions in Sacramento three months earlier. Two separate but related events will serve as a scale just to show how quickly things were moving and how much they had changed.

The black bourgeois politicians and endorsed spokesmen of the black community in California had put together what they called a Black Survival Conference that January in San Francisco. In June 1967, five months later, they held another one in Los Angeles. Both conferences were supposed to be a grassroots thing. That's how they were played off. In both of them, all phases of the political spectrum of the black community were involved, in one way or another, either on the inside or on the outside. At the one in San Francisco, black politicians and wheeler dealers, like Carleton Goodlett, the newspaper publisher from Northern California, were in control. In Los Angeles, it was the southern counterpart of that same clique that was dealing. Stokely Carmichael and Ron Karenga were there, as it were, to give voice to basic things like Black Power and Blackness. The black bourgeois media urged the black community as a whole to attend the conference, but then the manipulators of that event charged a five-dollar entrance fee at the door. This put a cold-blooded block on the grassroots delegates from San Francisco, Oakland, Richmond, and San Jose, who had been sent by their organizations—every kind of organization from welfare rights to fair housing and groups interested in the defense of the black community from racist violence and terror.

Kenny Freeman, who was the leader of the Black Panther Party of Northern California, kicked down the door and broke out a window, trying to storm the meeting. When all those people from miles around showed up at the conference and found themselves blocked at the door by a five-dollar sting, they held an impromptu caucus right there in the streets. It was unanimously decided to force the door. The cowardly niggers in control were not the problem. But would they call the pigs if we moved on them like that? It was decided that we should find out. So the door was kicked in. The niggers called the pigs and started pointing people out for the pigs to vamp on. So everybody cooled it at that point.

After much discussion, it was decided to discredit the conference by prevailing upon Stokely not to participate unless they dropped the five-dollar charge. A group of us went and explained the situation to Stokely. He said that he agreed with us on all points, except that he would like to deal with it in his own way—quietly, behind the scenes.

I looked at him. This is the same cat I had seen on TV while I was in Soledad. Then he had been dancing around a tent, scuffling with the pigs. I am not pretending to be objective now. I'm writing with malice toward certain people. When this shit was happening, Bunchy was alive. Now he is dead. And in a certain sense, what I am writing about is the shit that killed him. He was shot and killed by some of Ron Karenga's apes, on the campus of the University of California, in Los Angeles. All of my comrades of that day, the people with whom I was moving, are either dead, in jail, in exile, underground, or working with the pigs.

The conference was to last three days. The first day, the people were blocked at the door by five dollars. Inside, on that first day, the house niggers passed all their resolutions. Stokely got them to remove the cover charge for the second day. On the second day, the slick niggers read the resolutions to the audience and announced that they had been unanimously accepted the day before. The conference exploded, and there was a lot of shouting, as politician after politician got up in succession to explain the thing away and cool everybody out. Then they announced that Stokely would speak the next day. It went on and on like that.

Six months later, at the Black Survival Conference held in Los Angeles, Huey Newton and Bobby Seale were the dominant factors. At that moment, we still only had the parent branch of the party, in Oakland, but we were on the threshold of a heavy breakthrough, and we knew it. Between the first conference in San Francisco, and this one in Los Angeles, we had set the Bay Area on fire.

On one level, we had had a series of searing public confrontations with the pigs, and on another level, the shooting had already started. There were a lot of small groups of brothers moving on the pigs, sniping and bombing. California Highway patrolmen were being offed and downed regularly. Anything in a uniform was a target—police, firemen, bus drivers. Then Bobby and the other brothers went to jail. Although the influence of the party was getting strong, we still only had a small, stable membership of about 15 people, all brothers. There were no women in the party at that time.

That was when I learned that without Bobby, Huey was unable to function. Bobby worshipped Huey, and would state it openly, and I guess we all thought that he meant admiration, respect, trust—something like, that which people feel for their leaders, even love. Bobby submitted himself totally to Huey's will and became an instrument, like a walking cane, in his hand. Huey could place him wherever he willed. Bobby was like a microphone and loudspeaker for Huey. When we had rallies in the community, Huey would tell Bobby what to talk about and Bobby would get up and deal with it. Huey couldn't relate to too much speaking himself, and in another sense he was deliberately withdrawn. So, when Bobby went to jail, Huey began to flutter. Huey needed someone to be with him to help him organize his thoughts and to speak for him. After Bobby went to jail I started fulfilling this role, but it was not sufficient.

Huey broke off almost all party activity. He was besieged with invitations to speak. The demand was intense, especially in the Bay Area, but requests were beginning to come in from all over the country. People were springing up all over who wanted to organize branches of the party in their area. In those days, we'd ask people to fill out a membership form if they wanted to join the party. We had stacks and stacks of them. Black people, on a grassroots, mass level, wanted to get organized around the gun. This was a historic moment. Bobby Hutton, Reggie and Sherwin Forte, Oleander, John Sloan, Warren Tucker, and myself were the stable element around Huey, now that Bobby, Emory, Willie Thompson, and all the other good brothers were in jail. It was in this situation that Huey showed up one day with David Hilliard.

Huey had known David for a long time. David was working as a longshoreman on the San Francisco waterfront. On the side, David was dealing weed. Huey explained that David was in the party and that they were working together to turn over some weed to get some bread. We needed bread bad, but I had already gone to prison twice for dealing weed. If I ever went back again, it would not be for that! Besides, I knew that there were better ways of getting money. They gave me a can of weed for my own use and then split. Our lives became a ritual. At least once each day, the handful of us would get together, sometimes Huey would be there and sometimes he wouldn't. As time went by, Huey came around less and less.

But the pigs, particularly the Oakland pigs, were not taking into consideration that our group had stagnated. They had finally gotten a law passed outlawing the open carrying of guns in California, and armed with this law, they were tightening the circle around us. As far as the parole department was concerned, I had had it, and I expected them to try to vamp on me at any minute. Each time you went outside, you felt like a jackrabbit running across a farmer's field. We were trying to put out a newspaper, trying to accumulate guns, trying to expand our organization and contacts, and on the side, I was trying to write shit for *Ramparts*. It was really a holding action. It was at this low ebb that news flashed throughout Babylon that Huey was in the hospital, shot, and charged with killing one pig and wounding another. My telephone began a constant ring. Among those who called was Bunchy. He said that he was ready to go to work and asked me to come down to Los Angeles to speak to a group that he had organized.

Bunchy and a couple of other brothers met me at the Los Angeles International Airport, and we drove into the city. Los Angeles, the nut buster of the cities of Babylon. This was Chief Parker's city. Until the Watts uprising in 1965, Chief Parker was the heaviest pig in Babylon, on the local level, and he was often mentioned as the likeliest prospect to replace J. Edgar Hoover, when and if—if ever—he was officially pronounced dead. But Watts blew his shit away. The leading practioner of the philosophy of law and order, everything he ever said was contradicted in unanswerable terms when niggers in Watts rose up and expressed their point of view.

After the uprising quieted down and faded somewhat from the tip of everyone's tongue, some organization in Los Angeles gave the chief of police an award, supporting his actions with salutations for meritorious service. At the ceremony in his honor at which Parker was to officially accept the award and make a speech, Parker dropped dead on the spot of a heart attack. When the news that Parker had croaked came over the radio, I was lying on my bunk in Folsom Prison listening to it over a pair of earphones. The whole prison exploded with thunderous cheers as it sunk into heads that Parker had caused to be beaten, that he, Parker, was in the wind.

Parker took over the Los Angeles Police Department in 1947, in the wake of a scandal that sent the former chief of police, O'Dwyer, and most of his staff, to prison. It involved prostitutes, bribes, gambling, and the Mafia. Parker was called in to clean up, first the police department, and then the city. And L.A. was funky too. Naturally, everybody in town was uptight because Parker moved in as though everybody in town was under suspicion. He must have investigated everybody, because he scared everybody. There was no one around to whom he would not talk back to, in public, and it was common knowledge that he had a long shit list.

On a wall map in Parker's office the city itself was geographically laid out in something like a shit list. The black community and the Mexican community had red flags tacked onto them, to indicate war zones. Parker made a lot of noise about how he was going to bust everybody who gets down wrong, and then he started vamping on the black community and the Mexican community. There were no blacks or Mexicans in the crowd of pigs who got busted along with the chief of police, but it was against blacks and Mexicans that Parker moved when he came to town. He busted every two-dollar whore and petty reefer peddler in sight, and was demanding the death penalty for everything. In public, he would call Mexicans half-civilized savages out of the wild hills of Mexico. That is an almost direct quote that I'll never forget, because growing up in Los Angeles I can still remember the furor that it caused. It was legendary in L.A.

Manifested in the statistics of crimes committed, number of arrests and convictions, Parker won the reputation of the baddest town tamer since Wyatt Earp. In a very short span of time, Parker's police department was rated as the best, toughest, most efficient in Babylon. Personally, Parker would boast that he could have a police car on any corner of the city in two minutes. We who were actively engaged in crime in Los Angeles at the time knew that that was a goddamn lie, but we understood what he meant, because L.A. was, and always has been since Parker came in, hot.

For the black and Mexican communities, the situation was totalitarian. It was nothing for your door to get kicked down, or for you to get shot in the mouth by one of Parker's pigs if you were not careful. And any time a black person ventured out at night he was subjected to wake up the next day in jail, held on suspicion of—whatever. Years later, Parker was forced to draw a distinction between the doors of the black bourgeoisie and the just plain folk, because a crew of his storm troopers kicked in a door one night on Sugar Hill and caught the cream of L.A.'s black bourgeoisie playing poker. In spite of the outcry made by L.A.'s black bourgeoisie, principally through their mouthpiece, the *Los Angeles Sentinel,* Parker pressed charges against all those doctors, lawyers, and schoolteachers whom he caught dirty that night. Through a lot of be-hind-the-scenes maneuvering, the case was turned over to Judge David Williams, himself a sterling member of L.A.'s black bourgeoisie, and he threw the case out of court and denounced Parker and the LAPD for kicking down the wrong doors in the black community. Parker never admitted it in public, but he got the message. The black bourgeoisie laid off of him after that, until the Watts uprising, when Chief Parker arbitrarily included the West Side, along with the East Side and Watts, within the perimeter of the curfew area, and started treating all the niggers alike.

But the other blacks and Mexicans in Los Angeles hated Parker's guts. For them, there was no such thing as an arrest warrant or search warrant, and there might as well have been a pass law such as in South Africa. I doubt whether the average black person in South Africa was as much beneath the cruel mercy of the police as blacks and Mexicans in Los Angeles were. Parker had unleashed what amounted to death squads upon the blacks and Mexicans in Los Angeles, and they carried out a reign of terror from the time Parker went into office in 1947 throughout the decade of the 1950s. What struck terror into the hearts of blacks in those days were the teams of nigger pigs that Parker turned loose on the black community, sadistic fiends armed with a license to kill—niggers. When these cats decided to get you, you either split town or you had had it. Because they would do anything to you: shoot you, frame you, beat you, rob you—anything. This tactic, along with constant searches, seizures, and saturation patrols, was the status quo for niggers under Parker. Although Parker himself was dead, the machine of terror that he constructed remained.

It was this machine that Bunchy was organizing against. The racist, totalitarian Los Angeles Police Department that occupied the black community like foreign troops on conquered territory. And it was about the Los Angeles Police Department that I was to speak at the meeting that Bunchy had organized. This was a beautiful moment for Bunchy and me. This was just what we discussed, back in Soledad prison, for days and days, months and months. Wasn't this what we had dreamed of, moving against these pigs?

The War on Poverty and the Great Society had brought a flood of bullshit programs into the black community that were theoretically supposed to heal the wounds of centuries of slavery and oppression. Besides managing to put a few dirty dollars in the pockets of various political cliques in the black community, the only other thing that these programs did was to aggravate every grievance niggers ever had. Mostly because when niggers looked at that measly crumb tossed to them by the pigs, it was a simple process of multiplication to imagine what something whole would be like for a change.

One aspect of these antipoverty programs as applied in Los Angeles was a series of institutions called Teen Posts, scattered throughout the black community. They were supposed to provide centers where young people could gather, to keep them out of the streets, and give them some room in which to pull themselves up by their bootstraps. One of these Teen Posts, on Central Avenue, was run by an old sister named Mrs. Green. Absolutely unable to maintain any discipline over the young bloods who frequented her Teen Post, Mrs. Green was only too glad when Bunchy showed up one day and asked her to allow him to maintain discipline for her and be her sort of officer of the day. From Bunchy's point of view, it was a good deal, because it provided him with a cover for his parole officer's eyes, and at the same time it provided him with a physical facility in which he could begin to organize.

The first thing Bunchy did was to tell everybody that he only wanted people to come around if they were seriously interested in participating in the struggle for the liberation of our people. If they came around jiving, he told them, they could expect to get a good ass kicking, or worse, if that didn't work. Of course a few cats put Bunchy to the test, which he passed, but most of the people who came around were full of enthusiasm.

The Teen Post was a large, rusty brown, two-story building, with lots of rooms upstairs and downstairs. When we arrived, Bunchy took me upstairs to a room, where I was surprised to find waiting for me about a dozen niggers with every kind of gun you could imagine. Each of the brothers had on black shoes, black pants, and black turtleneck sweaters, where just over the heart there was the slashing yellow sign of the radical (the mathematical sign that indicates the square root $\sqrt{}$). The sight of those radical signs brought a warm glow to my heart as I thought back to how we had used it for our symbol in Soledad. We used to sit around in Soledad and speculate about the organization that we had dedicated ourselves to building once we got out, and we argued about everything, including the type of uniforms, if any, and the kinds of symbols we would use. One thing we had all agreed upon was the radical sign. Bunchy argued with me that day, too, as to whether we should use the radical sign or the Black Panther. But even as we argued we both knew that the Panther would be the thing, because it had already taken the leap into the future.

Bunchy took me up on the roof, where I could see on each surrounding rooftop that he pointed to, a brother with a rifle on sentry duty. Then we went downstairs to the large community meeting room where I rapped with the people who had turned out. To get to the meeting room from upstairs, it was necessary to go outside the building, then walk around to another door on the ground floor and the street you walked down was Central Avenue. As I walked out the door, Bunchy's troops formed lines on both sides of me and walked along with me, their guns at ready. This was the first time that what was to become the Los Angeles branch of the Black Panther Party hit the ground, armed. Between that day and that the day two years later, December 8, 1969, when the Los Angeles Police Department launched a military assault upon the party's headquarters, there was to be much shooting, much death.

On this first day, this maiden voyage, the brothers were so uptight and nervous with their pieces in their hands, and so determined to see it through to the end, that there was a possibility that one of them might have trembled off a shot. But I didn't care if they trembled off a shot or not, even if it had hit me, because it was beautiful to see strong black brothers armed, and I was beginning to see it everywhere I went, no matter in what state.

Niggers were getting it together and what I saw forming was an army, not yet conscious of what it was destined to become. It was at moments like this that all the people present felt the same way, and they sent out strong vibrations carrying a collective dare to the pigs to come down there and fuck with them. The pigs knew when to stay away. But I know that the pigs were there anyway because the next week my parole officer called me to his office and told me he had received a report from the L.A. office that I had been with some niggers with some guns. I told him that I wouldn't doubt it one bit if some of the people there had guns, considering how many black people get killed by the Los Angeles Police Department. But, I told him, I didn't see any guns myself.

"O.K., Cleaver," this cat probably said, "You make your own bed and you have to lay in it."

And if the truth were told, I would have had to answer: "Yeah, baby, and what I'm planting is roses."

By February 17, 1968, the Los Angeles branch of the Black Panther Party had consolidated its base. Centralized into one unit that had ripped off an office in the Black Congress building, but consisting in membership of niggers from throughout Southern California, as far south as San Diego, Bunchy was working feverishly to establish other units in his area. In a matter of months, Bunchy was to achieve this goal, but at that time, in February, Bunchy suffered a political shock that allowed him to gauge where the shit was at.

February 17 was Huey Newton's birthday. The date of his trial was drawing nearer. The mass mobilization that we initiated in October 1967, right after Huey was imprisoned, was reaching its peak. We decided to stage a huge rally, in the Oakland Auditorium, which was right across the street from the Alameda County Jail, where Huey was being held. Bobby Seale and I flew to Washington, D.C., to confer with Stokely, who had just returned from his famous world tour, including stops in Havana, Algiers, Moscow, Peking, Hanoi, etc., to persuade him to make his first public statement after returning to the USA at our rally in the Oakland Auditorium. Stokely readily agreed.

One of the main problems that we had to deal with was the fucked-up situation that the movement was facing after Stokely's year as the head of SNCC and the prophet of Black Power. We viewed the step that SNCC had taken in kicking the whites out of SNCC and spreading the concept of black control of black organizations as a welcome, positive event. Since the Black Panther Party never had any whites in it in the first place, our stance was a little different from that of SNCC and others who were caught up in the trickbag of integrated organizations and integrated political machinery. It seemed that they had carried Black Power to the point of mysticism and paranoia. White people were, as they always had been, a plague to blacks, and in the end, they could be guaranteed to fuck up any joint political activity undertaken. What it boiled down to was a form of stagnation, where people were immobilized by categorical definitions. And we were in a situation where we had to move, with no time for any bullshit.

On one level, the decision was made to fight Huey's case in court and to mobilize the people outside the court, around the demand that he be set free. I personally had quashed an alternative plan to break Huey out of the Alameda County Jail. I mention this because there were those who disagreed with me. But I made my decision based upon a personal knowledge of the Alameda County Jail, and my general experience with jails and prisons. In the best plan formulated for breaking Huey out, there were loopholes through which disaster would surely leap, and the time and the resources needed to pull that one off didn't exist for us, and to try it anyway, out of desperation and soul, seemed shortsighted. I realized that in making this decision, I shouldered a heavy burden, because what it meant was that Huey's life had to be guaranteed by other means.

I believed that we had the opportunity to kill a lot of birds with the same stone. There was a dead white policeman, another white policeman wounded and damn near dead. And there was Huey, wounded, imprisoned, but still alive. The basic position of the Black Panther Party, growing out of point no. seven in the party's platform and program, was that we were going to drive the occupying army of the police out of the black community. Huey had downed pig Frey in the center of Oakland's black ghetto, and it was clear that the people had said, Right On! Those who didn't say Right On! just didn't understand. The opportunity was at hand to extend organizational machinery throughout the country. Bunchy was my closest confident, and we both saw that shit could be elevated to a higher level throughout the country.

Huey was arrested October 28, 1967. Bobby Seale was still in jail and had been since the previous August. It would be a couple more months before he got out. How to move? Picking through the political thicket existing in the San Francisco–Oakland Bay Area, I was only interested in relating to people and organizations that were willing to help deal with this shit. Huey would have a jury trial, and it was not going to be an all-black jury, so some work had to done in the white community. After several disappointing experiences with the American Communist Party, the Socialist Workers Party, and a host of other monstrosities antedating the New Left, I only related to the student movement in the white community. If a person did not have roots in the student movement, roots that related to the new wave of protest growing out of the 1960s, I didn't want to deal with them.

In California, the students who had grown out of the Free Speech Movement on the UC Berkeley campus, the spirit of which spread throughout the state and then later throughout the country, had gone on, after leaving the campus, to organize the Peace and Freedom Party. Since 1968 was an election year that included a presidential contest, the Peace and Freedom Party was moving to qualify for the ballot, in order to field candidates on all levels, including a presidential candidate. What they needed, in order to obtain the number of signatures to get them officially on the ballot, were some signatures out of the black community. The Peace and Freedom Party was rooted on campus, going deep into the ranks of the anti-war activists and those who had actively participated in the civil rights movements' campaign of civil disobedience. Such people as Mario Savio and Jack Weinberg, who had been at the very heart of the Free Speech Movement at UC Berkeley, along with all of their friends, had an active, leading role in the Peace and Freedom Party. From prison, I had watched how these cats were moving, and I thought that they were sincere and would stand by their convictions.

But the word that Stokely had given stood as an interdiction against our relating to them. Seeing how Stokely's principles were being used, in practice, made his position, as far as I was concerned, untenable. It was impossible for the white members of the Peace and Freedom Party to come into the black community, unescorted, to canvas for votes. Their stated political goal was to field candidates and siphon off enough liberal and left votes to cause the candidates of the Democratic Party to lose to the Republicans. They wanted to so wreck the Democratic Party, on all levels, that after the tragedy they would suffer at the ballot box come November, what remained of the Democratic Party would have to sit down and deal with them politically.

The Democratic Party retaliated by giving a lot of money to the black members of the Democratic Party in California. One of their hired tasks was to block the Peace and Freedom Party from getting any signatures out of the black community. As an ideological weapon, these black Democrats picked up the rhetoric of Black Power, grew natural hairdos, and did everything they could to block the Peace and Freedom Party in the name of Black Power but for the benefit of the Democratic Party. And they had them blocked, too, until the Black Panther Party came on the scene. Also, the black Democrats who were on the make, like Ron Dellums, were interested in running for office in the same territory that the Peace and Freedom Party wanted to get into. Since the Peace and Freedom Party was interested in wrecking the political system, and Ron Dellums and his friends were interested in succeeding within it, the black Democrats viewed the Peace and Freedom Party as a dangerous adversary, even though the Peace and Freedom Party offered to support them in their political efforts if the black Democrats would leave and condemn the Democratic Party, whose chief was LBJ, for escalating the war both at home and abroad. Their very name, Peace and Freedom, meant peace in Vietnam and freedom for the Afro-American people. The black Democrats did not see any percentage in relating to that.

On one level, the black Democrats were able to run down a good line, but when it came to practice, they always felt forced to defeat themselves by hypocritically supporting the political machinery responsible for that against which they railed. Also, we had asked them to take public positions in support of Huey Newton, which most of them refused to do. Uniformly, those who already held elected offices were even afraid to talk with us, for fear that it might become known to the pigs and thus end their political careers. But those on the make, like Ron Dellums, were reading other cards.

Dellums had his eye on the 7th Congressional District seat, in Alameda County, which has at its core the community around the University of California in Berkeley, and in Oakland, the black ghetto. It was common knowledge that it was possible for either a black or a progressive white to win that seat. Bob Scheer, a left-liberal white journalist who had written some of the earliest exposés on what the Yanks were doing in Vietnam, and therefore had played a major role in kindling the spirit of rebellion on the Berkeley campus and surrounding community, had run for that same congressional seat as an independent candidate back in 1966 and had almost won. Statistics showed that had he gotten more votes out of the black community, he would have won by a handy margin. This knowledge whetted the lips of the black Democrats.

By working with the Peace and Freedom Party, there was a chance to deal with things on some interesting levels. I visited Huey at the Alameda County Jail, and explained to him how I proposed to move. Huey's mind just like everybody else's was blocked on the point of working with whites. He himself was trapped behind bars, couldn't move, and he had no ideas about what to do. His preference was to be broken out, to have a red-light trial, with the red lights flashing. Beyond that, he stood there looking at me through bars, like thousands of other convicts I had seen before. We both knew that the pigs in the state of California automatically put a nigger convicted of killing a policeman in the gas chamber, and in Alameda County, with a racist pig named Coakely for district attorney, it would take a miracle to beat the gas chamber. I pledged to Huey, through those bars in the Alameda County Jail, that the shit would be dealt with. These were Huey's words:

"O.K. Brother, deal with it."

By the time Bobby Seale got out of jail, at the end of December 1967, we had worked out a coalition with the Peace and Freedom Party. It had been difficult. At first, I was totally isolated, even inside the Black Panther Party, because by moving to a coalition with the white Peace and Freedom, the black Democrats started spreading the line throughout the black community that I was returning to integration. It was not a question of integrating anything except the American Revolution, which as far as I was concerned was born integrated. The question was how to deal with the situation that existed in reality and not in the figure of somebody's speech, in this case, Stokely's. I was not afraid that whites would end up in control of the Black Panther Party or of the black liberation struggle. In fact, where I was coming from, those days were gone forever and didn't even have to be discussed.

We drew blood from the black Democrats by announcing that we had made a coalition with the Peace and Freedom Party, that we would run members of the Black Panther Party for office on the Peace and Freedom Party ticket, and that we were going to bring the Peace and Freedom Party into the black community to get the signatures they needed to get on the ballot. After the Peace and Freedom Party had qualified for the ballot in the state of California and we announced that we were going to put Huey Newton up for Congress in the 7th Congressional District on the Peace and Freedom Party ticket, the black Democrats hit the ceiling.

Black Democrats throughout the state of California got uptight, along with white Democrats, because here came an unknown quantity. They had already decided, among themselves, that they were going to back a black lawyer, John George, for that seat, which meant that Ron Dellums, although he coveted that Congressional seat, would have to be content with being a member of the Berkeley City Council, which was based partly in the 7th Congressional District. And they already had a funky situation to deal with. Humphrey, Wallace, and Nixon were out there. Robert Kennedy had not gotten offed yet. Lyndon Johnson had not yet announced that he would not be a candidate, so the situation was a hairy one indeed.

I had several angry meetings with the black Democrats and clashed with them in community meetings. Once I confronted Ron Dellums at a meeting of people who were part of the base of the Peace and Freedom Party. Dellums hurled at them all the Carmichaelian imperatives that he could muster. Because they were white, they had no right to make any decisions affecting the black community. On the political level, they had to support the candidates put up by the black community, whether they, the whites, liked their politics or not. Otherwise, like a well-timed bomb, Dellums would drop the accusation that they were acting in a racist manner. This worked fine in the days when the black Democrats were the only force in the black community that put up candidates. But when the Black Panther Party put up alternatives, the shit caved in.

What remained to be done was to deal with SNCC. We thought that we had finished with SNCC's James Forman by this time. But we were wrong. Forman came back to haunt us. We saw the best solution was to get SNCC to merge their organization with ours. Since they also stood for the liberation of our people, they had no objective grounds for not merging with us. Besides that, as an organization, they were already dead. The members of SNCC knew this better than anybody else. So we moved on them like we were moving on a corpse. We already had the sisters inside SNCC on our side, not just because we were all pretty niggers, but because the sisters related to where we were coming from, and could dig it. It was mainly some of the cats, and not all of them, who felt that we cast them in a bad light. So I announced, in a speech, that the Black Panther Party and SNCC were going to merge. Coming after we had made the coalition with the Peace and Freedom Party, the announcement of the merger with SNCC confounded the black Democrats and fucked up their rhetoric. It also confounded Forman. Depending upon whom he was talking to, Forman would sometimes say that he supported the merger and at other times he would state that he didn't.

After he found out that Stokely was going to be the featured speaker at the climatic rally on Huey's birthday in the Oakland Auditorium,

Forman started saying that it was not really a merger after all, that it was an association of some brothers. When he found out that at that rally we were going to appoint Stokely prime minister of the Black Panther Party, Forman flew out to California and asked me not to do it. He wanted Rap Brown appointed to that position. We related heavily to Rap. It was a difficult decision. Forman saw that it was difficult, but when he learned that we were sticking by our position, he asked for a compromise: make Stokely and Rap both deputy prime ministers, but don't give Stokely a position above Rap. Rap is sensitive, Forman said, it would hurt him. What about our prime minister? I asked Forman. Make somebody else prime minister. Make Huey prime minister, or Bobby, or yourself, but not Stokely! We told him that it was not possible, that we would appoint Stokely prime minister, Rap minister of justice, and he himself would be appointed minister of foreign affairs.

Forman left furious, but powerless to block it. So he resorted to sabotage. He started wiring people up against us throughout the country. He was not able to make a dent in the San Francisco–Oakland Bay Area, because that was definitely our turf, but he went to Los Angeles, united with Ron Karenga, and together they hammered other members of the Black Congress, the preachers, and black politicians into a solid block against us. They all already hated us for various reasons, and Forman provided the leadership they needed. As a base for his activities in Los Angeles and California, he resurrected what he called Los Angeles SNCC, the same cats who had tried to rip off the name of the Black Panther Party by registering with the secretary of state.

The rally was scheduled in Oakland for February 17, and we scheduled another one for Los Angeles on February 18. Our position was that no one could speak at that rally if they did not support the demand that Huey be set free, and generally support the Black Panther Party. There were certain people whom we didn't want to speak at all—particularly Ron Karenga. It was then that I discovered what a master political manipulator Forman was!

In the first place, although we had made the proper applications and arrangements for the rally with the pigs who controlled the L.A. Sports Arena where we wanted to hold it, they acted like they were not going to allow us to use it. We didn't know for sure, up until the day that the rally was actually held, whether or not the pigs were going to allow us to have it. Stokely had selected a girl from Los Angeles to make all the arrangements for the rally: everything from the legal niceties of renting the auditorium, to the leaflets to be passed out in the community, to the spot announcements on the radio. She had prior experience in this business, and none of the hard niggers whom Bunchy had organized knew how to deal with that kind of shit. So we were delighted when Stokely cut us into this sister, Bobbi. What none of us knew, until it was too late, was that her old man, Babu, was uptight with the black Democrats.

Forman wired Babu up, and in turn got next to Bobbi. Forman was therefore in a position to wreck the rally unless we negotiated with him. His terms: Ron Karenga and Rev. Hartford Brookins had to speak at the rally. All of us, including Stokely, Forman, Karenga, and Bunchy had a meeting in the Black Congress building. The way that the shit stacked up was this: if we did not agree to allow Karenga and Brookins to speak at the rally, then the Black Congress would not support our attempt to force the city to allow us the use of the Sports Arena. On the other hand, if we accepted their speakers, the Black Congress would take the responsibility of getting the Sports Arena from the city.

The Black Congress representative, Walt Bremont, was kept busy running back and forth between the Black Congress building and City Hall. Our first position was that we would pick our own speakers, and if the city did not allow us to hold the rally inside the Sports Arena, then we would hold it in the streets. Stokely agreed that he would speak in the streets. We said that we would walk down Central Avenue from the East Side to Watts. When Bremont heard that, he jumped up and ran out of the Black Congress building, his black snake eyes gleaming as though he had seen his own grave being dug. We waited for him to come back. He told us that the whole thing was off, that they were not going to allow the rally in any shape, form, or fashion, and that was it. Furthermore, it would be best if all of us split town because the LAPD was sick of us.

Forman then proposed that Rev. Hartford Brookins be removed from the list, that another preacher, less odious because lesser known, be substituted for him. There was only Karenga to swallow. We regarded all these jacknapes as nuisances and stumbling blocks, because the two things we wanted out of the rally had nothing to do with them at all. Our first goal was to lock down support for Huey throughout Southern California, gain new recruits for the party, and get one up on the LAPD. We had demanded that no policemen come to the rally, that we did not want to see any of their uniforms, and that they were not welcome. We knew that they would come anyway, if they had to come naked, but there was a certain value we saw in challenging their authority, by stripping from them their aura of invincibility. If we could block them from controlling our rally, then many people would understand that, if properly organized, it was possible for the people to corral the police. We had already been successful in blocking the pigs out in Oakland, so we knew the value of it.

In the end, we had to compromise with Forman, accept the preacher and Karenga, because they brought to bear the telling argument that we were all outsiders, that Stokely, the principal speaker, was an outsider, and that the whole thing would fail if we did not have speakers from the local area. In addition, we had scheduled Reies Lopez Tierina, from Arizona, to speak for the Mexican Americans, so that we ran the risk of looking like a bunch of carpetbaggers. O.K., preacher, speak, but we've already heard all of your shit, and rejected it. You too, Ringo, as Bunchy called Karenga, go ahead and speak. After Stokely took the position that he thought Karenga should speak, we saw nothing else to do. But after that, Bunchy resolved that he would never find himself in that position again. He was going to work his ass off to see to that.

Bunchy and I both knew that we were living on borrowed time. We were both on parole and by now the pigs understood that we were working together in the party. Less than two months later, on April 4, 1968, Martin Luther King was assassinated. This event, more than any other, changed all our calculations. After the mammoth rallies staged in February, both in Oakland and Los Angeles, we felt that there was very little else to do on that level.

In the aftermath of the Oakland shoot-out on April 6, 1968, Eldridge Cleaver's parole was revoked and he was imprisoned at Vacaville in Solano County, to the north of the San Francisco Bay Area. While there, he wrote the following affidavit as a document to be used in his legal defense. It was later published by Ramparts *magazine.*

AFFIDAVIT NO. 1:

I AM 33 YEARS OLD

I am thirty-three years old. My first fifteen years were given to learning how to cope with the world and developing my approach to life. I blundered in my choices and set off down a road that was a dead end. Long years of incarceration is what I found on that road, from Juvenile Hall at the beginning to San Quentin, Folsom, and Soledad State Prisons at the end. From my sixteenth year, I spent the next fifteen years in and out of prison, the last time being an unbroken stay of nine years.

During my last stay in prison, I made the desperate decision to abandon completely the criminal path and to redirect my life. While in prison, I concentrated on developing the skills of a writer and I wrote a book which a publisher bought while I was still in prison and which was published after I was out on parole.

It looked like smooth sailing for me. I had fallen in love with a beautiful girl and got married; my book was soon to be published, and I had a good job as a staff writer with *Ramparts* magazine in San Francisco. I had broken completely with my old life. Having gone to jail each time out of Los Angeles, I had also put Los Angeles behind me, taking my parole to the Bay Area. I had a totally new set of friends and, indeed, I had a brand new life.

The thought of indulging in any "criminal activity" was as absurd and irrelevant as the thought of sprouting wings and flying to the moon. Besides, I was too busy. I joined the Black Panther Party, and because of my writing skills and interest in communications, became the editor of the party's newspaper, *The Black Panther.* In this I found harmony with my wife, Kathleen, who had worked in the communications department of SNCC in Atlanta, Georgia, and who, after our marriage, moved to San Francisco, joined the Black Panther Party, and became our Communications Secretary. Also, she is our party's candidate for the 18th Assembly District seat in San Francisco, running on the Peace and Freedom Party ticket. With my job at *Ramparts,* my political activity, editing the newspaper, and work on a new book, I had more to do than I could handle. My life was an endless round of speeches, organizational meetings, and a few hours snatched here and there on my typewriter.

I thought that the parole authorities would be pleased with my new life because in terms of complying with the rules governing conduct on parole, I was a model parolee. But such was not the case. My case was designated a "Special Study Case," which required that I see my parole agent four times each month, once at home, once at my job, once "in the field," and once in his office. My parole agent, Mr. R. L. Bilideau, was white, but his boss, Mr. Isaac Rivers, was a black man. Together these two gentlemen were my contact with the parole authorities. On a personal level, we got along very well together, and we spent many moments talking about the world and its problems. However, I could never believe in them as sincere friends, because they were organization men and experience had taught me that, on receiving orders from above, they would snap into line and close ranks against me.

The first time this happened was when, on April 15, 1967, I made a speech at Kezar Stadium criticizing this country's role in the war in Vietnam. The speech was part of the program of the Spring Mobilization Against the War in Vietnam, during the International Days of Protest. There were demonstrations from coast to coast. Dr. Martin Luther King spoke at the rally in New York and his wife at our rally at Kezar. The crowd was estimated at about 65,000 and the speeches were shown on television. Members of the parole authority, who don't like me, I was told, saw excerpts of my speech on TV and launched their campaign to have my parole revoked, but failed. Even though I had a perfect right to free speech, Mr. Rivers and Mr. Bilideau said there were those in the State Capital who, for political purposes, were clamoring to have my parole revoked and me returned to prison. They advised me to cool it and forsake my rights in the interest of not antagonizing those in Sacramento who did not like my politics. From then on, I was under constant pressure through them to keep my mouth shut and my pen still on any subject that might arouse a negative reaction in certain circles in Sacramento. Because I was violating neither any law of the land nor any rule of parole, upon being assured by my attorney that I was strictly within my rights, I decided not to accept these warnings and continued exercising my right to free speech and to write what was on my mind.

The next crisis occurred two weeks later when I was arrested in Sacramento with a delegation of armed Black Panthers, who visited the Capitol in this manner as a shrewd political and publicity gesture. The news media, heavily concentrated in the Capitol, gave the Black Panthers a million dollars' worth of publicity and helped spread the Panther message to black people that they should arm themselves against a racist country that was becoming increasingly repressive. Although I was there as a reporter, with an assignment from my magazine, and with the advance permission of my parole agent, I was arrested by the Sacramento police; and then the parole authority slapped a "Hold" on me so that I could not get out on bail. To the surprise of both the cops and the parole authority, their investigations proved that my press credentials were in order, that I was indeed there on an assignment, and that I had permission from my parole agent—also, that I had been armed with nothing more lethal than a camera and a ball point pen. Still the Sacramento cops would not drop the charges and the parole authority would not lift its "Hold" until the judge, citing the obvious "mistake" on the part of the cops, released me on my own recognizance. Then, magnanimously, the parole authority lifted its "Hold."

When I returned to San Francisco, I was again told about the clamor in Sacramento to have my parole revoked. My enemies, I was told, had stayed up all night scanning TV film footage, trying to find a shot of me with a gun in my hands. No luck. But anyhow, severe new restrictions were to be imposed. 1) I was not to go outside a seven mile area; specifically, I was not to cross the Bay Bridge. 2) I was to keep my name out of the news for the next six months; specifically, my face was not to appear on any TV screen. 3) I was not to make any more speeches. 4) And I was not to write anything critical of the California Department of Corrections or any California politician. In short, I was to play dead, or I would be sent back to prison. "All that Governor Reagan has to do," I was told, "is sign his name on a dotted line and you are dead, with no appeal." Knowing that this was true and with my back thus to the wall, I decided to play it cool and go along with them, as I didn't see what else I could do. My attorneys said that we could challenge it in court, but that I would probably have to pound the Big Yard in San Quentin for a couple of years, waiting for the court to hand down a decision. I was in a bad bag.

Things stayed like that, but after a couple of months the travel ban was lifted with all the other restrictions remaining in force.

Then, on October 28, 1967, Huey Newton, Minister of Defense and leader of our party, was shot down in the streets by an Oakland cop and was arrested and charged with the murder of one Oakland cop and the wounding of another. Bobby Seale, Chairman of our party, was serving a six months' jail sentence for the Sacramento incident, and I was the only other effective public speaker that we had. A campaign to mobilize support in Huey's defense had to be launched immediately. So in November, 1967, I started making speeches again and writing in Huey's defense. The political nature of the case, and the fact that it involved a frame-up by the Oakland Police Department and the D.A.'s office, dictated that I had not only to criticize politicians but also the police. Well, helping Huey stay out of the gas chamber was more important than my staying out of San Quentin, so I went for broke. TV, radio, newspapers, magazines, the works. I missed no opportunity to speak out with Huey's side of the story. Mr. Rivers and Mr. Bilideau told me that the decision had already been made above to revoke my parole at the first pretext. Living thus on borrowed time, I tried to get as much done as I possibly could before time ran out.

In the latter part of December 1967, Bobby Seale's sentence ran out and he was free to speak. Mass public support for Huey had developed. Our party had formed a coalition with the new Peace and Freedom Party, demanding that Huey be set free. In addition, we arranged to run Huey for Congress in the 7th Congressional District of Alameda County, to run Bobby Seale for the 17th Assembly District, and, as I have mentioned, to run my wife, Kathleen, for the 18th Assembly seat in San Francisco.

With such a forum and with the assurance that we had already stimulated overwhelming support for Huey, I decided to back up a little. Maybe it was possible to stay the hand of the parole authority. I cut back drastically on my public speaking.

In January, the Police departments of Oakland, Berkeley and San Francisco unleashed a terror and arrest campaign against the Black Panther Party. Members of the party were being arrested and harassed constantly. On January 15, 1968, at 3 A.M. the Special Tactical Squad of San Francisco's Police Department kicked down the door of my home, terrorizing my wife, myself, and our party's Revolutionary Artist, Emory Douglass, who was our guest that night.

On February 17, which was Huey Newton's twenty-sixth birthday, we staged a huge rally at the Oakland Auditorium, featuring Stokely Carmichael and his first public speech following his triumphal tour of the revolutionary countries of the world, and also featuring, as a surprise guest, H. Rap Brown, along with the venerable James Forman, who took the occasion to announce the merger of SNCC and the Black Panther Party. Held in the shadow of the Alameda County jail wherein Huey is confined, the theme of the rally was "Come See About Huey." Over five thousand people showed up, a shattering and unequivocal demonstration of the broad support built up for the Minister of Defense. A similar rally was held in Los Angeles the next day, and altogether Stokely spent nine days in California beating the drums for Huey.

Every time we turned around Bobby Seale was getting arrested on frivolous, trumped-up charges. On February 22, 1968, a posse of Berkeley police kicked down Bobby's door, dragging him and his wife, Artie, from bed and arresting them on a sensational charge of conspiracy to commit murder. The same night, six other members of the party were arrested on the same charge. The ridiculous charge of conspiracy to commit murder was quickly dropped, but all arrested were held to answer on various gun law violations, all of which were unfounded. All in all, during that hectic week, sixteen members of our party were arrested gratuitously and charged with offenses that had never been committed. Although we know that we will ultimately beat all of these cases in court, they constitute a serious drain on our time, energy, and financial resources, the last of which have always been virtually non-existent.

During these hectic days, public sentiment throughout the Bay Area swung heavily in our favor because it was obvious to a blind man that we were being openly persecuted by the police.

In the midst of all this, McGraw-Hill Publishing Co., on February 28, 1968, published my book, *Soul on Ice,* and a lot of publicity was focused on me as a result. By this time, my parole agent had virtually given up coming to see me, sending for me, or even calling me on the phone, a development that kept my nerves on edge. Was this the calm before the storm?

I was out of the state most of the month of March, filling TV appearances with my book, mostly in New York.

On April 3, 1968, the Oakland Police Department invaded the regular meeting of our party at St. Augustine's Church at 27th and West Street. Led by a captain, brandishing shotguns, and accompanied by a white monsignor and a black preacher, about a dozen of them burst through the door. Neither Bobby Seale nor myself was at that particular meeting (Bobby was in L.A. and I had left minutes before the raid in response to an urgent call). Our National Captain, David Hilliard, was in charge. David said that the cops came in with their shotguns leveled, but that when they saw him in charge they looked confused and disappointed. Mumbling incoherently, they lowered their weapons and stalked out.

Father Neil, whose church it is, happened to be present to witness the entire event. Theretofore, criticism of the police had been just that, and although he was inclined to believe that there was some validity to all the complaints, it was all still pretty abstract to him because he had never witnessed anything with his own eyes. Well, he had witnessed it now, and in his own church—with ugly shotguns thrown down on innocent, unarmed people who were holding a quiet peaceful assembly. Father Neil was outraged. He called a press conference the next day at which he denounced the Oakland Police Department for behaving like Nazi storm troopers inside his church. However, Father Neil's press conference was upstaged by the fact that earlier in the day, his brother of the cloth, Martin Luther King, had got assassinated in Memphis, Tennessee. An ugly cloud boding evil settled over the nation.

A few days prior to the assassination of Martin Luther King, Marlon Brando had flown up from Hollywood to find out for himself what the hell was going on in the Bay Area. We took him to my pad and talked and argued with him all night long, explaining to him our side of the story. We had to wade through the history of the world before everything was placed in perspective and Brando could see where the Black Panther Party was coming from. When Brando split back to Hollywood, after accompanying Bobby Seale to court the next day, we felt that we had gained a sincere friend and valuable ally in the struggle.

On the third night following the raid on St. Augustine's church, members of the Oakland Police Department tried to kill me. They did kill my companion, Little Bobby Hutton, Treasurer of our party and the first Black Panther recruited by Huey Newton and Bobby Seale when they organized the party in October 1966. They murdered Little Bobby in cold blood. I saw them shoot him, with fifty guns aimed at my head. I did get shot in the leg.

I am convinced that I was marked for death that night, and the only reason I was not killed was that there were too many beautiful black people crowded around demanding that the cops not shoot me, too many witnesses for even the brazen, contemptuous and contemptible Oakland Pigs.

A few hours later at 4 A.M. on April 7, someone somewhere in the shadowy secret world of the California Adult Authority ordered my parole revoked. While I was still in the emergency ward of Highland Hospital, three Oakland cops kept saying to me: "You're going home to San Quentin tonight!" Before the sun rose on a new day, charged with attempted murder after watching Little Bobby being murdered and almost joining him, I was shackled hand and foot and taken by Lieutenant Snellgrove and two other employees of the Department of Corrections to San Quentin.

Lieutenant Snellgrove, whom I knew very well from my stay at San Quentin and who remembered me, looked at me and said, while we rode in the back seat of the car headed for San Quentin, "Bad night, huh?" He was not being facetious—what else could he say—and neither was I. "Yeah," I said. "About the baddest yet."

Further, Affiant sayeth not.

April 19, 1968

When the California Adult Authority announced its intention of having Cleaver's parole revoked again, Playboy dispatched Nat Hentoff to interview the embattled activist in San Francisco before he was once again incommunicado behind bars.

Returning to New York with the longest and most searching interview Cleaver has ever granted, Hentoff wrote of his subject:

> Having corresponded briefly with him while he was in prison a few years ago and having read Soul on Ice, I was aware of the probing, resourceful quality of Cleaver's mind. But I wondered if some of the flamboyant rhetoric of his public statements since he'd become prominent indicated a change in the man—his constant use of the word "pigs" to describe police, for example; the incendiary tone of a recent Yippie-Panther Manifesto, signed by Cleaver and three leaders of the white student group, which in effect declared war on the establishment; and statements like: "The cities of America have tasted the first flames of revolution. But a hotter fire rages in the heart of black people today: total liberty for black people or total destruction for America." Was he turning into a demagogue?

> We met in the office of his . . . attorney, Charles Garry. . . . The bearded Cleaver, in black leather jacket, black pants and an open shirt, was initially reserved and preoccupied.

> Leaving the office, he and Kathleen drove me through the black Fillmore district of San Francisco, where he was frequently recognized and waved at—particularly by the young. Dropping Kathleen off, Cleaver and I went to a white friend's house overlooking San Francisco Bay.

> We started talking in the afternoon and continued late into the night. Cleaver gradually relaxed, but not entirely. Tautness remained, a reflection of the constant tension under which he works. I remembered, as we talked, the conversations I'd had with Malcolm X; both were intrigued with ideas and their ramifications, but both were impatient with theoretical formulations that did not have application to immediate reality.

> As the interview went on, I was more and more impressed with Eldridge Cleaver—with the quality of his mind, with the depth of his determination, with the totality of his commitment to his role as a leader in the new stage of the black movement for liberation. It was on the question of this new stage and the kind of leadership he's convinced it requires that the interview began.

PLAYBOY INTERVIEW

Excerpt from the Playboy Interview: Eldridge Cleaver, Playboy *magazine (December 1968). Copyright © 1968 by Playboy. Reprinted with permission. All rights reserved.*

PLAYBOY: You have written that "a new black leadership with its own distinct style and philosophy will now come into its own, to center stage. Nothing can stop this leadership from taking over, because it is based on charisma, has the allegiance and support of the black masses, is conscious of its self and its position and is prepared to shoot its way to power if the need arises." As one who is increasingly regarded as among the pivotal figures in this new black leadership, how do you distinguish the new breed from those—such as Roy Wilkins and Whitney Young—most Americans consider the established Negro spokesmen?

CLEAVER: The so-called leaders you name have been willing to work within the framework of the rules laid down by the white establishment. They have tried to bring change within the system as it now is—without violence. Although Martin Luther King was the leader-spokesman for the nonviolent theme, all the rest condemn violence, too. Furthermore, all are careful to remind everybody that they're Americans as well as "Negroes," that the prestige of this country is as important to them as it is to whites. By contrast, the new black leadership identifies first and foremost with the best interests of the masses of *black* people, and we don't care about preserving the dignity of a country that has no regard for ours. We don't give a damn about any embarrassments we may cause the United States on an international level. . . .

PLAYBOY: So far—apart from your willingness to resort to violence in achieving that goal—you haven't proposed anything specific, or different from the aims of the traditional Negro leadership.

CLEAVER: OK, the best way to be specific is to list the ten points of the Black Panther Party. They make clear that we are not willing to accept the rules of the white establishment. One: We want freedom;

we want power to determine the destiny of our black communities. Two: We want full employment for our people. Three: We want housing fit for the shelter of human beings. Four: We want all black men to be exempt from military service. Five: We want decent education for black people—education that teaches us the true nature of this decadent, racist society and that teaches young black brothers and sisters their rightful place in society; for if they don't know their place in society and the world, they can't relate to anything else. Six: We want an end to the robbery of black people in their own communities by white-racist businessmen. Seven: We want an immediate end to police brutality and murder of black people. Eight: We want all black men held in city, county, state and federal jails to be released, because they haven't had fair trials; they've been tried by all-white juries, and that's like being a Jew tried in Nazi Germany. Nine: We want black people accused of crimes to be tried by members of their peer group—a peer being one who comes from the same economic, social, religious, historical and racial community. Black people, in other words, would have to compose the jury in any trial of a black person. And ten: We want land, we want money, we want housing, we want clothing, we want education, we want justice, we want peace.

PLAYBOY: Peace? But you've written that "the genie of black revolutionary violence is here."

CLEAVER: Yes, but put that into context. I've said that war will come only if these basic demands are not met. Not just a race war, which in itself would destroy this country, but a guerrilla resistance movement that will amount to a second Civil War, with thousands of white John Browns fighting on the side of the blacks, plunging America into the depths of its most desperate nightmare on the way to realizing the American Dream.

PLAYBOY: How much time is there for these demands to be met before this takes place?

CLEAVER: . . . How long do you expect black people, who are already fed up, to endure the continued indifference of the federal government to their needs? How long will they endure the continued escalation of police force and brutality? I can't give you an exact answer, but surely they will not wait indefinitely if their demands are not met—particularly since we think that the United States has already decided where its next campaign is going to be after the war in Vietnam is over. We think the government has already picked this new target area, and it's black America. A lot of black people are very uptight about what they see in terms of preparations for the suppression of the black liberation struggle in this country. We don't work on a timetable, but we do say that the situation is deteriorating rapidly. There have been more and more armed clashes and violent encounters with the police departments that occupy black communities. Who can tell at which point any one of the dozens of incidents that take place every day will just boil over and break out into an irrevocable war? Let me make myself clear. I don't dig violence. Guns are ugly. People are what's beautiful; and when you use a gun to kill someone, you're doing something ugly. But there are two forms of violence: violence directed at you to keep you in your place and violence to defend yourself against that suppression and to win your freedom. . . .

PLAYBOY: But other black militants, such as the leaders of CORE, are working now for black capitalism. They even helped draft a bill introduced in Congress last summer to set up neighborhood-controlled corporations. Federal funds would be channeled through those corporations and private firms would be given tax incentives to set up businesses in black neighborhoods—businesses that would eventually be turned over to ghetto residents through the corporations.

CLEAVER: I know. It's part of a big move across the country to convince black people that this way, they can finally get into the economic system. But we don't feel it's going to work, because it won't go far enough and deep enough to give the masses of black people real community control of all their institutions. Remember how the War on Poverty looked on paper and how it worked out? You may recall that of all the organizations around then, it was CORE that rushed in most enthusiastically to embrace that delusion; in some cities, they formed a large part of the staff. But they didn't have the decisive control, and that's where it's at. They can call these new devices "community" corporations, but those private firms from the outside can always pull out and Congress can always cut down on the federal funds they put in, just as happened in the War on Poverty.

. . . A man finally reaches a point where he sees he's been tricked over and over again, and then he moves for ultimate liberation. But for the masses to achieve that, they will have to be organized so that they can make their collective weight felt, so that they themselves make the final decisions in their communities—from control of the police department to command over all social and economic programs that have to do with them. The struggle we're in now is on two levels—getting people together locally to implement our demands and organizing black people nationally into a unified body. We want black people to be represented by leaders of their choice who, with the power of the masses behind them, will be able to go into the political arena, set forth the desires and needs of black people and have those desires and needs acted upon.

PLAYBOY: But we repeat—isn't this already happening—at least on a small scale? There's a black mayor of Cleveland, Carl Stokes, and a black mayor of Gary, Richard Hatcher.

CLEAVER: You're talking about black personalities, not about basic changes in the system. There is a large and deepening layer of black people in this country who cannot be tricked anymore by having a few black faces put up front. Let me make this very clear. We are demanding structural changes in society, and that means a real redistribution of power, so that we have control over our own lives. Having a black mayor in the present situation doesn't begin to accomplish that. And this is a question of more than breaking out of poverty. I know there are a lot of people in this country, particularly in urban ghettos, who are going hungry, who are deprived on all levels; but, obviously, it's not a matter of rampant famine. The people we deal with in the Black Panther Party are not literally dying of hunger; they're not going around in rags. But they are people who are tired of having their lives controlled and manipulated by outsiders and by people hostile to them. They're moving into a psychological and spiritual awareness of oppression, and they won't sit still for any more of it. Where we are now is in the final stages of a process with all our cards on the table. We've learned how to play cards; we know the game and we're just not going to be tricked any more. That's what seems so difficult to get across to people.

PLAYBOY: Is it a trick, however, when Senator Eugene McCarthy, among others, says that since more and more industry and, therefore, jobs, are moving out to the suburbs, more blacks will have to move there, too, with accompanying desegregation of housing in the suburbs and massive funds for improved transportation facilities? Isn't that a sincere analysis of a current trend?

CLEAVER: We feel that a lot of these attempts to relocate black people are essentially hostile moves to break up the concentration of blacks, because in that concentration of numbers, we have potential political power. We didn't choose to be packed into ghettos, but since that's where we are, we're not going to get any real power over our lives unless we use what we have—our strength as a bloc. A lot of people in the Republican and Democratic Parties are worried about all this potential black voting power in the cities; that's why, under the guise of bettering the conditions of black people, they're trying to break us up.
  . . . The issue and the dilemma [is] how to find a revolutionary mode of moving in this most complicated of all situations. The people who supported McCarthy found out *that* wasn't the way. I'm not saying we, the Black Panthers, have the answer, either, but we're trying to find the way. One thing we do know is that we have to bring a lot of these loosely connected elements of opposition into an organizational framework. You can't have an amorphous thing pulling in all directions and realistically call it a "revolutionary movement." That's why we're organizing among blacks and intend the Panthers to be *the* black national movement. At the same time, it makes no sense to holler for freedom for the black community and have no interconnection with white groups who also recognize the need for fundamental change. It's by coalition that we intend to bring together all the elements for liberation—by force, if all the alternatives are exhausted.

PLAYBOY: Are they exhausted, in your opinion?

CLEAVER: Not yet, but time is running out. It may still be possible, barely possible, to revolutionize this society—to get fundamental structural changes—without resorting to civil war, but only if we get enough power before it's too late.

PLAYBOY: Police and federal agencies have shown great skill in infiltrating radical movements—including the Panthers. If conditions became such that you decided guerrilla warfare was the only alternative, isn't it likely that your group and all its potential allies—with or without the help of black veterans—would be instantly neutralized from within, because the government would know every move you planned?

CLEAVER: As for the Panthers, we have always worked on the assumption that we're under constant surveillance and have long been infiltrated. But we figure this is something you just have to live with. In any case, the destruction of a particular organization will not destroy the will to freedom among any oppressed people. Nor will it destroy the certainty that they'll act to win it. Sure, we try to take precautions to make sure we're not including hostile elements in our organization, but we don't spend all our time worrying about it. If we go under—and that could easily be done with police frame-ups right now—there'll be others to take our place.

PLAYBOY: Have you considered the possibility that you could be wrong about the chances of waging a successful guerrilla war? Don't you run the risk that all your efforts toward that end—even if they don't escalate beyond rhetoric—could invite a massive wave of repression that would result in a black blood bath and turn the country's ghettos into concentration camps?

CLEAVER: It seems to me a strange assumption that black people could just be killed or cooped up into concentration camps and that would be the end of it. This isn't the 1930s. We're not going to play Jews. The whole world is different now from what it was then. Not only would black people resist, with the help of white people, but we would also have the help of those around the world who are just waiting for some kind of extreme crisis within this country so that they can move for their own liberation from American repression abroad. This government does not have unlimited forces of repression; it can't hold the whole world down—not at home *and* abroad. Eventually, it will be able to control the racial situation here only by ignoring its military "commitments" overseas. That might stop *our* movement for a while, but think what would be happening in Latin America, Asia and Africa. In that event, there would be a net gain for freedom in the world. We see our struggle as inextricably bound up with the struggle of all op-pressed peoples, and there is no telling what sacrifices we in this coun-try may have to make before that struggle is won.

PLAYBOY: Do you think you have any real chance of winning that struggle—even without government repression—as long as the ma-jority of white Americans, who outnumber blacks ten to one, remain hostile or indifferent to black aspirations? According to the indica-tions of recent public-opinion surveys, they deplore even *nonviolent* demonstrations on behalf of civil rights.

CLEAVER: At the present stage, the majority of white people are indif-ferent and complacent simply because their own lives have remained more or less intact and as remote from the lives of most blacks as the old French aristocracy was from "the great unwashed." It's disturbing to them to hear about Hough burning, Watts burning, the black community in Newark burning. But they don't really understand why it's happening, and they don't really care, as long as *their* homes and *their* places of work—or the schools to which they send their chil-dren—aren't burning, too. So for most whites, what's happened up to now has been something like a spectator sport. There may be a lot more of them than there are of us, but they're not really involved; and there are millions and millions of black people in this country who *are*—more than the census shows. Maybe 30 million, maybe more. A lot of black people never get counted in the census. It's not going to be easy to deal with that large a number, and it won't be possible to indefinitely limit the burning to black neighborhoods—even with all the tanks, tear gas, riot guns, paddy wagons and fire trucks in this country. But if it does come to massive repression of blacks, I don't think the majority of whites are going to either approve it or remain silent. If a situation breaks out in which soldiers are hunting down and killing black people obviously and openly, we don't think the ma-jority will accept that for long. It could go on for a while, but at some point, we think large numbers of whites would become so revolted that leaders would arise in the white community and offer other solutions. So we don't accept the analysis that we're doomed because we're in a minority. We don't believe that the majority in this country would permit concentration camps and genocide.

PLAYBOY: Suppose you're right in claiming that most whites, for whatever reason, would not support massive repression of blacks in this country. These same whites, however, don't want black violence, either—but as you point out, most don't fully grasp the dimensions of the injustices against which that violence is a rebellion, nor do they understand why it continues in the wake of several milestone civil rights laws and Supreme Court decisions. The familiar question is: "What more do they want?" How would you answer it?

CLEAVER: I can only answer with what Malcolm X said. If you've had a knife in my back for four hundred years, am I supposed to thank you for pulling it out? Because that's all those laws and decisions have accomplished. The very least of your responsibility now is to compensate me, however inadequately, for centuries of degradation and disenfranchisement by granting peacefully—before I take them forcefully—the same rights and opportunities for a decent life that you've taken for granted as an American birthright. This isn't a request but a *demand,* and the ten points of that demand are set down with crystal clarity in the Black Panther Party platform.

PLAYBOY: Many would doubt that you're serious about some of them. Point four, for instance: "We want all black men to be exempt from military service."

CLEAVER: We couldn't be more serious about that point. As a colonized people, we consider it absurd to fight the wars of the mother country against other colonized peoples, as in Vietnam right now. The conviction that no black man should be forced to fight for the system that's suppressing him is growing among more and more black people, outside the Black Panther Party as well as in it. And as we can organize masses of black people behind that demand for exemption, it will have to be taken seriously.

PLAYBOY: Are you equally serious about point eight, which demands that all black prisoners held in city, county, state and federal jails be released because they haven't had fair trials; and about point nine, which demands that the black defendants be tried by all black juries?

CLEAVER: We think the day will come when these demands, too, will receive serious attention, because they deserve it. Take point eight. All the social sciences—criminology, sociology, psychology, economics—point out that if you subject people to deprivation and inhuman living conditions, you can predict that they will rebel against those conditions. What we have in this country is a system organized against black people in such a way that many are forced to rebel and turn to forms of behavior that are called criminal in order to get the things they need to survive. Consider the basic contradiction here. You subject people to conditions that make rebellion inevitable and then you punish them for rebelling. Now, under those circumstances, does the black convict owe a debt to society or does society owe a debt to the black convict? Since the social, economic and political system is so rigged against black people, we feel the burden of the indictment should rest on the system and not on us. Therefore, black people should not be confined in jails and prisons for rebelling against that system—even though the rebellion might express itself in some unfortunate ways. And this idea can be taken further, to apply also to those white people who have been subjected to a disgusting system for so long that they resort to disgusting forms of behavior. This is part of our fundamental critique of the way this society, under its present system of organization, molds the character of its second-class citizens.

PLAYBOY: Have you considered the consequences to society of opening the prisons and setting all the inmates free? Their behavior may in one sense be society's fault, but they're still criminals.

CLEAVER: We don't feel that there's any black man or any white man in any prison in this country who could be compared in terms of criminality with Lyndon Johnson. No mass murderer in any penitentiary in America or in any other country comes anywhere close to the thousands and thousands of deaths for which Johnson is responsible.

PLAYBOY: Do you think that analogy is valid? After all, Johnson has been waging a war, however misguidedly, in the belief that his cause is just.

CLEAVER: Many murderers feel exactly the same way about *their* crimes. But let me give you another example: Compare the thieves in our prisons with the big-businessmen of this country, who are in control of a system that is depriving millions of people of a decent life. These people—the men who run the government and the corporations—are much more dangerous than the guy who walks into a store with a pistol and robs somebody of a few dollars. The men in control are robbing the entire world of billions and billions of dollars.

PLAYBOY: *All* the men in control?

CLEAVER: That's what I said: and they're not only stealing money, they're robbing people of life itself. When you talk about criminals, you have to recognize the vastly different degrees of criminality.

PLAYBOY: You still haven't answered our question about the social consequences of releasing all those now behind bars.

CLEAVER: Those who are now in prison could be put through a process of real rehabilitation before their release—not caged like animals, as they are now, thus guaranteeing that they'll be hardened criminals when they get out if they weren't when they went in. By rehabilitation I mean they would be trained for jobs that would not be an insult to their dignity, that would give them some sense of security, that would allow them to achieve some brotherly connection with their fellow man. But for this kind of rehabilitation to happen on a large scale would entail the complete reorganization of society, not to mention the prison system. It would call for the teaching of a new set of ethics, based on the principle of cooperation, as opposed to the presently dominating principle of competition. It would require the transformation of the entire moral fabric of this country into a way of being that would make these former criminals feel more obligated to their fellow man than they do now. The way things are today, however, what reasons do these victims of society have for feeling an obligation to their fellow man? I look with respect on a guy who has walked the streets because he's been unable to find a job in a system that's rigged against him, who doesn't go around begging and instead walks into a store and says, "Stick 'em up, motherfucker!" I prefer that man to the Uncle Tom who does nothing but just shrink into himself and accept any shit that's thrown into his face.

PLAYBOY: Would you feel that way if it were *your* store that got held up?

CLEAVER: That's inconceivable; I wouldn't own a store. But for the sake of argument, let's say I did. I'd still respect the guy who came in and robbed me more than the panhandler who mooched a dime from me in the street.

PLAYBOY: But would you feel he was *justified* in robbing you because of his disadvantaged social background?

CLEAVER: Yes, I would—and this form of social rebellion is on the rise. When I went to San Quentin in 1958, black people constituted about 30 percent of the prison population. Recently, I was back at San Quentin, and the blacks are now in the majority. There's an incredible number of black people coming in with each new load of prisoners. Moreover, I've talked to a lot of other people who've been in different prisons, and the percentage of black inmates there, too, is indisputably climbing. And within that growing number, the percentage of *young* black prisoners is increasing most of all. Youngsters from the ages of eighteen to twenty-three are clearly in the majority of the new people who come to prison. The reason is that for a lot of black people, including the young, jobs are almost non-existent, and the feeling of rebellion is particularly powerful among the young. Take a guy who was four years old in 1954, when the Supreme Court decision on school desegregation was handed down, a decision that was supposed to herald a whole new era. Obviously, it didn't, but it did accelerate agitation and unrest. So this guy, who was four then, has had a lifetime of hearing grievances articulated very sharply but of seeing nothing changed. By the time he's eighteen or nineteen, he's very, very uptight. He's very turned off to the system and he has it in his mind that he's justified in moving against so unjust a system in any way he sees fit.

PLAYBOY: Can that be the whole explanation for the growing number of young black prisoners? Are they all in conscious rebellion against the white power structure?

CLEAVER: That's not the whole explanation, of course, but it would be a mistake to underestimate that rising mood of rebellion. Whatever their conscious motivation, though, every one of them is in prison because of the injustice of society itself. White people are able to get away with a lot of things black people can't begin to get away with; cops are much quicker to make busts in black neighborhoods. And even when they're arrested, whites are ahead because more of them can afford attorneys. A lot of black cats end up in prison solely because they didn't have someone to really present their cases in court. They're left with the public defenders, whom prison inmates quite accurately call "penitentiary deliverers." I'll tell you what usually happens. It's the common practice of the police to file ten or so charges on you, and then the public defender comes and says, "Look, we can't beat them all, so the best thing you can do is plead guilty on one count. If you do that, I can get the others dropped." So a black cat is sitting there without real legal help, without any money, and he knows that if he's convicted of all ten counts, he'll get a thousand years. He's in a stupor of confusion and winds up taking the advice of the public defender. He doesn't know the law. He doesn't know how to make legal motions. He doesn't really know what's going on in that courtroom. So he goes along, wakes up in the penitentiary, starts exchanging experiences with other guys who have been through the same mill; and if he wasn't a rebel when he went in, he'll be a revolutionary by the time he gets out.

PLAYBOY: What happens to the ordinary black inmate who has no special talent that earns him a reputation—and influential supporters— outside of prison?

CLEAVER: When I was in the guidance center at San Quentin last spring, I saw a lot of people like that—people I've known for years. Two of them had been in Los Angeles Juvenile Hall with me the first time I was ever arrested—some eighteen years ago. Since then, they had done some time and been paroled, and here they were back in San Quentin on bullshit charges of parole violation. That's a device used all the time to keep sending people back to prison. These guys had done nothing more than have personality clashes with their parole officers, who were empowered to send them back up on their own arbitrary decision. This would never have happened if these guys had had any decent legal help. But neither had anybody outside but their mothers and fathers. And they were just two among hundreds of kids in that guidance center who'd been sent back on parole violations, for no better reason. They hadn't committed felonies; they hadn't done anything that would get the average white man hauled into court. The only conclusion one can draw is that the parole system is a procedure devised primarily for the purpose of running people in and out of jail—most of them black—in order to create and maintain a lot of jobs for the white prison system. In California, which I know best—and I'm sure it's the same in other states—there are thousands and thousands of people who draw their living directly or indirectly from the prison system: all the clerks, all the guards, all the bailiffs, all the people who sell goods to the prisons. They regard the inmates as a sort of product from which they all draw their livelihood, and the part of the crop they keep exploiting most are the black inmates.

PLAYBOY: You seem to alternate between advocating revolutionary violence and allowing for the possibility of social reform without violence. Which is it going to be?

CLEAVER: What happens, as I've said, will depend on the continuing dynamics of the situation. What we're doing now is telling the government that if it does not do its duty, then we will see to it ourselves that justice is done. Again, I can't tell you when we may have to start defending ourselves by violence from continued violence against us. That will depend on what is done against us and on whether real change can be accomplished non-violently within the system. We'd much rather do it that way, because we don't feel it would be a healthy situation to have even black revolutionaries going around distributing justice. I'd much prefer a society in which we wouldn't have to use—or even carry—guns, but that means the pigs would have to be disarmed, too. In the meantime, as long as this remains an unjust and unsafe society for black people, we're faced with a situation in which our survival is at stake. We will do whatever we must to protect our lives and to redeem the lives of our people—without too much concern for the niceties of a system that is rigged against us.

PLAYBOY: Some black militants say there is an alternative to revolution or capitulation: the formation of a separate black nation within the United States. At a meeting in Detroit last March, a group of black nationalists proposed the creation of a state called New Africa, encompassing all the territory now occupied by Alabama, Georgia, Louisiana, Mississippi and South Carolina. Do you think that's a viable plan?

CLEAVER: I don't have any sympathy with that approach, but the Black Panthers feel that it's a proposal black people should be polled on. There have been too many people and too many organizations in the past who claimed to speak for the ultimate destiny of black people. Some call for a new state; some have insisted that black people should go back to Africa. We Black Panthers, on the other hand, don't feel we should speak for all black people. We say that black people deserve an opportunity to record their own national will.

PLAYBOY: Few, if any, colonized peoples have the support of a contingent of the colonizing power; yet the Black Panthers have formed a working coalition with the Peace and Freedom Party in California—a group that is predominantly white. Isn't there an ideological inconsistency in such a coalition—despite what you've said about the good will and dedication of many sympathetic young whites—at a time when other militant black organizations, such as SNCC, pointedly reject all white allies as agents of the white power structure?

CLEAVER: There is no inconsistency if you don't confuse coalitions with mergers. We believe black people should be in full control of their organizations; the Black Panthers have always been. You may remember that Stokely Carmichael, when he came out for an all-black SNCC, also said that the role of whites was to go into their own communities and organize, so that there could be a basis for eventual coalitions. We've now reached a point where many white people have, in fact, organized in their own communities; therefore, we see no reason to maintain an alienated posture and to refuse to work with such groups.

PLAYBOY: One of the passages in *Soul on Ice* had particular impact on many young white people who felt they had been drummed out of "the movement." You wrote: "There is in America today a generation of white youth that is truly worthy of a black man's respect, and this is a rare event in the foul annals of American history." Having since worked in collaboration with the Peace and Freedom Party, do you still think as highly of the new generation of white youth?

CLEAVER: I'm even more convinced it's true than when I wrote those lines. We work with these young people all the time, and we've had nothing but encouraging experiences with them. These young white people aren't hung up battling to maintain the status quo like some of the older people who think they'll become extinct if the system changes. They're adventurous: they're willing to experiment with new forms; they're willing to confront life. And I don't mean only those on college campuses. A lot who aren't in college share with their college counterparts an ability to welcome and work for change.

PLAYBOY: Do you agree with those who feel that this generation of youth is going to "sell out" to the status quo as it moves into middle age?

CLEAVER: I expect all of us will become somewhat less resilient as we get into our forties and fifties—if we live that long—and I'm sure that those who come after us will look back on us as being conservative. Even us Panthers. But I don't think this generation will become as rigid as the ones before; and, for that matter, I don't write off all older people right now. There are a lot of older whites and blacks who keep working for change. So there are people over thirty I trust. *I'm* over thirty, and I trust *me*.

PLAYBOY: Specifically, what can they do, what must they do, to earn your respect and trust?

CLEAVER: There are a whole lot of things they can do. They can organize white people so that together we can go into the halls of government, demand our rights—and get them. They can organize politically and get rid of all the clods and racists in the legislatures around the country. They can help keep the police from rioting. They can help make public servants recognize that they *are* public servants, that the public—black and white—pays their salaries and that they don't own the people and must be responsive to them. What can whites do? Just be Americans, as the rhetoric claims Americans are supposed to be. Just stand up for liberty everywhere. Stand up for justice everywhere—especially right here in their own country. Stand up for the underdog; that's supposed to be the American way. Make this *really* the home of the free. But that will never happen unless they help us conduct a thorough housecleaning of the political and economic arenas. Now is the time for whites to help us get the machinery together, to organize themselves and then form coalitions with black groups and Mexican and Puerto Rican groups that also want to bring about social change—and then act to do just that.

PLAYBOY: What about whites—undoubtedly a much larger number—who are just not revolutionaries but still want to work for positive change?

CLEAVER: That's simple, too. Find out which white organizations are for real and join them. Many whites can help educate other whites about the true nature of the system. And they can help black people—in the courts, in the social clubs, in the Congress, in the city councils, in the board rooms—win their demands for justice. The number-one problem right now, as we see it, is that of repression by the police. Whites should become aware of what the police are doing and why the Black Panther Party, to name only one group, has got so hung-up over this crucial question. It's not just police brutality and crimes; it's police intimidation of black communities. When we started, it became very clear to us that the reason black people don't come out to meetings, don't join organizations working for real change, is that they're afraid of various forms of retaliation from the police. They're afraid of being identified as members of a militant organization. So we recognized that the first thing we had to do was to expose and deal with the Gestapo power of the police. Once we've done that, we can move to mobilize people who will then be free to come out and start discussing and articulating their grievances, as well as proposing various changes and solutions. We are doing that in the Bay Area and in other areas where the Black Panther Party is now active. But there are many places where the police continue to intimidate, and it would be a great help for white people to start their own local organizations or to form local chapters of the Peace and Freedom Party. They could then focus community attention on what the police actually do—as opposed to what the police and the city administrations *claim* they do—and work with black people who are trying to break free. That kind of organized activity is really the only hope for this country.

PLAYBOY: If whites were to do this, wouldn't they have a lot to lose, even if they themselves don't become the victims of police repression? Radicals keep telling them that if they're really going to join in the struggle they can't go on living as they do now; that they can't expect to continue enjoying the material comforts of a system they intend to confront; that anyone who "breaks free" is going to have to change his entire style of life. Do you agree?

CLEAVER: Well, they're certainly going to have to give up those privileges that are based on the oppression and exploitation of other people. Most whites today are in the position of being the recipients of stolen property. This country was *built*, in large part, on the sweat of slaves. The standard of living most white people enjoy today is a direct result of the historical exploitation of blacks, and of the Third World, by the imperialist nations, of which America is now the leader. But thanks to technological advances, even if that exploitation were stopped and there were just distribution of wealth abroad and at home, whites wouldn't really have to suffer materially. If the money now used for bombs and airplanes were redirected to build more houses and better schools—as even the white man's Kerner Commission recommended—I can't see how white people would have to make any sacrifices at all. And think of how much more wholesome—and peaceful—a social environment there'd be for everybody. It seems to me the only whites who would be losing anything are those irretrievably committed, emotionally or economically, to the continued subordination of non-whites. But those whites who are not wedded to exploitation and oppression can only benefit if basic change comes.

PLAYBOY: . . . But how do you reconcile such expressions of hope with a statement you wrote for *Ramparts* shortly after the murder of Martin Luther King? "There is a holocaust coming . . . the war has begun. The violent phase of the black liberation struggle is here, and it will spread. From that shot, from that blood, America will be painted red. Dead bodies will litter the streets and the scenes will be reminiscent of the disgusting, terrifying, nightmarish news reports coming out of Algeria during the height of the general violence right before the final breakdown of the French colonial regime." If you really believe that, what's the point of talking about black-white coalitions?

CLEAVER: Let me emphasize again that I try to be realistic. I keep working for change, in the hope that violence will not be necessary; but I cannot pretend, in the face of the currently deteriorating situation, that a holocaust is not very possible, even likely. Perhaps if enough people recognize how possible it is, they'll work all the harder for the basic changes that can prevent it. Obviously, there have already been dead bodies on the streets since the murder of King; and at some point, there can occur an eruption that will escalate beyond control. But let me also make clear that I do not justify shooting the wrong people. If the holocaust comes, the bodies on the streets would be those of the oppressors: those who control the corporations that profiteer off the poor, that oil the war machine, that traffic with racist nations like South Africa; those who use the economic and military power of the U.S. to exploit and exterminate the disenfranchised in this country and around the world; and, above all, those politicians who use their public trust to kill social reform and perpetuate injustice. The rest are just part of the machinery. They're not making decisions. They're not manipulating the masses. They're being manipulated themselves by the criminals who run the country.

PLAYBOY: In everything you say, there are the intertwining themes of vengeance and forgiveness, of violent revolution and nonviolent social reform; and that leads to a good deal of confusion among many whites as to what the Black Panthers are really for. On the one hand, you write of the coming holocaust and of bodies littering the streets. And yet the day before you wrote that article, you were at a junior high school in Oakland, where the black kids had decided to burn down the school in anger at the murder of Dr. King, and you talked them out of it. Similarly, you and other Panthers speak of a black revolutionary generation that has the courage to kill; yet when a group of seventh and eighth graders at another Oakland school tried to emulate what they thought the Panthers stood for by turning into a gang and beating up other kids, several Panther leaders went to the school at the invitation of the principal and told the kids they were in the wrong bag. The Panthers' advice was for black youngsters to study hard, so that they could be in a better position to help their brothers. They also told them not to hate whites but to learn to work with them. Which is the *real* Black Panther philosophy?

CLEAVER: There is no contradiction between what we say and what we do. We are for responsible action. That's why we don't advocate people going around inventing hostilities and burning down schools and thereby depriving youngsters of a place to learn. What we do advocate is that hostilities in the black community be focused on specific targets. The police are a specific target. As I said before, we are engaged in organizing black communities so that they will have the power to stop the police from wanton harassment and killing of black people. And that also means self-defense, if necessary. Beyond that, it means getting enough power so that we can have autonomous black departments of safety in black communities. We have the courage—and the good sense—to defend ourselves, but we are not about to engage in the kind of random violence that will give the pigs an opportunity to destroy us. We are revolutionary, but that means we're disciplined, that we're working out programs, that we intend to create a radical political machinery in coalition with whites that will uproot this decadent society, transform its politics and economics and build a structure fit to exist on a civilized planet inhabited by *humanized* beings.

PLAYBOY: You say the police are a prime target for Panther hostility. Is this, perhaps, because the reverse is also true? Police departments in all the cities in which the Panthers have organized claim that your group is a public menace—engaged in beatings, shakedowns, thefts, shootings, fire bombings and other criminal activities.

CLEAVER: Who are the criminals? I know about these rumors of what Panthers are supposed to be doing, but that's all they are—false reports spread by racist cops. They'd like the public to forget that it was Black Panthers in Brooklyn who were attacked by off-duty *police* outside a courtroom last September. Who were the criminals there? And who shot up the Black Panther office in Oakland in a drunken orgy, riddling pictures of Huey Newton and me—and a picture of Bobby Hutton, whom they had already killed? Two pigs from the Oakland Police Department. Of course, they're going to spread these false rumors about us; it's one of the ways they're trying to destroy us before we destroy them with the truth about their own lawlessness.

PLAYBOY: Granted there have been conflicts between the Panthers and the police; but aren't you exaggerating their intent when you claim, as you did recently, that they're out to "systematically eliminate our leadership"?

CLEAVER: Not in the least. We are a great threat to the police and to the whole white power structure in Alameda County and in Oakland, where the Panthers were born. The police are the agents of the power structure, in trying to destroy us. Let me give you the background. When Bobby Seale and Huey Newton organized the Black Panther Party in October 1966, they initiated armed black patrols. Each car, which had four men, would follow the police around, observing them. When police accosted a citizen on the street and started doing something wrong to him, the patrol would be there as witnesses and to tell the person being mistreated what his rights were. In this way, the Panthers focused community attention on the police and the people learned they didn't have to submit to the kind of oppressive, arbitrary brutality that had been directed against the black people in Oakland for a long time.

When the Panthers started to educate the community, those in power were afraid that blacks would go on to organize and exercise real political power. And the police were told to prevent this. They tried to do this first by multiple arrests. Anyone known to be a Panther would be rousted on ridiculous charges that couldn't stand up in court but that led to our having to spend a lot of money on bail and legal fees. That didn't work. They couldn't intimidate us. Then in October 1967, they finally got Huey Newton into a position where a shoot-out occurred. Huey was wounded, a cop was killed and another was wounded. Murder charges were filed against Huey; he was eventually convicted and sentenced to two to fifteen years, and that case is now on appeal. After the shoot-out and the arrest of Huey, the whole Black Panther Party became involved in mobilizing community awareness of the political aspects of that case.

We had such great effect in that effort that the police tried even harder to stifle us. They moved against just about everyone who had taken an active part in speaking and mobilizing for Huey. To give you some examples, on January 15 of this year, our national captain, David Hilliard, was arrested while passing out leaflets at Oakland Tech. The next day, police broke down the door of my apartment and searched it without a warrant. On February 5, a Panther and his girl-friend were arrested for "disturbing the peace" after a rally at which Dr. Spock had spoken. They were beaten in jail. On February 24, Panther Jimmy Charley approached a policeman who was assaulting a black person. He questioned the officer and was immediately arrested and charged with "resisting arrest." On February 25, at 3:30 in the morning, police broke down the door of Bobby Seale's home. Again, there was no warrant. During the third and fourth weeks of February, there was a rash of arrests of black men either in the Panthers or identified with them. And on and on.

PLAYBOY: You've also been a spokesman for the Peace and Freedom Party, of which you were this year's Presidential nominee. How significant do you consider that kind of political activity, in terms of your plans for the growth of the Black Panthers?

CLEAVER: Well, I never exactly dreamed of waking up in the White House after the November election, but I took part in that campaign because I think it's necessary to pull a lot of people together, black and white. Certainly, we're concerned with building the Black Panther Party, but we also have to build a national coalition between white activists and black activists. We have to build some machinery so that they can work on a coordinated basis. Right now, you have thousands and thousands of young activists, black and white, who are working at cross-purposes, who don't communicate with one another, who are isolated and alienated from one another. But they could be a source of mutual strength and support. I believe that if we can simultaneously move forward the liberation struggle that's going on in the black colonies of this country and the revolutionary struggle that's going on in the mother country, we can amass the strength and numbers needed to change the course of American history.

PLAYBOY: There are those who believe that this vision of yours is just another of those fugitive illusions that appear from time to time among radicals, black and white. Michael Harris, a reporter for the *San Francisco Chronicle,* wrote in *The Nation* last July, quoting a law-enforcement agent who had infiltrated the Panthers: "If the federal government makes a serious effort to pump lots of money into the ghetto, you can likely kiss the Panthers goodbye. You simply can't agitate happy people." Do you think that's likely to happen?

CLEAVER: If the federal government moved to honor all the grievances of black people, not merely to alleviate but eliminate oppression, we'd be delighted to fold the whole thing up and call it a day. There are many other—and certainly safer—things we'd prefer to be doing with our lives. But until the government moves to undo all the injustices—every one of them, every last shadow of colonialism—no amount of bribes, brutality, threats or promises is going to deter us from our cause. There will be no compromise, no surrender and no sell-out; we will accept nothing less than total victory. That's why more and more black people have faith in us—because we offer a totally inflexible program in terms of our demands for black people, yet we have steered clear of doing this in a racist manner, as the Muslims have done. People are turning not to Muslims, not to the NAACP, not to CORE or SNCC but to the Black Panther Party.

PLAYBOY: You went back to prison in 1958 for a fourteen-year sentence, after being convicted of assault with intent to kill and rape. During the nine years you served, what changed you to the point at which you admitted, in *Soul on Ice,* that you were wrong? "I had gone astray," you wrote, "astray not so much from the white man's law as from being human, civilized—for I could not approve my own motivations, I did not feel justified. I lost my self-respect. My pride as a man dissolved and my whole fragile moral structure seemed to collapse, completely shattered."

CLEAVER: I came to realize that the particular women I had victimized had not been involved in actively oppressing me or other black people. I was taking revenge on them for what the whole system was responsible for. And as I thought about it, I felt I had become less than human. I also came to see that the price of hating other human beings is loving oneself less. But this didn't happen all at once; beginning to write was an important part of getting myself together. In fact, looking back, I started writing to save myself.

PLAYBOY: In none of your own writing so far have you gone into any detail about your formative years and about whether the pressures on you as a boy in the ghetto were representative, in your view, of the pressures on young black people throughout the society. Were they?

CLEAVER: So much so that I realized very soon after getting out of prison how little progress—if any—had been made in the nine years since I was sent up. What struck me more than anything else was the fact that the police still practice a systematic program to limit the opportunities in life for black cats by giving them a police record at an early age. In my own set, we were always being stopped and written up by the cops, even when we hadn't done anything. We'd just be walking down the street and the pigs would stop us and call in to see if we were wanted—all of which would serve to amass a file on us at headquarters. It's a general practice in this country that a young black gets put through this demeaning routine. But it's only one facet of the institutionalized conspiracy against black men in this country—to tame them, to break their spirit. As soon as he becomes aware of his environment, a black kid has to gauge his conduct and interpret his experiences in the context of his color and he has to orient himself to his environment in terms of how to survive as a black in a racist nation. But at least there's been one improvement in the years since I was a kid: Nowadays, being black—thanks to increasing white oppression—has been turned from a burden into an asset. Out there on the grade school and high school levels, young blacks are no longer uptight about their color. They're proud of it.

PLAYBOY: W. H. Ferry of the Center for the Study of Democratic Institutions maintains that "integration does not seem likely in the

United States now or in the future. Americans are afraid of living with differences." Do you agree?

CLEAVER: Well, talking about the future, I'd say that's up to white people. What black people want now is relief from being controlled and manipulated by white people. That could take the form of separation if white people continue to create conditions that make blacks convinced that total separation is the only alternative. If, on the other hand, conditions change sufficiently to end all exploitation and oppression of black people, then there is a possibility of integration in the long run for those who choose it. But we're a very long way from that.

PLAYBOY: In which direction would you like to see America go— toward separation or integration?

CLEAVER: Keeping in mind that we're talking about the very long view, it seems to me we're living in a world that has become virtually a neighborhood. If the world is not to destroy itself, the concept of people going their totally separate ways is really something that can't continue indefinitely. When you start speaking in ultimate terms, I don't see any way in which the world can be administered for the best interests of mankind without having a form of world government that would be responsive and responsible to *all* the people of the world—a world government that would function so that the welfare of no one segment of the population would be sacrificed for the enrichment of another.

PLAYBOY: How do you feel about Roy Wilkins' claim that America's black people really want what the white middle class already has under capitalism—split-level homes and all the accouterments of the affluent life?

CLEAVER: There's no question that black people want these things and have a right to them. The question is how to go about getting them. Many feel that they can get these things by entering into the mainstream of American society and becoming black capitalists. But to others, including myself, it's clear that in order for black people to have the best that society and technology are capable of providing, we need a new kind of society and a new kind of economic system. The goal must be to make possible a more equitable distribution of goods and services—but also to have a different set of values, so that things themselves don't become a substitute for life itself. In order to achieve that dual goal, we're going to have to move toward a new form of socialism. As long as there is so much stress on private property, we're going to have a society of competition rather than cooperation; we're going to have the exploited and the exploiters. Consider all these deeds, for example, that give people ownership of the productive and natural resources of this country. If there's going to be any burning, let's burn up these deeds, because everybody comes into this world the same way— naked, crying, without ownership of anything. The earth is here; it's given, like air and water, and I believe everyone should have equal access to its resources.

I want to see a society purged of Madison Avenue mind-benders who propagandize people into a mad pursuit of gadgets. They've conned people into believing that their lives depend on having an electric toothbrush, two cars and a color-television set in every room. We've got to rid ourselves of this dreadful and all-consuming hunger for *things,* this mindless substitution of the rat race for a humane life. Only then will people become capable of relating to other people on the basis of individual merit, rather than on the basis of status, property and wealth. The values I'm for are really quite traditional and simple—like respecting your fellow man, respecting your parents, respecting your leaders if they're true leaders. These revolutionary goals are as old as time itself: Let people be. Let them fulfill their capacities.

PLAYBOY: The ultimate society you envision, in *Soul on Ice,* is one in which male and female will "realize their true nature," thereby closing the present "fissure of society into antagonistic classes" and regenerating "a dying culture and civilization alienated from its biology." But some critics of the book felt that you seemed to reserve this new Garden of Eden for black people, who, you claim, are "the wealth of a nation, an abundant supply of unexhausted, unde-essenced human raw material upon which the future of the society depends and with which, through the implacable march of history to an ever-broader base of democracy and equality, the society will renew and transform itself."

CLEAVER: No, it's not limited to black people. Black or white, the male-female principle is toward unity. Both black and white people have to get out of the bags they're in to be natural again. White people have to disabuse themselves of the illusion that it's their job to rule and that the black man's job is to produce labor. And black men have to use their minds and acquire confidence in the products of their minds. This doesn't mean the white man has to let *his* mind fall into disuse, but he also has to relate to his body again, as the black man does. What I'm saying is that everyone needs a new understanding of his total nature, mental and physical. Only when people, black and white, start seeing themselves and acting as total individuals, with bodies and minds, will they stop assigning exclusive mental roles to one set of people and exclusive physical roles to another. Only then will the primary thrust of life—the fusion of male and female—be freed of sociological obstacles. That's the base of the kind of social system I want to see, a society in which a man and a woman can come as close as possible to total unity on the basis of natural attraction. In my own life, the more totally I've been able to relate to a particular woman, the more fulfilled I've been.

PLAYBOY: Have you ever been tempted to withdraw from the front lines of the revolutionary social struggle to pursue that process of self-fulfillment in private life, by writing and raising a family with your wife Kathleen?

CLEAVER: I could do that. I could withdraw. I've got enough money from the book so that I could get myself a pad away from all this shit. I could go down to my parole officer and say, "Look, man, I don't want to go back to prison. I'm going to stop talking revolution. I'm going to start writing poetry and fairy tales the way you want me to and I won't be a problem anymore. So how about re-evaluating my case and leaving me alone? Live and let live." I know they'd go for that, and I wouldn't need much money to do it because I'm not hung up on material things. But the fact is that I feel *good* working with my people and with the brothers of the Black Panther Party. I'd feel miserable doing anything else. Hell, most of my life has been involved in conflicts with authority, and now that I've politicized that conflict, I'm very content to be working for black liberation. I couldn't conceive of myself playing any other role—not even if I have to go back to prison for it. I'm going to do everything I can *not* to go back to prison, but I can't compromise my beliefs. I'd rather be dead than do that. And I may have a violent end, anyway. I'm hearing more and more these days from people telling me to be careful, because they feel my life's in danger. They may be right, but I say fuck it.

PLAYBOY: If you are imprisoned or killed, how much confidence do you have that the Black Panther Party or any succeeding group in the revolutionary struggle will ultimately prevail?

CLEAVER: I have confidence that people learn from experiences of others. Every time a black man is murdered for speaking out against oppression, his death is fuel for the struggle to continue. When Malcolm was killed, that didn't frighten people; his death created more disciples. I can only hope that if what I'm doing has any constructive value, others will take up the fight and continue it if I'm killed. Che Guevara put it the way I feel, when he said: "Wherever death may surprise us, let it be welcome, provided that this, our battle cry, may have reached some receptive ear and another hand may be extended to wield our weapons." That's all I ask for.

PLAYBOY: How do you rate your chances of survival?

CLEAVER: I plan to be around for quite a while.

October, 1968

When this article was first published in The Black Panther *in 1969, it was briefly introduced with the statement: "The following article introduces a new series of articles on the ideology of the Black Panther Party by our Minister of Information, Eldridge Cleaver."*

ON THE IDEOLOGY OF THE BLACK PANTHER PARTY

PART I

ONE OF THE GREAT CONTRIBUTIONS OF HUEY P. NEWTON IS THAT HE GAVE THE BLACK PANTHER PARTY A FIRM IDEOLOGICAL FOUNDATION THAT FREES US FROM IDEOLOGICAL FLUNKEYISM AND OPENS UP THE PATH TO THE FUTURE.

Eldridge Cleaver
Minister of Information

We have said: the ideology of the Black Panther Party is the historical experience of Black people and the wisdom gained by Black people in their 400 year long struggle against the system of racist oppression and economic exploitation in Babylon, interpreted through the prism of the Marxist-Leninist analysis by our Minister of Defense, Huey P. Newton.

However, we must place heavy emphasis upon the last part of that definition—'*interpreted . . . by our Minister of Defense. . . .*' The world of Marxism-Leninism has become a jungle of opinion in which conflicting interpretations, from Right Revisionism to Left Dogmatism, foist off their reactionary and blind philosophies as revolutionary Marxism-Leninism. Around the world and in every nation people, all who call themselves

Marxist-Leninists, are at each other's throats. Such a situation presents serious problems to a young party, such as ours, that is still in the process of refining its ideology.

When we say that we are Marxist-Leninists, we mean that we have studied and understood the classical principles of scientific socialism and that we have adapted these principles to our own situation for ourselves. However, we do not move with a closed mind to new ideas or information. At the same time, we know that we must rely upon our own brains in solving ideological problems as they relate to us.

For too long Black people have relied upon the analyses and ideological perspectives of others. Our struggle has reached a point now where it would be absolutely suicidal for us to continue this posture of dependency. No other people in the world are in the same position as we are, and no other people in the world can get us out of it except ourselves. There are those who are all too willing to do our thinking for us, even if it gets us killed. However, they are not willing to follow through and do our dying for us. If thoughts bring about our deaths, let them at least be our own thoughts, so that we will have broken, once and for all, with the flunkeyism of dying for every cause and every error—except our own.

One of the great contributions of Huey P. Newton is that he gave the Black Panther Party a firm ideological foundation that frees us from ideological flunkeyism and opens up the path to the future—a future to which we must provide new ideological formulations to fit our ever changing situation.

Much—*most*—of the teachings of Huey P. Newton are unknown to the people because Huey has been placed in a position where it is impossible for him to really communicate with us. And much that he taught while he was free has gotten distorted and watered down precisely because the Black Panther Party has been too hung up in relating to the courts and trying to put on a good face in order to help lawyers convince juries of the justice of our cause. This whole court hang-up has created much confusion.

For instance, many people confuse the Black Panther Party with the Free Huey Movement or the many other mass activities that we have been forced to indulge in in order to build mass support for our comrades who have gotten captured by the pigs. We are absolutely correct in indulging in such mass activity. But we are wrong when we confuse our mass line with our party line.

Essentially, what Huey did was to provide the ideology and the methodology for organizing the Black Urban Lumpenproletariat.

Armed with this ideological perspective and method, Huey transformed the Black Lumpenproletariat from the forgotten people at the bottom of society into the vanguard of the proletariat.

There is a lot of confusion over whether we are members of the Working Class or whether we are Lumpenproletariat. It is necessary to confront this confusion, because it has a great deal to do with the strategy and tactics that we follow and with our strained relations with the White radicals from the oppressor section of Babylon.

Some so-called Marxist-Leninists will attack us for what we have to say, but that is a good thing and not a bad thing because some people call themselves Marxist-Leninists who are the downright enemies of Black people. Later for them. We want them to step boldly forward, as they will do—blinded by their own stupidity and racist arrogance—so that it will be easier for us to deal with them in the future.

We make these criticisms in a fraternal spirit of how some Marxist-Leninists apply the classical principles to the specific situation that exists in the United States because we believe in the need for a unified revolutionary movement in the United States, a movement that is informed by the revolutionary principles of scientific socialism. Huey P. Newton says that "power is the ability to define phenomena and make it act in a desired manner." And we need power, desperately, to counter the power of the pigs that now bears so heavily upon us.

Ideology is a comprehensive definition of a status quo that takes into account both the history and the future of that status quo and serves as the social glue that holds a people together and through which a people relate to the world and other groups of people in the world. The correct ideology is an invincible weapon against the oppressor in our struggle for freedom and liberation.

Marx defined the epoch of the bourgeoisie and laid bare the direction of the Proletarian future. He analyzed Capitalism and defined the method of its doom: VIOLENT REVOLUTION BY THE PROLETARIAT AGAINST THE BOURGEOIS STATE APPARATUS OF CLASS OPPRESSION AND REPRESSION. REVOLUTIONARY VIOLENCE AGAINST THE COUNTER-REVOLUTIONARY CLASS VIOLENCE PERPETRATED THROUGH THE SPECIAL REPRESSIVE FORCE OF THE ARMED TENTACLES OF THE STATE.

This great definition by Marx and Engels became the mightiest weapon in the hands of oppressed people in the history of ideology. It marks a gigantic advance for all mankind. And since Marx's time, his definition has been strengthened, further elaborated, illumined, and further refined.

But Marxism has never really dealt with the United States of America. There have been some very nice attempts. People have done the best that they know how. However, in the past, Marxist-Leninists in the United States have relied too heavily upon foreign, imported analyses and have seriously distorted the realities of the American scene. We might say that the Marxism-Leninism of the past belongs to the gestation period of Marxism-Leninism in the United States, and that now is the time when a new, strictly American ideological synthesis will arise, springing up from the hearts and souls of the oppressed people inside Babylon, and uniting these people and hurling them mightily, from the force of their struggle, into the future. The swiftly developing revolution in America is like the gathering of a mighty storm, and nothing can stop that storm from finally bursting, inside America, washing away the pigs of the power structure and all their foul, oppressive works. And the children of the pigs and the oppressed people will dance and spit upon the common graves of these pigs.

There are some Black people in the United States who are absolutely happy, who do not feel themselves to be oppressed, and who think that they are free. Some even believe that the President wouldn't lie, and that he is more or less an honest man; that Supreme Court decisions were almost written by god in person; that the Police are Guardians of the Law; and that people who do not have jobs are just plain lazy and good-for nothing and should be severely punished. These are like crabs that must be left to boil a little longer in the pot of oppression before they will be ready and willing to relate. But the overwhelming majority of Black people are uptight, know that they are oppressed and not free; and they wouldn't believe Nixon if he confessed to being a pig; they don't relate to the Supreme Court or any other court; and they know that the racist pig cops are their sworn enemies. As for poverty, they know what it is all about.

These millions of Black people have no political representation, they are unorganized, and they do not own or control any of the natural resources; they neither own nor control any of the industrial machinery, and their daily life is a hustle to make it by any means necessary in the struggle to survive.

Every Black person knows that the wind may change at any given moment and that the Lynch Mob, made up of White members of the "Working Class," might come breathing down his neck if not kicking down his door. It is because of these factors that when we begin to talk about being Marxist-Leninists, we must be very careful to make it absolutely clear just what we are talking about.

On the subject of racism, Marxism-Leninism offers us very little assistance. In fact, there is much evidence that Marx and Engels were themselves racists—just like their White brothers and sisters of their era, and just as many Marxist-Leninists of our own time are also racists. Historically, Marxism-Leninism has been an outgrowth of European problems and it has been primarily preoccupied with finding solutions to European problems.

With the founding of the Democratic People's Republic of Korea in 1948 and the People's Republic of China in 1949, something new was injected into Marxism-Leninism, and it ceased to be just a narrow, exclusively European phenomenon. Comrade Kim Il Sung and Comrade Mao Tse-tung applied the classical principles of Marxism-Leninism to the conditions in their own countries and thereby made the ideology into something useful for their people. But they rejected that part of the analysis that was not beneficial to them and had only to do with the welfare of Europe.

Given the racist history of the United States, it is very difficult for Black people to comfortably call themselves Marxist-Leninists or anything else that takes its name from White people. It's like praying to Jesus, a White man. We must emphasize the fact that Marx and Lenin didn't invent Socialism. They only added their contributions, enriching the doctrine, just as many others did before them and after them. And we must remember that Marx and Lenin didn't organize the Black Panther Party. Huey P. Newton and Bobby Seale did.

Not until we reach Fanon do we find a major Marxist-Leninist theoretician who was primarily concerned about the problems of Black people, wherever they may be found. And even Fanon, in his published works, was primarily focused on Africa. It is only indirectly that his works are beneficial to Afro-Americans. It is just easier to relate to Fanon because he is clearly free of that racist bias that blocks out so much about the Black man in the hands of Whites who are primarily interested in themselves and the problems of their own people. But even though we are able to relate heavily to Fanon, he has not given us the last word on applying the Marxist-Leninist analysis to our problems inside the United States. No one is going to do this for us because no one can. We have to do it ourselves, and until we do, we are going to be uptight.

We must take the teachings of Huey P. Newton as our foundation and go from there. Any other course will bring us to a sorry and regrettable end.

Fanon delivered a devastating attack upon Marxism-Leninism for its narrow preoccupation with Europe and the affairs and salvation of White folks, while lumping all third world peoples into the category of the Lumpenproletariat and then forgetting them there; Fanon unearthed the category of the Lumpenproletariat and began to deal with it, recognizing that vast majorities of the colonized people fall into that category. It is because of the fact that Black people in the United States are also colonized that Fanon's analysis is so relevant to us.

After studying Fanon, Huey P. Newton and Bobby Seale began to apply his analysis of colonized people to Black people in the United States. They adopted the Fanonian perspective, but they gave it a uniquely Afro-American content.

Just as we must make the distinctions between the mother country and the colony when dealing with Black people and White people as a whole, we must also make this distinction when we deal with the categories of the Working Class and the Lumpenproletariat.

We have, in the United States, a "Mother Country Working Class" and a "Working Class from the Black Colony." We also have a Mother Country Lumpenproletariat and a Lumpenproletariat from the Black Colony. Inside the Mother Country, these categories are fairly stable, but when we look at the Black Colony, we find that the hard and fast distinctions melt away. This is because of the leveling effect of the colonial process and the fact that all Black people are colonized, even if some of them occupy favored positions in the schemes of the Mother Country colonizing exploiters.

There is a difference between the problems of the Mother Country Working Class and the Working Class from the Black Colony. There is also a difference between the Mother Country Lumpen and the Lumpen from the Black Colony. We have nothing to gain from trying to smooth over these differences as though they don't exist, because they are objective facts that must be dealt with. To make this point clear, we have only to look at the long and bitter history of the struggles of Black Colony Workers fighting for democracy inside Mother Country Labor Unions.

Historically, we have fallen into the trap of criticizing Mother Country Labor Unions and workers for the racism as an explanation for the way they treat Black workers. Of course, they are racist, but this is not the full explanation.

White workers belong to a totally different world than that of Black workers. They are caught up in a totally different economic, political, and social reality, and on the basis of this distinct reality, the pigs of the power structure and treacherous labor leaders find it very easy to manipulate them with Babylonian racism.

This complex reality presents us with many problems, and only through proper analysis can these problems be solved. The lack of a proper analysis is responsible for the ridiculous approach to these problems that we find among Mother Country Marxist-Leninists. And their improper analysis leads them to advocate solutions that are doomed to failure in advance. The key area of the confusion has to do with falsely assuming the existence of one All-American Proletariat; one All-American Working Class; and one All-American Lumpenproletariat.

O.K. We are Lumpen. Right on. The Lumpenproletariat are all those who have no secure relationship or vested interest in the means of production and the institutions of capitalist society. That part of the "Industrial Reserve Army" held perpetually in reserve; who have never worked and never will; who can't find a job; who are unskilled and unfit; who have been displaced by machines, automation, and cybernation, and were never "retained or invested with new skills"; all those on Welfare or receiving State Aid.

Also the so-called "Criminal Element," those who live by their wits, existing off that which they rip off, who stick guns in the faces of businessmen and say "stick'em up," or "give it up"! Those who don't even want a job, who hate to work and can't relate to punching some pig's time clock, who would rather punch a pig in the mouth and rob him than punch that same pig's time clock and work for him, those whom Huey P. Newton calls "the illegitimate capitalists." In short, all those who simply have been locked out of the economy and robbed of their rightful social heritage.

But even though we are Lumpen, we are still members of the Proletariat, a category which theoretically cuts across national boundaries but which in practice leaves something to be desired.

CONTRADICTIONS WITHIN
THE PROLETARIAT OF THE USA

In both the Mother Country and the Black Colony, the Working Class is the Right Wing of the Proletariat, and the Lumpenproletariat is the Left Wing. Within the Working Class itself, we have a major contradiction between the Unemployed and the Employed. And we definitely have a major contradiction between the Working Class and the Lumpen.

Some blind so-called Marxist-Leninists accuse the Lumpen of being parasites upon the Working Class. This is a stupid charge derived from reading too many of Marx's footnotes and taking some of his offhand scurrilous remarks for holy writ. In reality, it is accurate to say that the Working Class, particularly the American Working Class, is a parasite upon the heritage of mankind, of which the Lumpen has been totally robbed by the rigged system of Capitalism which in turn, has thrown the majority of mankind upon the junkheap while it buys off a percentage with jobs and security.

The Working Class that we must deal with today shows little resemblance to the Working Class of Marx's day. In the days of its infancy, insecurity, and instability, the Working Class was very revolutionary and carried forward the struggle against the bourgeoisie. But through long and bitter struggles, the Working Class has made some inroads into the Capitalist system, carving out a comfortable niche for itself. The advent of Labor Unions, Collective Bargaining, the Union Shop, Social Security, and other special protective legislation has castrated the Working Class, transforming it into the bought-off Labor Movement—a most un-revolutionary, reformist minded movement that is only interested in higher wages and more job security. The Labor Movement has abandoned all basic criticism of the Capitalist system of exploitation itself. The George Meanys, Walter Reuthers, and A. Phillip Randolphs may correctly be labelled traitors to the proletariat as a whole, but they accurately reflect and embody the outlook and aspirations of the Working Class. The Communist Party of the United States of America, at its poorly attended meetings, may raise the roof with its proclamations of being the Vanguard of the Working Class, but the Working Class itself looks upon the Democratic Party as the legitimate vehicle of its political salvation.

As a matter of fact, the Working Class of our time has become a new industrial elite, resembling more the chauvinistic elites of the selfish craft and trade guilds of Marx's time than the toiling masses ground down in abject poverty. Every job on the market in the American Economy today demands as high a complexity of skills as did the jobs in the elite trade and craft guilds of Marx's time.

In a highly mechanized economy, it cannot be said that the fantastically high productivity is the product solely of the Working Class. Machines and computers are not members of the Working Class, although some spokesmen for the Working Class, particularly some Marxist-Leninists, seem to think like machines and computers.

The flames of revolution, which once raged like an inferno in the heart of the Working Class, in our day have dwindled into a flickering candle light, only powerful enough to bounce the Working Class back and forth like a ping pong ball between the Democratic Party and the Republican Party every four years, never once even glancing at the alternatives on the Left.

WHO SPEAKS FOR THE LUMPEN PROLETARIAT?

Some Marxist-Leninists are guilty of that class egotism and hypocrisy often displayed by superior classes to those beneath them on the social scale. On the one hand, they freely admit that their organizations are specifically designed to represent the interests of the Working Class. But then they go beyond that to say that by representing the interests of the Working Class, they represent the interest of the Proletariat as a whole. This is clearly not true. This is a fallacious assumption based upon the egotism of these organizations and is partly responsible for their miserable failure to make a revolution in Babylon.

And since there clearly is a contradiction between the right wing and the left wing of the Proletariat, just as the right wing has created its own organizations, it is necessary for the left wing to have its form of organization to represent its interests against all hostile classes—including the Working Class.

The contradiction between the Lumpen and the Working Class is very serious because it even dictates a different strategy and set of tactics. The students focus their rebellions on the campuses, and the Working Class focuses its rebellions on the factories and picket lines. But the Lumpen finds itself in the peculiar position of being unable to find a job and therefore is unable to attend the Universities. The Lumpen has no choice but to manifest its rebellion in the University of the Streets.

It's very important to recognize that the streets belong to the Lumpen, and that it is in the streets that the Lumpen will make their rebellion.

One outstanding characteristic of the liberation struggle of Black people in the United States has been that most of the activity has taken place in the streets. This is because, by and large, the rebellions have been spear-headed by Black Lumpen.

It is because of Black people's Lumpen relationship to the means of production and the institutions of the society that they are unable to manifest their rebellion around those means of production and institutions. But this does not mean that the rebellions that take place in the streets are not legitimate expressions of an oppressed people. These are the means of rebellion left open to the Lumpen.

The Lumpen have been locked outside of the economy. And when the Lumpen does engage in direct action against the system of oppression, it is often greeted by hoots and howls from the spokesmen of the Working Class in chorus with the mouthpieces of the bourgeoisie. These talkers like to put down the struggles of the Lumpen as being "spontaneous" (perhaps because they themselves did not order the actions!), "unorganized," and "chaotic and undirected." But these are only prejudiced analyses made from the narrow perspective of the Working Class. But the Lumpen moves anyway, refusing to be straight-jacketed or controlled by the tactics dictated by the conditions of life and the relationship to the means of production of the Working Class.

The Lumpen finds itself in the position where it is very difficult for it to manifest its complaints against the system. The Working Class has the possibility of calling a strike against the factory and the employer and through the mechanism of Labor Unions they can have some arbitration or some process through which its grievances are manifested. Collective bargaining is the way out of the pit of oppression and exploitation discovered by the Working Class, but the Lumpen has no opportunity to do any collective bargaining. The Lumpen has no institutionalized focus in Capitalist society. It has no immediate oppressor except perhaps the Pig Police with which it is confronted daily.

So that the very conditions of life of the Lumpen dictate the so-called spontaneous reactions against the system, and because the Lumpen is in this extremely oppressed condition, it therefore has an extreme reaction against the system as a whole. It sees itself as being bypassed by all of the organizations, even by the Labor Unions, and even by the Communist Parties that despise it and look down upon it and consider it to be, in the words of Karl Marx, the father of Communist Parties, "The Scum Layer of the Society." The Lumpen is forced to create its own forms of rebellion that are consistent with its condition in life and with its relationship to the means of production and the institutions of society. That is, to strike out at all the structures around it, including at the reactionary Right Wing of the Proletariat when it gets in the way of revolution.

The faulty analyses which the ideologies of the Working Class have made, of the true nature of the Lumpen, are greatly responsible for the retardation of the development of the revolution in urban situations. It can be said that the true revolutionaries in the urban centers of the world have been analyzed out of the revolution by some Marxist-Leninists.

After the California Appeals Court overruled Judge Sherwin's writ of habeas corpus, Eldridge Clever was ordered to surrender to the prison authorities on November 27, 1968. Five days before that date, Cleaver spoke at a San Francisco meeting held at California Hall on behalf of his defense. This turned out to be his last public appearance before he became a "fugitive" from California, and then wanted by the FBI. It is reprinted from the book Eldridge Cleaver: Post-Prison Writings and Speeches *(1969), which has been out of print for decades.*

FAREWELL ADDRESS

Good evening, everybody. Kind of stuck for words tonight. I don't know whether this is a hello or a goodbye. I talked to my parole officer today, and he told me that on Wednesday the 27th he wanted me to call him up about 8:30 in the morning, so he could tell me where to meet him so he could transport me to San Quentin. They want to have a parole revocation hearing, and I guess they think they have a right to do that. They certainly are proceeding as though they have a right. Having had some experience with them, I know that when they have you in their clutches, they proceed with what they want to do whether they have a right or not.

A lot of people don't know anything about the prison system. I think they make the same mistake looking at prison officials as they do with cops: they think that in some sense they are guardians of the law; that they're there to protect society, and everything they say is the truth; that there's nothing wrong with what they're into, and nothing wrong with what they're doing. Well, I know. Not so much in my own case, but from the cases of others that I've observed in the various prisons in the State of California. There are a whole lot of people behind those walls who don't belong there. And everybody behind those walls is being subjected to programs that are not authorized, nor related to the reasons for which they were sent there.

Rehabilitation in the State of California is less than a bad joke. I don't even know how to relate to that word, "rehabilitation." It presupposes that at one time one was "habilitated," and that somehow he got off the right track and was sent to this garage, or repair shop, to be dealt with and then released. Rehabilitated, and placed back on the right track. Well, I guess that the right track has to be this scene out here: the free world. Convicts call us out here the "free world." After you're behind those walls for a while, I guess it starts looking like the Garden of Eden. They can't see all of the little conflicts that are going on out here. Alioto [San Francisco Mayor Joseph Alioto] doesn't look as much like Al Capone from that distance. That's right. Al Capone, Alioto—Big Al. Alley-oop Oto. You know. People yearn, people *yearn,* behind those walls, to return to the free world. To return to society. To be free, and not to be returned to the penitentiary.

Now, when I went into the penitentiary I made a decision. I took a long hard look at myself and I said, well, you've been walking this trip for a little too long, you've tired of it. It's very clear that what you had going for yourself before you came in was not adequate. While you're here you're going to have to work with yourself, deal with yourself, so that when you get out of here you're going to stay out. Because it was pretty clear to me that that was my last go-round, that I could not relate to prison any more. So I guess I developed something of a social conscience. I decided to come out here and work with social problems, get involved with the Movement and make whatever contribution I possibly could. When I made that decision, I thought that the parole authorities would be tickled pink with me, because they were always telling me to do exactly that. They would tell me I was selfish. They would ask me why I didn't start relating to other people, and looking beyond the horizons of myself.

So I did that, you know. And I just want to tell you this. I've had more trouble out of parole officers and the Department of Corrections simply because I've been relating to the Movement than I had when I was committing robberies, rapes and other things that I didn't get caught for. That's the truth. If I was on the carpet for having committed a robbery, well, there would be a few people uptight about that. But it seemed to be localized. It didn't seem to affect the entire prison system or the entire parole board. They didn't seem to have much time to discuss it, you know. They run you through their meetings very, very briefly. You feel that your case is not even being considered. But I know that now my case is constantly on their desks, and my parole officer doesn't have very much to do except keep track of me. He wants to know where I go, how much money I make each month, where I'm living, when I'm going to go out of town, phone him up when I get back to town, and ask his permission to do this and that.

There's something more dangerous about attacking the pigs of the power structure verbally than there is in walking into the Bank of America with a gun and attacking it forthrightly. Bankers hate armed robbery, but someone who stands up and directly challenges their racist system, that drives them crazy. I don't know if there are any bankers in the audience tonight, but I hope that there are. I hope that there's at least one, or a friend of one, or somebody who will carry the message to one. And I hope particularly that there's one here from the Bank of America. I heard today on the news that brother Cesar Chavez has declared war on the Bank of America. The Bank of America is Alioto's bank. My wife told me this evening that she received a phone call from the Bank of America saying that they were going to repossess our car because we were three months behind in our payments. That's not true, but I wished that I had never paid a penny for it. I wished that I could have just walked onto that lot and said, "Stick 'em up, motherfucker! I'm taking this." Because that's how I felt about it. That's how I feel about it now. I don't relate to this system of credit—see it now, take it home, pay later . . . but make sure you pay.

It was only out of consideration for the atmosphere that I would need in order to do the other things I wanted to do that I didn't rip it off. Or that I haven't walked into the Bank of America. Or that I haven't walked into any other establishment and repossessed the loot that they have in there. So I don't know what they expect from me, see? I haven't committed any crimes, I don't feel there's a need for rehabilitation. I don't feel the need of going back to Dirty Red's penitentiary. Warden Nelson [Warden of San Quentin] The prison guards call him Big Red, but the convicts call him Dirty Red. He's sitting over there across the bay and he's waiting for me, because we have a little history of friction. He doesn't like me. My parole officer doesn't like me. He tells the newspaper writers, "Yeah, I think he's a real nice fellow. I think he's made an excellent adjustment. If it wasn't for this particular indictment brought against him, I'd be perfectly willing to have him as my parolee from now on." Yet if you go down to the parole department and ask them to let you see my file, you will find just one charge against me, other than those lodged against me in Alameda County, which are yet to be adjudicated. I haven't gone to trial for those. I have pleaded "Not Guilty" to them. The one legitimate charge they have is "failing to cooperate with the parole agent."

The first time I saw that, I couldn't understand what it meant, because I bent over backwards to cooperate with that punk. So I asked him, "just what does that mean? What's the substance of that?" Now this is going to really surprise you. He said, "Do you remember when you went to New York to tape the *David Susskind Show?*" I said, "Yes, I remember doing that."

"Remember I told you that when you got back you should give me a phone call and let me know you were back in town?"

"Yes, and I did that, didn't I?"

"No, you didn't do it. That's against the rules."

And that's the only thing that they have in my file that is even debatable. All the other things that they are hostile towards me for, they can't put in the files because it's against the law. It's contrary to the Constitution and they would be ashamed to write it down on paper and place it in my file. They probably have another file that they smuggle around between them. But they cannot come out and tell you one thing that I've done that would justify returning me to the penitentiary.

I just have to say that I didn't leave anything in that penitentiary except half of my mind and half of my soul, and that's dead there, I have no use for it. It's theirs. They can have that. That's my debt to them. That's my debt to society, and I don't owe them a motherfucking thing! They don't have anything coming. Everything they get from now on, they have to take! I believe that our time has come. A point has been reached where a line just has to be drawn, because the power structure of this country has been thoroughly exposed. There is no right on their side. We know that they're moving against people for political purposes.

There's a favorite line of mine. It says that there is a point where caution ends and cowardice begins. Everybody is scared of the pigs, of the power structure. The people have reason to be concerned about them because they have these gestapo forces that they issue orders to. They come in with their clubs and their guns, and they will exterminate you, if that's what it takes to carry out the will of their bosses.

I don't know how to go about waiting until people start practicing what they preach. I don't know how to go about waiting on that. Because all I see is a very critical situation, a chaotic situation where there's pain, there's suffering, there's death, and I see no justification for waiting until tomorrow to say what you could say tonight. I see no justification for waiting until other people get ready. I see no justification for not moving even if I have to move by myself. I think of my attitude towards these criminals—my parole officer included—who control the prison system, who control the parole board. I can't reconcile things with them because for so long I've watched them shove shit down people's throats. I knew there was something wrong with the way that they were treating people. I knew that by no stretch of the imagination could that be right. It took me a long time to put my finger on it, at least to my own satisfaction. And after seeing that they were the opposite of what they were supposed to be, I got extremely angry at them. I don't want to see them get away with anything. I want to see them in the penitentiary. They belong in there because they've committed so many crimes against the human rights of the people. They belong in the penitentiary!

When you focus on the adult penitentiaries, you're looking at the end of the line, trying to see where a process begins. But if you really want to understand and see what's behind the prison system, you have to look at Juvenile Hall. You have to go down to Juvenile Hall. That's where I started my career, at about the age of twelve, for some charge. I don't know what it was—vandalism. I think I ripped off a bicycle, maybe two or three bicycles. Maybe I had a bicycle business, I don't remember. But it related to bicycles. They took me to Juvenile Hall, and it took me about six months to get out again. While I was there I met a lot of people. I met a lot of *real, nice, groovy* cats who were very active, very healthy people, who had stolen bicycles and things like that. Then I moved up the ladder from Juvenile Hall to Whittier Reform School for youngsters. I graduated from there with honors and went to another one a little higher, Preston School of Industries. I graduated from that one and they jumped me up to the big leagues, to the adult penitentiary system.

I noticed that every time I went back to jail, the same guys who were in Juvenile Hall with me were also there again. They arrived there soon after I got there, or a little bit before I left. They always seemed to make the scene. In the California prison system, they carry you from Juvenile Hall to the old folks' colony, down in San Luis Obispo, and wait for you to die. Then they bury you there, if you don't have anyone outside to claim your body, and most people down there don't. I noticed these waves, these generations. I had a chance to watch other generations that came be-hind me, and I talked with them. I'd ask them if they'd been in jail before. You will find graduating classes moving up from Juvenile Hall, all the way up. It occurred to me that this was a social failure, one that cannot be jus-tified by any stretch of the imagination. Not by any stretch of the imagi-nation can the children in the Juvenile Halls be condemned, because they're innocent, and they're processed by an environment that they have no control over.

If you look at the adult prisons, you can't make head or tail out of them. By the time these men get there, they're in for murder, rape, rob-bery and all the high crimes. But when you look into their pasts, you find Juvenile Hall. You have to ask yourself, why is there not in this country a program for young people that will interest them? That will actively involve them and will process them to be healthy individuals leading healthy lives. Until someone answers that question for me, the only attitude I can have towards the prison system, including Juvenile Hall, is tear those walls down and let those people out of there. That's the only question. How do we tear those walls down and let those peo-ple *out* of there?

People look at the point in the Black Panther Party program that calls for freedom for all black men and women held in federal, state, county and municipal jails. They find it hard to accept that particular point. They can relate to running the police out of the community, but they say, "Those people in those prisons committed crimes. They're con-victed of crimes. How can you even talk about bringing them out? If you did get them out; would you, in the black community, take them and put them on trial and send them back again?" I don't know how to deal with that. It's just no. NO! Let them out and leave them alone! Let them out because they're hip to all of us out here now. Turn them over to the Black Panther Party. Give them to us. We will redeem them from the promises of the Statue of Liberty that were never fulfilled. We have a program for them that will keep them active—twenty-four hours a day. And I don't mean eight big strong men in a big conspicuous truck robbing a jive gas station for $75.* When I sit down to conspire to com-mit a robbery, it's going to be the Bank of America, or Chase Manhat-tan Bank, or Brinks.

I've been working with Bobby Seale on the biography of Huey P. Newton. Bob Scheer and I took Bobby Seale down to Carmel-by-the-Sea. But we went away from the sea. We went into a little cabin, and we got a fifth of Scotch, a couple of chasers, a tape recorder and a large stack of blank tapes. We said, "Bobby, take the fifth, and talk about brother Huey P. Newton." And Bobby started talking about Huey. One of the things that just blew my mind was when he mentioned that prior to organizing the Black Panther Party, he and Huey had been planning a gigantic bank robbery. They put their minds to work on that because they recognized that they needed money for the Movement. So they sat down and started trying to put together a key to open the vault. But as they thought about it, they thought about the implications. Bobby tells how one day while they were discussing this, Huey jumped up and said, "Later for a bank. What we're talking about is politics. What we're talking about essentially is the liberation of our people. So later for one jive bank. Let's organize the brothers and put this together. Let's arm them for defense of the black community, and it will be like walking up to the White House and saying, "Stick 'em up, motherfucker. We want what's ours."

So there's a very interesting and a very key connection between insurrection and acts carried out by oneself, a private, personal civil war. We define a civil war as when a society splits down the middle and you have two opposing sides. Does that have to be the definition? Can 5,000 people launch a civil war? Can 4,000, 3,000, two or one? Or one-half of 1,000? Or half of that? Can one person? Can one person engage in civil war? I'm not a lawyer. I'm definitely not a judge, but I would say that one person acting alone could in fact be engaged in a civil war against an oppressive system. That's how I look upon those cats in those penitentiaries. I don't care what they're in for—robbery, burglary, rape, murder, kidnap, anything. A response to a situation. A response to an environment. Any social science book will tell you that if you subject people to an unpleasant environment, you can predict that they will rebel against it. That gives rise to a contradiction. When you have a social unit organized in such a way that people are moved to rebel against it in large numbers, how, then, do you come behind them and tell them that they owe a debt to society? I say that society owes a debt to them. And society doesn't look as though it wants to pay.

There's a young brother over at Juvenile Hall in Alameda County right now by the name of Gregory Harrison. He's about fourteen or fifteen years old and he's the leader of the Black Students Union at Oakland Tech High School. At this moment they have him over there charged with insurrection. They've charged him with insurrection because the

Black Students Union on that campus wants black history added to the curriculum. They want an environment created on their campus—not one that will teach black people how to be black, but one that will remove the restraints, so that they can just be themselves, and their blackness will automatically flourish. Like you don't have to teach a rose how to turn red, or teach a tree how to grow leaves. You just leave it alone and don't pour salt on its roots, and it will be a rose, or it will be a tree.

This piggish, criminal system. This system that is the enemy of people. This very system that we live in and function in every day. This system that we are in and under at this very moment. *Our* system! Each and every one of your systems. If you happen to be from another country, it's still your system, because the system in your country is part of this. This system is *evil.* It is criminal; it is murderous. And it is in control. It is in power. It is arrogant. It is crazy. And it looks upon the people as its property. So much so that *cops,* who are public servants, feel justified in going onto a campus, a college campus or high school campus, and spraying mace in the faces of the people. They beat people with those clubs, and even shoot people, if it takes that to enforce the will of the likes of Ronald Reagan, Jesse Unruh, or Mussolini Alioto.

Have you ever seen Alioto on television? When you see him will you swear that he doesn't frighten you, or that he doesn't look like Al Capone? Alioto reminds me of convicts that I know in Folsom Prison. And this is not a contradiction. When I speak up for convicts, I don't say that every convict is going to come out here and join the Peace and Freedom Party. I'm not saying that. Or that he would be nice to people out here. I'm not saying that. Yet I call for the freedom of even those who are so alienated from society that they hate everybody. Cats who tattoo on their chest, "Born to Hate," "Born to Lose." I know a cat who tattooed across his forehead, "Born to Kill." He needs to be released also. Because whereas Lyndon B. Johnson doesn't have any tattoos on his head, he has blood dripping from his fingers. LBJ has killed more people than any man who has ever been in any prison in the United States of America from the beginning of it to the end. He has murdered. And people like prison officials, policemen, mayors, chiefs of police—they endorse it. They even call for escalation, meaning: kill more people. I don't want it. The people who are here tonight, because I see so many faces that I recognize, I could say that I know you don't want it either. There's only one way that we're going to get rid of it. That's by standing up and drawing a firm line, a distinct and firm line, and standing on our side of the line, and defending that line by whatever means necessary, including laying down our lives. Not in sacrifice, but by taking pigs with us. Taking pigs with us.

I cannot relate to spending the next four years in the penitentiary, not with madmen with supreme power in their hands. Not with Ronald Reagan the head of the Department of Corrections, as he is the head of every other state agency. Not with Dirty Red's being the warden. If they made Dr. Shapiro [San Francisco psychiatrist and long-time supporter of the Panthers] the warden of San Quentin, I'd go right now. But while they have sadistic fiends, mean men, cruel men, in control of that apparatus, I say that my interest is elsewhere. My heart is out here with the people who are trying to improve our environment.

You're even a bigger fool than I know you are if you could go through all of these abstract and ridiculous charges, all of these overt political maneuvers, and think that I'm going to relate to that. Talk all this shit that you want to, issue all the orders that you want to issue. I'm charged with a crime in Alameda County and I'm anxious to go to trial because we can deal with it. We're going to tell the truth, and the pigs are going to have to tell lies and that's hard for them to do, especially when we have with us technicians such as the Honorable Charles R. Garry [Huey Newton's attorney]. I'm not afraid to walk in any courtroom in this land with a lawyer like Garry, because he can deal with the judge and the prosecutor. But don't you come up to me telling me that you're going to revoke my parole on a charge for which I put in nine years behind the walls, and for which I was supposed to receive my discharge next month. Don't you come up to me talking that shit because I don't want to hear it.

November 22, 1968

* Two days before this speech, eight Panthers had been arrested following a gas station robbery in San Francisco. Charges against five of them have since been dropped.

PART THREE EXILE

Eldridge Cleaver at a guerilla camp of Angolan revolutionaries in Cabinda, Africa, 1971. Photograph by William Stevens.

THE AUTOBIOGRAPHY
OF ELDRIDGE CLEAVER

CHAPTER FOUR

I arrived in Cuba Christmas morning, 1968. I felt very proud of myself for slipping past the FBI and the CIA, even the Northwest Mounted Police in Canada, who claim always to get their man. They didn't get me.

When I landed, the Cubans came onto the boat, bringing me a uniform that fit me just right, a pistol, and an AK–47 machine gun. I had always loved guns, ever since I started sneaking my father's pistol out of the house as a child. When I sailed, the Cubans wouldn't let me carry any weapons with me, but they assured me that as soon as I landed on Cuban soil they would provide me with guns and I would be allowed to carry them. They kept that promise.

Castro gave me the red-carpet treatment, setting me up in a Havana penthouse with two military security guards, a white one and a black one. They gave me a combination cook and maid. The penthouse was stocked with plenty of food, rum, and cigars. I felt more than a little puffed up with all that royal treatment.

They began to teach me about Cuba, including Cuban history, and started taking me on visits to all parts of the island. I had an audience with Fidel Castro, shook his big hand. I thought everything was going to be wonderful.

But after I had been around the island several times, I was ready to get to work, but they insisted on taking me on more tours, and giving me more lectures and instruction.

I wanted to get started on the revolutionary training center for American Black Panthers I expected to set up. There were people in the States ready to join me as soon as I gave the word, so I was anxious to get going. It was a matter of urgency with me. But I spent four months going back and forth from one end of Cuba to the other, and was getting sick and tired of guided tours. The island is not that big and there's not that much to see, so I felt I didn't need to continue doing that. As the weeks became months the situation became intolerable for me.

The next time they announced a tour, I told them I didn't want any more tours. They insisted, so I demanded to see Fidel Castro. Because he'd told me when I arrived that if I had any problems, I should see him personally.

As a result of my demands, the situation changed dramatically. I was taken to a dinner meeting where I was verbally attacked by a number of people. They said the Black Panther Party was infiltrated by the CIA and they couldn't trust us. Then they accused me of attending secret Black Power meetings in Havana.

I was stunned because I hadn't done anything like that. In fact, I didn't even know there was a Black Power movement in the so-called people's paradise where they said everyone had equal economic opportunity. They claimed they had a witness who had seen me at one of the Black Power meetings. They said I was interfering in the internal affairs of Cuba, and because of that they would not allow me to carry out the mission I had come to Cuba to accomplish.

I told them they were lying. The dinner meeting ended on a very bitter note. I left with the thought that maybe they did mistake someone else for me at one of those secret meetings.

I began to seek out the Black Power organizations. As I made contacts, the other side of Castro's Cuban paradise became visible. I heard horror stories of torture and murder. It was almost too much to believe. I thought maybe I was being tested or something. But I heard so many stories over a period of several months that I couldn't deny that terrible things were actually happening. I had observed Cuba from top to bottom, and decided that if this was communism, it wasn't the kind I was looking for. I had a very disappointing opinion of what was supposed to be a utopian society, an ideal society of the future.

My relationship with the Cuban authorities continued to deteriorate, until I began to fear for my safety. At the end of eight months I decided to leave.

Cuba posed the first serious challenge to my Communist beliefs, but it did not turn me against the Communist doctrine. I just thought that the Cubans were doing it wrong. I felt that by going to another part of the world I would experience true Communism. I told my friends I was leaving Cuba and going to Algeria. I sent word to my wife to meet me there.

Ericka Huggins, the widow of Los Angeles Black Panther leader Jon Huggins, murdered on January 17, 1969, moved from Los Angeles to his hometown of New Haven, Connecticut where she decided to fulfill his desire to start a chapter of the Black Panther Party. In late May 1969 the leaders and members of the New Haven chapter of the Black Panther Party were swooped into prison on charges of conspiracy to commit murder in connection with the death of Alex Rackley, a Black Panther from New York City. Chairman Bobby Seale was also charged with participation in this conspiracy, and imprisoned in New Haven for the duration of the trial. These events happened in the midst of a ferocious campaign of raids, arrests, denunciations, and killings of Black Panthers across the United States, which were later revealed to be part of a coordinated FBI program called COINTELPRO.

Although "underground" and forced to keep silent about his whereabouts, Eldridge Cleaver sent Ericka this message of encouragement, which was first published in the party newspaper, The Black Panther. *When the case went to trial the following year, thousands upon thousands of supporters turned out on the New Haven Green to protest what was happening to the Panthers. The support garnered national attention when Yale President Kingman Brewster was attributed with saying that it was impossible for a black revolutionary to get a fair trial.*

MESSAGE TO SISTER ERICKA HUGGINS
OF THE BLACK PANTHER PARTY

Excerpt from Tape of Eldridge Breaking His Silence
from Somewhere in the Third World

I'd like to send a very special word to sister Ericka Huggins, the wife of our slain, murdered Deputy Minister of Information, Jon Huggins, who was murdered along with our Deputy Minister of Defense, Brother Alprentice "Bunchy" Carter. He's Bunchy to me.

And now, the pigs have compounded this by taking this woman, this black woman, this sister, after inflicting this horrible pain upon her by murdering the father of her newborn child. Taking her away from her child and placing her behind bars [in Connecticut] on some trumped-up charges.

I know Ericka, and I know that she's a very strong sister. But I know that she is now being subjected to a form of torture that is horrible. I know that she is strong and that she will endure and sister Ericka, be strong sister.

We must not rest until this sister is liberated, and if she is not out at this moment, then she should be out just as rapidly as it is possible for us to get her out. And an example to all of us, let it be a lesson and an example to all of the sisters, particularly to all of the brothers, that we must understand that our women are suffering strongly and enthusiastically as we are participating in the struggle. And I'm aware that it has been a problem in all organizations in Babylon to structure our struggle in such a way that our sisters, our women are liberated and made equal in our struggle and in regard to sister Ericka, I know that the Minister of Defense, Huey P. Newton, has spoken out many times that the male chauvinism that is rampant in Babylon in general is also rampant in our own ranks.

The incarceration and the suffering of Sister Ericka should be a stinging rebuke to all manifestations of male chauvinism within our ranks. That we must purge our ranks and our hearts, and our minds, and our understanding of any chauvinism, chauvinistic behavior or disrespectful behavior toward women. That we must too recognize that a woman can be just as revolutionary as a man and that she has equal stature, that, along with men, and that we cannot prejudice her in any manner, that we cannot relegate her to an inferior position. That we have to recognize our women as our equals and that revolutionary standards of principles demand that we go to great lengths to see to it that disciplinary action is taken on all levels against those who manifest male chauvinism behavior.

Because the liberation of women is one of the most important issues facing the world today. Great efforts have been made in various parts of the world to do something about this, but I know from my own experience that the smoldering and the burning of the flame, the demand for liberation of women in Babylon, is the issue that is going to explode, and if we're not careful it's going to destroy our ranks, destroy our organization, because women want to be liberated just as all oppressed people want to be liberated.

So if we want to go around and call ourselves a vanguard organization, then we've got to be the vanguard in all our behaviour, and to be the vanguard also in the area of women's liberation and set an example in that area, and all of us to start being respectful and not condescending and patronizing, but to really understand and look upon this question, recognize, that women are our other half, they're not our weaker half, they're not our stronger half, but they are our other half and that we sell ourselves out, we sell our children out, and we sell our women out when we treat them in any other manner.

We have to be very careful about that, and Sister Ericka Huggins is a shining example of a revolutionary woman who's been meted out the same kind of injustice from the pig power structure that a revolutionary man receives. So they didn't put her in a powder puffed cell. They did not make life easy for her. But the pigs recognized a revolutionary woman to be just as much a threat as a revolutionary man.

And so we recognize that we also have a duty to stop inflicting injustices of misuse of women. We have to be very careful about that, and we all know the problem. But I'm saying that it's mandatory, the Minster of Defense Huey P. Newton has said that it is mandatory that all manifestations of male chauvinism be excluded from our ranks and that sisters have a duty and the right to do whatever they want to do in order to see to it that they are not relegated to an inferior position, and that they're not treated as though they are not equal members of the Party and equal in all regards. And that they're not subjected to male practices.

And Sister Ericka Huggins is a good example of a revolutionary woman who has sacrificed everything, including her husband. So Sister Ericka—Right On.

ALL POWER TO THE PEOPLE.

—The Black Panther, July 5, 1969

In late May 1969, Eldridge Cleaver traveled clandestinely from Havana to Algiers with the help of Cuban diplomats, with whom he soon found himself at odds. Representatives of Southern African liberation struggles based in Algiers came to Cleaver's assistance and facilitated his effort to remain in Algeria. No longer required to be silent, Cleaver wrote these three articles for publication in Ramparts, *where he remained on the editorial staff, and reasserted his connection to the political movements back in the United States.*

THREE NOTES FROM EXILE

1) A NOTE TO MY FRIENDS

At the moment, I'm sitting in a little pad on the beach, about 200 yards from the water, and there are people passing by my window speaking in a language that I do not understand—the language is *not* Spanish and this land is *not* Cuba.

My wife, Kathleen, is lying in another room, her belly swollen with another problem for the pigs. The sky is overcast and a pretty strong wind is working up, driving all the people from the beach and past my window. We are here, but our minds, hearts, and souls are there, in Babylon.

It has come to my attention that there are some Yankees in Babylon who feel that they have both the right and the power to tell others that they are no longer American citizens. They even go so far as to designate the outcast person a citizen of another country, without consulting either the person involved or the government of the country in question. In my case, I hear that I have been declared a Cuban by pigs who sit in ivory towers in Washington, D.C., oinking at the world and its problems and apparently convinced that they are still working out of a brand new bag.

I can't recall ever finding myself in agreement with these hot-shots on any subject, and I see no reason to start agreeing with them now. So, just to keep the record straight, I'd like to say that I am an American citizen—Afro-American, to be sure—and this latest oink is nothing but a whistle from some pig's ass.

I started working for RAMPARTS in 1966, while I was still in prison, and since that time I've often found myself in situations from which it has been difficult to do my job. However, through our joint efforts we have managed to make things hang together. For my part, I will continue to function as best I can and I have no intention of giving up my citizenship at RAMPARTS either.

Exiles always say that they are going to return, and perhaps at the moment of saying it they really mean it and have every intention of doing so. But something happens and they get locked into this bag, this cold bag of fleeing from the furies of the State. At other times, the situation flips over, turns inside out, and the exiles return. Then the pigs, who thought themselves secure, who went on oinking until the last minute, have to grab their hats and split. And it is not unusual that at such times the former exiles are among those who help put out the all-points bulletins for the pigs. I prefer to think of myself as falling in the latter category, that of those who shall return.

Since leaving Babylon, I have been in about eight countries, and in each place I've found much to love; people are beautiful everywhere, and those whom I've been among, including the people with whom I find myself right now, are among the poorest in the world, the victims of centuries of colonialism and exploitation. I find myself repeating, beneath my breath, "this shit has to be ended, this shit has to be stopped." And all the while I know that the United States of America is the chief culprit. All this suffering, by all these beautiful people, for whose benefit? Mussolini Alioto, Mickey Mouse Reagan, Milquetoast Nixon, and Bulldog Hoover? No! Not just them, and not just for the puppet masters who pull their strings. But for every Babylonian, even those who are oppressed in Babylon. It seems to me now, after seeing this deep shit, that those who are being squashed in Babylon are being squashed between two pieces of silk.

Other people are being destroyed, starved and killed in our name; it is this that should piss us off most of all. It is no use to say that we were not consulted, that it is all happening against our will, and that we do not have any power. Others have dipped our hands in the blood for us.

The point is that the blood is still there, and we are all Babylonians. For my part, I feel guilty about this shit, principally because I know that I have not done enough to bring it to an end. As long as I am alive and this system which creates all this suffering, all this pain, is also alive, I will know that I have not done enough, I will not have given my all to destroy it. And it has to be destroyed in its lair—in Babylon. It is for that reason that I must return. But that is not the only reason I want to return. There is so much there that I love. But why speak of love . . . except that Che was quoted to have said that we must hate our enemies with a revolutionary love. . . .

One last word. I think that we have all been sold a trick—this shit about us being powerless—by the pigs who benefit from the sale. In the formal sense, yes, we have been organized out of the power structure. But we still have the ultimate power: the power to overturn systems, to smash power structures, and to bring pigs to justice. We have that power, and the pigs tremble when they think of it because they know it's true, even if we don't.

[POSTSCRIPT: ON SURFACING]

July 17, 1969. 4 P.M. Algiers, Algeria.
So now it is official. I was starting to think that perhaps it never would be. For the past eight months, I've been scooting around the globe as a non-person, ducking into doorways at the sight of a camera, avoiding English-speaking people like the plague. I used so many names that my own was out of focus. I trained myself not to react if I heard the name Eldridge Cleaver called, and learned instead to respond naturally, spontaneously, to my cover names. Anyone who thinks this is easy to do should try it. For my part, I'm glad that it is over.

This morning we held a press conference, thus putting an end to all the hocus-pocus. Two days ago, the Algerian government announced that I had arrived here to participate in the historic First Pan-African Cultural Festival. After that, there was no longer any reason not to reach for the telephone and call home, so the first thing I did was to call my mother in Los Angeles: "Boy, where are you at?" she asked. It sounded as though she expected me to answer, "Right around the corner, mom," or "Up here in San Francisco," so that when I said I was in Africa, in Algeria, it was clear that her mind was blown, for her response was, "Africa? You can't make no phone call from Africa!" That's my mom. She doesn't relate to all this shit about phone calls across the ocean when there are no phone poles. She has both her feet on the ground, and it is clear that she intends to keep them there.

It is clear to me now that there are forms of imprisonment other than the kind I left Babylon to avoid, for immediately upon splitting that scene I found myself incarcerated in an anonymity, the walls of which were every bit as thick as those of Folsom Prison. I discovered, to my surprise, that it is impossible to hold a decent conversation without making frequent references to one's past. So I found myself creating personal histories spontaneously, off the top of my head, and I felt bad about that because I know that I left many people standing around scratching their heads. The shit that I had to run down to them just didn't add up.

Now all that is over. So what? What has really changed? Alioto is still crazy and mayor, Ronald Reagan is still Mickey Mouse, Nixon is in the White House and the McClellan Committee is investigating the Black Panther Party. And Huey P. Newton is still in prison. I cannot make light of this shit because it is getting deeper. And here we are in Algeria. What is a cat from Arkansas, who calls San Francisco home, doing in Algeria? And listen to Kathleen behind me talking over the telephone in French. With a little loosening of the will, I could easily flip out right now!

I've always been amazed at the audacity of people who, when you criticize the United States government, or aspects of the society with which you disagree and which you would like to see changed, say to you, "Why don't you go to Russia, or China, or Cuba?"—or whatever country happens to be on the State Department's shit list at the moment. Just like that, off the tip of their lips, and I suppose they think they are being cute or taking a sound position. Many of the reporters who have been calling me up on the telephone from the United States have fallen into that pattern. "I hear you're homesick, and you want to return to the U.S." And then they go on, and this is the part that gets next to my rage: "Well, since you criticized the U.S. so strongly while you were here, why do you want to come back?" Is that a good question? I think not. To me it represents the worst smug, self-satisfied strain in the Babylonian mentality.

Well, it just happens that that is the kind of nigger this nigger just happens to be. And when I say that I'm homesick, it is not in the spirit of recantation, but in the spirit of focusing in, ever more finely, on the

Babylonian contempt for the rights of others that stands between me and where I want to be.

And so I say to these reporters that there is one question to consider: What will be the form of my return to Babylon? Inside my skull I know of only three possibilities: Rescind the decision of the California Adult Authority ordering me returned to prison, and I will catch the first plane out of here, or wherever else I may happen to be when I get the word. Restore my right to my day in court on the charges for which I was indicted in Oakland, and I will be there when some pig of a judge bangs his gavel down and calls the court to order. That is my choice, and I think it is what every man deserves. If not that, then J. Edgar Hoover has to catch me and drag me back, but this, obviously, will be vigorously opposed. What's left is the quiet passage back, and just as the pigs were unable to prevent me from leaving, they are unable to prevent me from returning, not knowing when, where, or how.

I don't know any other way of dealing with all this, and I can't help it if I'm obsessed with the idea that the madness in America does not have to last forever, that it can be grappled with and changed. I believe that the American revolution can and will be made in my lifetime, and I know that I want to help make it. I know that I would die of a broken heart were I to remain outside of Babylon and neglect the sense of duty that I have toward my people, toward my compatriots and toward the land in which I was born. I am not going to turn my back on America and I am not going to allow America to turn its back on me. All that has happened thus far I regard as neither a victory nor a defeat, but rather a flanking action from which to move again.

During the days of my blindness, of my evil deeds, I played with my life and risked it for the wind. But in these good days when I know that I am not fucking over anybody, but rather doing what I can in the movement to stop people from being fucked over, I dig the gamble involved. I know that I have bet my life—with no regrets, but with a relish that comes from knowing that I am doing my thing and that I dig doing it.

So I have to return to Babylon, to live or die in Babylon—but to fight, as it is only human to do. And the adversaries to be confronted are not super-beings from another planet. They are only other cats and other chicks who are in a pig bag.

In the meantime, the Pan-African Cultural Festival is about to begin. Folks are streaming in from all over the world to participate, to look at each other, and perhaps to conceive or communicate fantastic thoughts. The Chief of Staff of the Black Panther Party, David Hilliard, is here, and so is Emory Douglas, our Minister of Culture, who will put on an exhibit of his revolutionary art. Bob Scheer, editor of RAMPARTS magazine, is here, and so is one of my attorneys; others will be coming. (Is the CIA/FBI already here or coming? Fuck them!) Ex-Prime Minister Stokely Carmichael, rumor has it, is arriving tomorrow. Yesterday, rumor had it he was arriving today. Miriam Makeba is coming with Stokely, and I wonder if I will get a chance to see her perform, or will I be barred, blocked by some strange wisdom that will blow my mind? My mind is already blown, wide open, because I dig life. And when I die, my death will be the price I paid to live. Right on! Power to the people. Oink to the pigs.

2) AN OPEN LETTER TO STOKELY CARMICHAEL

Stokely Carmichael, Conakry, Guinea.

Your letter of resignation as Prime Minster of the Black Panther Party came, I think, about one year too late. As a matter of fact, since the day of your appointment to that position—February 17, 1968—events have proven that you were not cut out for the job in the first place. Even then it was clear that your position on coalition with revolutionary white organizations was in conflict with that of the Black Panther Party. But we thought that, in time, even you would be able to shake the SNCC paranoia about white control and get on with the business of building the type of revolutionary machinery that we need in the United States in order to unite all the revolutionary forces in the country to overthrow the system of Capitalism, Imperialism and Racism.

I know these terms are kicked around like lifeless bodies and that it is easy to allow the grisly realities behind them to become obscured by too frequent repetition. But when you see the squalor in which people live as a result of the policies of the exploiters, when you see the effects of exploitation on the emaciated bodies of little children, when you see the hunger and desperation, then these terms come alive in a new way. Since you've made this trip yourself and seen it all with your own eyes, you should know that suffering is colorblind, that the victims of Imperialism, Racism, and Colonialism, and Neo-colonialism come in all colors, and that they need a unity based on revolutionary principles rather than skin color.

The other charges which you make in your letter—about our new-found ideology, our dogmatism, our arm-twisting, etc.—seem to me to be of secondary importance, because, with the exception, perhaps, of the honorable Elijah Muhammad, you are the most dogmatic cat on the scene today, and I've never known you to be opposed to twisting arms or, for that matter, necks. In many ways your letter struck me as being an echo and rehash of the charges brought against the party by the bootlickers before the McClellan Committee. And since you chose this moment to denounce the party, we—and I'm sure many other people outside the party—must look upon your letter in this light. The only point in your letter that I think is really you is the one about coalition with whites, because it has been this point on which our differences have turned from the very beginning.

You have never been able to distinguish the history of the Black Panther Party from the history of the organization of which you were once the chairman—the Student Non-Violent Coordinating Committee. It is understandable that you can have such fears of black organizations being controlled, or partly controlled, by whites, because most of your years in SNCC were spent under precisely those conditions. But the Black Panther Party has never been in that situation. Because we have never had to wrest control of our organization out of the hands of whites, we have not been shackled with the type of paranoid fear that was developed by you cats in SNCC. Therefore we are able to sit down with whites and hammer out solutions to our common problems without trembling in our boots about whether or not we might get taken over in the process. It has always seemed to me that you belittle the intelligence of your black brothers and sisters when you constantly warn them that they had better beware of white folks. After all, you are not the only black person out of Babylon who has been victimized by white racism. But you sound as though you are scared of white people, as though you are still running away from slave-catchers who will lay hands on your body and dump you in a bag.

As a matter of fact, it has been precisely your nebulous enunciation of Black Power that has provided the power structure with its new weapon against our people. The Black Panther Party tried to give you a chance to rescue Black Power from the pigs who have seized upon it and turned it into the rationale for Black Capitalism. With James Farmer in the Nixon Administration to preside over the implementation of Black Capitalism under the slogan of Black Power, what value does that slogan now have to our people's struggle for liberation? Is denouncing the Black Panther party the best you can do to combat this evil? I would think that your responsibility goes a little further than that. Even though you were right when you said that LBJ would never stand up and call for Black Power, Nixon has done so and he's bankrolling it with millions of dollars. So now your old Black Power buddies are cashing in on your slogan. In effect, your cry for Black Power has become the grease to ease the black bourgeoisie into the power structure.

By giving you the position of Prime Minister of the Black Panther Party, we were trying to rescue you from the black bourgeoisie that had latched on to your coat tails and was riding you like a mule. Now they have stolen your football and run away for a touchdown: six points for Richard Milhous Nixon.

In February 1968, at the Free Huey Birthday Rally in Oakland, California, where you made your first public speech after returning to the United States from your triumphant tour of the revolutionary countries of the Third World, you took the occasion to denounce the coalition that the Black Panther Party had made with the white Peace and Freedom Party. What you called for instead was a Black United Front that would unite all the forces in the black community from left to right, close ranks against the whites, and all go skipping off to freedom. Within the ranks of your Black United front you wanted to include the Cultural nationalists, the Black Capitalists, and the Professional Uncle Toms, even though it was precisely these three groups who were working to murder your shit even before it broke wind. (Remember what Ron Karenga did to your meeting in Los Angeles?)

You had great dreams in those days, Stokely, and your visions, on the top side, were heroic. On the bottom side, when it came to the details of reality, your vision was blind. You were unable to distinguish your friends from your enemies because all you could see was the color of the cat's skin. It was this blindness that led you to the defense of Adam Clayton Powell, that Jackal from Harlem, when he came under attack by his brother jackals in congress. And it was this blindness that led you to the defense of that black cop in Washington, D.C., who was being fucked over by the whites above him in the Police Department for whom he carried his gun as he patrolled the black community. In short, your habit of looking at the world through black-colored glasses would lead you, on the domestic level, to close ranks with such enemies of the black people as James Farmer, Whitney Young, Roy Wilkins and Ron Karenga; and on the international level you would end up in the same bag with Papa Doc Duvalier, Joseph Mobutu, and Haile Selassie. Yes, we opposed that shit then and we oppose it now even more strongly, especially since the Nixon Administration has stolen your program from you and, I think, included you out.

And now you are going to liberate Africa! Where are you going to start, Ghana? The Congo? Biafra? Angola? Mozambique? South Africa? If you are not aware of it, I think that you should know that the brothers in Africa who are involved in armed struggle against the Colonialists would like nothing better than for you to pack up your suitcase full of African souvenirs and split back to Babylon. They have never forgiven the fat-mouthing you did in Dar-es-Salaam when you presumed to tell them how to conduct their business. It seems to me that you are now trapped between the extremes of your own rhetoric. On the one hand, you have cut yourself off from the struggle in Babylon, and on the other hand, you are not about to become the Redeemer of Mother Africa.

The enemies of black people have learned something from history even if you haven't, and they are discovering new ways to divide us faster than we are discovering new ways to unite. One thing they know, and we know, that seems to escape you, is that there is not going to be any revolution or black liberation in the United States as long as revolutionary blacks, whites, Mexicans, Puerto Ricans, Indians, Chinese and Eskimos are unwilling or unable to unite into some functional machinery that can cope with the situation. Your talk and fears about premature coalition are absurd, because no coalition against oppression by forces possessing revolutionary integrity can ever be premature. If anything, it is too late, because the forces of counterrevolution are sweeping the world, and this is happening precisely because in the past people have been united on a basis that perpetuates disunity among races and ignores basic revolutionary principles and analyses.

You are peeved because the Black Panther Party informs itself with the revolutionary principles of Marxism-Leninism, but if you look around the world you will see that the only countries which have liberated themselves and managed to withstand the tide of the counterrevolution are precisely those countries that have strong Marxist-Leninists parties. All those countries that have fought for their liberation solely on the basis of nationalism have fallen victims to capitalism and neo-colonialism, and in many cases now find themselves under tyrannies equally as oppressive as the former colonial regimes.

That you know nothing about the revolutionary process is clear; that you know even less about the United States and its people is clearer; and that you know still less about humanity than you do about the rest is even clearer. You speak about an "undying love for black people." An undying love for black people that denies the humanity of other people is doomed. It was an undying love of white people for each other which led them to deny the humanity of colored people and which has stripped white people of humanity itself. It would seem to me that an undying love for our people would, at the very least, lead you to a strategy that would aid our struggle for liberation instead of leading you into a coalition of purpose with McClellan committee in its attempt to destroy the Black Panther Party.

Well, so long, Stokely, and take care. And beware of some white folks and some black folks, because I assure you that some of the both of them have teeth that will bite. Remember what Brother Malcolm said in his Autobiography: "We had the best organization that the black man has ever had in the United States—and niggers ruined it! POWER TO THE PEOPLE!"

ELDRIDGE CLEAVER,
Minister of Information, Black Panther Party, July, 1969

3) ON MEETING THE NEEDS OF THE PEOPLE

Back during the days when I was still running around in Babylon talking crazy about the pigs, if anyone had told me that someday I'd find myself in this exile situation trying to send a message back about the Black Panther Party's Breakfast for Children program and the white radicals of Berkeley with their People's Park, I probably would have taken it as a put-down. But it's all for real, and what is more I find myself very enthusiastic about these developments.

Both of these actions expose the contradiction between the pretenses of the system and the needs of the people. They stand as an assertion that the pigs of the power structure are not fulfilling their duties and that the people are moving, directly, to fill their own needs and redress their grievances. And the pigs in turn, with their hostile response to both of these programs, clearly expose themselves as enemies of the people.

Breakfast for Children and the People's Park are qualitatively different types of actions from anything we have been into in the past. They represent a move from theory to practice and implementation. The pigs cannot argue against the substance of these programs, even though they hate the forces that have brought them about. In fact, they will move to co-opt the programs and to drive a wedge between the programs and the vanguard forces that launched them. This has been the strategy of ruling classes all through history, because they really have no other choice—given their determination to hang on to power until it is wrenched from their grasp—and even this never really works, except to buy them time. It can only be tragic when the vanguard forces allow themselves to get co-opted. On the one hand, the pigs will pressure the vanguard—they will make liberal use of the Big Stick—but at the same time they will use the carrot. For instance, they will try to get Jerry Rubin to become the director of a City Park, and Bobby Seale to become the headwaiter in a state-wide Nutrition Supplement program.

I have a question: Will my child ever be able to sit down to a Black Panther breakfast, and will Kathleen and I, with our child—and I'm counting this Panther before he claws his way out of the womb—ever be able to visit the People's Park? What we need is some liberated territory in Babylon that we are willing and prepared to defend, so that all the exiles, fugitives, draft-dodgers, and runaway slaves can return to help finish the job.

The black and white communities are controlled by the same ruling class. Towards black people this ruling class uses racism as a tool of oppression, turning this oppression into a National Question. In the white community, oppression is a Class Question, provoking the response of Class Struggle. And when we see clearly that we're only dealing with Dr. Jekyll and Mr. Hyde, we recognize the beauty of the response of the people. We recognize that the Breakfast for Children program and the People's Park are authentic and accurate responses to the situations of black people and white people in Babylon.

Breakfast for Children pulls people out of the system and organizes them into an alternative. Black children who go to school hungry each morning have been organized into their poverty, and the Panther program liberates them, frees them from that aspect of their poverty. This is liberation in practice. In the white mother country where class struggle is the appropriate tactic and expropriation of the expropriators the proper means to revolution, the act of seizing that land and establishing a People's Park could not have been more to the point. So it is clear that the people are always able to discover a way of moving. Out of their practice they develop new theory that sheds light on future ways of moving.

If we can understand Breakfast for Children, can we not also understand Lunch for Children, and Dinner for Children, and Clothing for Children, and Education for Children, and Medical Care for Children? And if we can understand that, why can't we understand not only a People's Park, but People's Housing, and People's Transportation, and People's Industry, and People's Banks? And why can't we understand a People's Government?

It is very curious that the Breakfast for Children program was born in West Oakland, which can be categorized as one of the most oppressed areas in Babylon, and that the People's Park, on the other hand, was born in Berkeley, which can be categorized as one of the least oppressed areas. I think this is how we have traditionally looked upon these two contrasting areas. Of white people, those in Berkeley thought that they were amongst the freest in the land, and of black people, those in West Oakland knew that they were amongst the most oppressed. So we have these two very significant developments, one in the most oppressed area and the other in the least oppressed area. And it's very instructive to notice that on the one hand there is an attempt to fill the emptiness of want, of need, and of deprivation that the system of oppression and colonization leaves in the lives of a people. Here people are fighting for the essentials of survival, fighting for food for children, fighting for what it takes just to survive. On the other hand, in the least oppressed area, we see a fight which at a superficial glance can be mistaken for a fight for leisure. But we must look upon the fight for the People's Park as an in-road into the system, because it poses the question of basic rearrangements in the system itself. And this is really the crucial question in our overall struggle, for in Babylon there is not really a scarcity of goods, and there is, objectively, no real reason why there can't be people's parks, because the land is available and the wherewithal to build such parks is there in abundance. But the capitalists, who must first see the prospects of a profit before they make any distribution of the resources, do not see a profit in a park for the people. And they see no percentage, beyond underwriting some marginal goodwill in the community or good public relations, in the Breakfast for Children program. They see this program as a threat, as cutting into the goods that are under their control. They see it as cutting into the expendable portion of their possessions. These two questions pose the basic problem that radicals have to deal with in Babylon; ultimately, they both pose precisely the same question. It is only because they start from such divergent sources that they give the appearance of being worlds apart. One springs from needs that are obvious and basic, and people can relate to them on that basis, while the other springs from an area that we are not accustomed to looking upon as basic to survival. People can readily relate to the need to eat breakfast, but it is possible that they cannot see the need for a park. They can see life continuing without a park but they would be more concerned about attempting to perpetuate life without food.

Revolution, in its essence, means precisely the rearrangement of a system. Many people think of revolution only as overt violence—as guns shooting and conflagrations, as flames leaping into the air, bodies in the streets and the uprising masses storming city hall. This is only one phase of the revolutionary process, and the violence is not an end in itself but only the means through which the necessary power is seized so that the rearrangements in the system can be carried out. It is the means for expropriating the land, the natural resources, the machines, all the means of production, the institutions of society—for taking them out of the control, out of the hands of those who now have them and who have abused them, who have perverted these things and have converted them into instruments with which to pursue their own private gain at the expense of the wider public good.

Ironically, many of the oppressed people themselves do not feel that they have a right to the things that a revolutionary program demands in their name. They have guilt feelings about it. They recognize and relate to people having food to eat and a park for their children to play in. But when the pigs of the power structure oink their lying tears, bemoaning the outlaw nature of the movement, these politically unaware people who are not firm in their ideology will get up-tight and feel guilty. They can even be made to feel that they are doing something wrong or something that is immoral, and they can be manipulated because of this feeling. It is necessary to dispel this feeling, because what it flows from is indoctrination with the myth of private property, the myth and the cluster of beliefs that have been spawned by the soothsayers of greed in order to sanctify their possession of the earth under the guise of private property.

We are trapped between our visions of what life could be like and what it really is: a People's Government in which a rational arrangement is made, and the present reality—helicopters dispatched over college campuses to spread clouds of noxious gasses in order to intimidate the people and to stifle their protests; troops marching in battle formation down our streets; sharpshooters in the uniforms of the guardians of the law, taking aim, taking deadly aim, at citizens, actually aiming at vital spots of the body, actually pulling triggers, and actually killing people. And we stare dumbly, and we wonder, and we feel impotent and intimidated because we know that they have the guns, and they have the courts, and they have the prisons.

In a recent issue of the Black Panther Party newspaper which reported on the first casualty of the battle for the People's Park, an essential question was raised: "The white mother country radicals have demonstrated that they are willing to lay down their lives in the struggle, but the question still begs an answer—are they willing to pick up the gun?" This gives rise to another question. After picking up the gun, whom do we shoot?

We must get it clear in our minds that we will shoot anyone who uses a gun, or causes others to use guns, to defend the system of oppression, racism, and exploitation. And the issues of the People's Park and the Breakfast for Children program clearly convey that we are moving beyond the racist pig cops to confront the avaricious businessmen and the demagogic politicians, because we have to ask ourselves who sends the cops and the National Guard, and who they are there to protect.

We have nothing to gain by deluding ourselves or by seeking ways to evade the reality, the terrible reality, that confronts us. We must face the fact that we are at war in America. Not everyone realizes that there is a war going on. Some of us understand theoretically that in a capitalistic economy the relationship between the ruling class and the ruled has been defined as a relationship of struggle, of war, but even so it is as though we have been reading some mysterious sociological poetry that stimulates the fat inside our skulls and gives us some sort of secret thrill. Others of us are so nit-pickingly fanatical that we cannot assess the reality before our very eyes—the reality in which we ourselves are participants and which our own work has helped bring about—unless we can read it in a book written a hundred years ago in another country, under vastly different circumstances which do not begin to approximate the gigantic proportions of the task which rests so smotheringly upon our shoulders.

The principles that have been learned from our experience with the People's Park and the Breakfast for Children program, I think, will take root in the minds of radicals all over the United States. Myself, I'm tired of using the terms "radicals" and "militants," and I prefer to use the term "revolutionaries," because if we are not involved in a Revolution, and if we don't understand ourselves to be revolutionaries, then there is very little that we can really hope to do. But if we understand ourselves to be revolutionaries, and if we accept our historic task, then we can move beyond the halting steps that we've been taking, beyond the Stupid Revolution, and gain the revolutionary audacity to take the actions needed to unlock and focus the great revolutionary spirit of the people. All they need is to get their teeth into a pig's ass, or to see the ace up the avaricious businessman's sleeve or the lies in the teeth of the demagogic politicians. Then there will be a new day in Babylon, there will be a housecleaning in Babylon, and we can halt the machinery of oppression, purge our institutions of racism, and put the oppressors up against the wall—or maybe more appropriately, up against the fence that they have built around the People's Park.

POWER TO THE PEOPLE!

THE AUTOBIOGRAPHY OF ELDRIDGE CLEAVER

CHAPTER FIVE

Upon arrival in Algeria I was taken to a hotel and given the room number where I could find my wife. I went to the room and knocked on the door, and when it opened there was a fat lady standing there. She had my wife's hair.

"What happened?" I asked, still shocked by her appearance.

"Remember when I told you I thought we were expecting a baby? Well, we really are, next month," she said.

That's when I realized I had been in Cuba for exactly eight months.

It was so good to be with her again. Other friends joined us there. They were there with me when I had to rush Kathleen to the hospital.

The hospitals in Algeria aren't like the American ones, where they let fathers participate in the birthing process. They kicked me out and wouldn't let me around while my baby was being born.

I had just arrived back at my hotel room when the hospital called to say I had a new son. I was so happy. I had always wanted to have a son first, then a daughter, and that was just the way it was working out.

Taking a few of my buddies with me, we went to the hospital to see what the little guy looked like. When I saw the little fellow, I was appalled at how white he looked. His hair was straight. Even his eyes looked blue. They explained that his appearance was a result of him just arriving, and soon he would get acclimatized and take on the desirable colors, the hair would begin to curl, and everything would be just fine.

I looked at his face, hoping to see some mark, like a mole or big ears, something he could have inherited from me. His face looked just like a crumpled-up dish rag. My buddies looked at him and said he looked just like me.

I was so pleased, and just wanted him to hurry up and grow, and be like me. I'll never forget the feeling of becoming a father for the first time.

We stayed in Algeria for four years, which at that time was the haven for people involved in revolutionary movements from Africa, the Middle East, Latin America, as well as Canada and the United States. All roads led to Algeria.

We had about 24 people arrive in Algiers to join us, mostly from America, including the pope of dope Timothy Leary. We had our own little colony, including prison escapees, skyjackers, terrorists, and revolutionaries. Whomever we sponsored, the government would let in.

I visited the Soviet Union many times, Czechoslovakia, East Germany. In Asia we visited the People's Republic of China, North Vietnam, and North Korea. Those years we traveled extensively throughout the Communist world and Africa became for me a laboratory for checking references and learning first hand how the Communist revolution was progressing. We visited these countries, saw how they were organized, how the people lived, and tried to get ideas that could help us carry out a revolutionary struggle. I would get the information I gathered about the Communist struggles going on in the world back to my comrades in the United States. In return they would send me information about what was going on back home, and I would relay that information to the Communist world.

During one of the trips to North Korea our second child was born, a little girl. She's the one that ended up with the mark of the Cleavers, the outturned ears, just like mine. While she was growing up she thought her ears were ugly, and she wanted an operation to straighten them out. I like things natural, even if they are misshaped a little. She wanted them pinned down.

"Look Joju," I said, "Don't worry about your ears, because as you grow older they will stop growing and your head will catch up, and everything will work out fine."

She looked at me and said, "Yours didn't."

She hasn't said anything in recent years, and she is very beautiful, so I think that problem has worked itself out.

From his earliest days in the Black Panther Party, Eldridge Cleaver was engaged in editing and expanding the party's newspaper, The Black Panther. *By 1971, its circulation had reached into the thousands, which made it a significant target of the FBI's COINTELPO actions to sabotage and destroy the Black Panther Party. The division this covert operation instigated within the Black Panther Party's Central Committee ultimately pitted Huey Newton against Eldridge Cleaver and led to the break-up of the organization; chapters and individual members aligned with Cleaver were expelled along with him. This chaotic period during 1971, dubbed in the media as "the split" in the Black Panther Party, was hailed by FBI agents as a victory.*

In New York City, where several Black Panther leaders had already been expelled for public criticism of Newton's policies, a new newspaper was started that enabled the so-called "Cleaver faction," no longer part of the national Black Panther Party organization, to express their revolutionary views. Eldridge Cleaver was intimately involved with editing and publishing that newspaper, initially named Babylon *(and then changed to* Right On!*) In the summer of 1971,* Babylon *published Cleaver's article "Towards a People's Army."*

TOWARDS A PEOPLE'S ARMY

The decisive moment in the Afro-American peoples' struggle for their freedom and liberation will be when the fascists of Babylon, in order to tactically cope with the Afro-American Peoples' Army, move, in one form or another, to run down the Concentration Camp/Strategic Hamlet bit on us. This is a battle that we dare not lose. For if we as a people allow ourselves to be thus totally fettered again, as during the time of slavery, it is clear that we might as well kiss life and the planet earth good-bye. Already, white racists are busy regretting that they did not kill off all black people when they had the earth under their heel. The trends in the world today dictate that we, as a people, if we truly intend to survive, must snap to attention immediately, unite immediately, and deal decisively with the forces that are preparing a final genocide for us.

We must understand this fact: at this very moment, men are discussing and negotiating a fundamental deal that will perhaps shape human destiny for the next 1,000 years. Various countries, which we thought were our friends and allies to the end, are now making a separate peace with our sworn enemy, the fascist imperialist U.S. government and ruling class. The coming into view of the dialogue and negotiations between the United States government and the government of the Peoples Republic of China should be the final signal necessary for each and every one of us to sit up and take notice.

Already the Western Imperialist powers—England, France, West Germany, Belgium, etc., etc.,—have united into the Common Market and NATO. Eastern European so-called socialist countries have united in the Warsaw Pact. Discussions have been underway on how to merge the Warsaw Pact countries and the NATO countries into a unified command. They are quickly resolving contradictions between capitalism and socialism, between Christians and Jews, between Catholics and Protestants. Their continued support for the racist colonialism of Portugal in Africa, their stepped up aid and support to South Africa and Southern Rhodesia, and added to this is our own experience, bloody and brutal, which clearly indicates that the long-range plan of the fascists for Afro-Americans has nothing to do with any peace, harmony and brotherhood.

While they do everything in their power to keep our people weak, disorganized, confused and disunited, they are moving at a feverish pace to strengthen each other, tighten each others organizational machinery, and wipe away their disagreements for a perfect harmony.

The ruling class of the United States is unfolding a global plan to carve up the planet in such a way that when the deal goes down the Afro-American people will find themselves trapped inside and at the mercy of a white racist empire uniting the customary grouping of Western Capitalist sweetheart nations, and including Spain, Portugal, South Africa, Southern Rhodesia, and Israel. In return for this the United States is going to pull its forces out of Asia—South Korea, Indochina, Japan, the Philippines, Thailand and Taiwan, etc.

To cope with this situation, we have one and only one path open to us: to arm and organize ourselves into a powerful, deadly, invincible block inside the United States so that the United States cannot do anything of which we do not approve. There is no other path open to us. Only an Afro-American People's Army can guarantee us against another plateau of control, such as was done to us after the Civil War. Our first battle is for the right to organize our People's Army. We can never get the enemy's permission to do this. Our People's Army must guarantee its own existence through its own strength. Again, there is no other way. Our People's Army must come into being through combat, fighting from its inception for its right to be.

There are those, I know, who feel let down at this point, because here I go again talking about guns. But whether we like it or not, the world that we live in is controlled with guns, organized and controlled by those who rule. This is the basic fact that we have to deal with. Those who cannot move beyond that point—I don't know what to say to them. I would hope that Attica speaks louder than words. Kent State and Attica, unless we look upon these as freak incidents that more than likely will not repeat themselves, should make it clear to all where the ruling class is coming from and how readily they turn the guns upon the people. In both of these cases, what must be taken careful note of is the eagerness with which policemen, state troopers and national guardsmen did their killing. Backed up as they were by politicans in the highest seats of authority, these murderers of the people knew that what they did would be written off as justifiable homicide. The line that was drawn, with the blood of the people, defines both the nature of our movement and the lengths to which the enemy will go to contain our struggle. What Frederick Douglass said a hundred years ago is still true today.

An unarmed people is subject to slavery at any given moment.

We have the choice of moving now, or waiting, on CP Time, to make a final rush for the door when it begins to close. The door is already closed. Our task is to open it. What our enemy is doing is trying to seal that door forever. In concrete terms, we must, over-night, pull together some political machinery and back it up with guns. When I say "political machinery," I'm not talking about the Republican or the Democratic Parties. We must come together in a United Front organized on a community by community, city by city, state by state basis. We must pool our strength, through organizational machinery, with all the other oppressed people inside Babylon and the world who have not made their separate peace with the enemy and continue to struggle for their human rights. This must be backed up with guns so that the uncle toms and traitors cannot destroy it from within and the enemy cannot smash it from without.

There is a world of difference between 30 million unarmed niggers and 30 million niggers armed to the gills.

The poem "Gangster Cigarettes," which Cleaver self-published in his palm sized chapbook series in 1984, draws on his experiences leading an anti-imperialist delegation of radical Americans to visit Pyongyang, Peking, and Hanoi during the summer of 1970.

GANGSTER CIGARETTES

I led the forbidden exploration
To mysterious Asia Major
By the U.S. Peoples
Anti-Imperialist Delegation,
A flock of peaceful geese
Sowing seeds against the war,
And resurrecting broken bridges
Over broken faith between
Wicked West and Inscrutable East.

We were thirteen altogether
In our Anti-War band
Meant to be a crosscut
From each section of our land.
There were four Jewish women
And half a Jewish man.

"One half a Jewish man?" you ask.
"Are you picking on the Jews?"

His parents were born in Germany
There was nothing they could do.
His father was an Aryan
His mother was a Jew.
His father followed Hitler
His mother, big with child,
Sailed into New York harbor
To bear him free and wild.

Sometimes he hates the Germans

Sometimes he hates the Jews
Rarely he sings with laughter
Always crying the Blues.
He sings more Blues than a black man
Soliciting sympathy on all hands.
He wants Creation to know
How it hurts him so
To be torn between Judea and Reichland.

There was one black woman
With vampire blood
Who quenched Satan's fire
And caused the flood.
She entered my life on her knees
And under cover of darkness
Stole my keys.
She had my keys duplicated
And passed them to a man who waited
In a stingy brim hat and a three piece suit
Underneath a tree.
And my best friend was shot in the back
When she walked round the corner.
I'll remember her face till the day I die
And one of these days I'll tell you why.
One of these days I'll tell you where,
And one of these days I'll tell you when.

One by one I'll tell you who.
Step by step I'll show you how,
One of these days. Not now.

An uptight Japanese woman,
And a laid back Chinese man,
Were superstars
In the constellation
Of handpicked Delegation.

There were two white women
With Anglo-Saxon roots
And one such man
Dying in his boots.

We assembled our Delegation
In a Moscow Hotel
"No rubles, no soup," said the waiter.

We said, "Go to hell!"

We had to pay the rubles
Before he'd give the soup,
Most un-Proletarian,
We thought, lousy soup,
To boot.

From Moscow to Pyongyang,
We flew, to Kim Il Sung's Domain,
The Democratic Peoples Republic of Korea,
You understand.
When we hit Pyongyang
And were barely there
The Japanese girl stuck her nose in the air,
Said, "Asia is It! The West is Nowhere!"
Refused to talk, refused to look
Spent all her time writing in her book.

She recorded all we said and did
Including what was best left hid
All the stupid things,
Like when our 1/2 Jewish man
Discovered Women's Lib to be
A Jewish women's conspiracy
Against Jewish men.

We all began to fear her book
And some began to hate the girl
And call her Jap behind her back
The way Koreans did.
I believe they would have killed
Her, if I hadn't confiscated
That which through her
Had been created.

In Hanoi, where poet premier Pham Van Dong,
Had the grace to say—
With a saki toast
On a blazing night
Of reds, and greens, and khaki,
With winds that howled like demons in the sky—
"In the West, you are a black in the shadow.
Here, you are a black in the sun!"
While Richard Nixon bombed the land,

His work of death undone.

When we first saw the Great Wall of China
From 10,000 feet in the sky
Our Frisco Chinaman shrieked
"I made it!" and began to cry.
China was an endless feast
For Body, Mind, and Spirit,
And I could see the ideology
Of China is its culture.
We had duck at a Peking restaurant
Over 3,000 years old,
It had burnt down thrice,
Been bombed out twice
And still was a pot of gold.

We studied Asian politics
We studied Asia's magic tricks
Its history, arts, science, and its wars,
And just when I had all I could handle
Of yin/yang thoughts in a thousand sing-song tongues
I broke out an abstract parachute
Which I'd neatly tucked away
In concentric interstices of my style,
Five Gangster Cigarettes
I'd been saving for a while.
Dynamite Moroccan buds,
Princess of the harvest skimmed
Off the top that year,
A connoisseur's treasure trove
For such a time.

I wanted to be able
Over or under the table,
At a later date, of course,
To claim the fame
And make a Guinness Book of Records boast
That I'm the first to blast
From the same bag of goods
  In Moscow
  In Pyonyang
  In Hanoi
  And two in Peking.
Just another untamed vato,
From Rose Hill, East L.A.,

Sharing the faith of my neighborhood
And my choice of sacred treat,
While the Dictatorship raged
Like a dragon in the streets.
Proletarian Destroyers
With their brothers in their keep.

I thought I'd make a statement
In the silence of the night,
That they can jail
And they can kill
And burn our bodies in public squares,
But they can't stop
Riders like me
Who just don't know
How not to be free.
So I kicked back
On rough dry State Owned sheets,
And fired up a gangster cigarette
And blew a twirling cloud
Of destabilizing smoke
Into the disapproving eyes
Of the official portrait
Of the local Ozymandias
On the wall.

Originally published in October 1971 in the journal The Black Scholar, *this essay articulates the insights Eldridge Cleaver drew from a visit to the Peoples Republic of the Congo, in the heart of Black Africa, also known then as Congo-Brazzaville. Cleaver directed the analysis here toward regaining the momentum and unity within the black liberation struggle lost from what he called the divergence between "the cultural aspects of our Africanness and the revolutionary aspects."*

"Culture and Revolution: Their Synthesis in Africa." Reprinted by permission of The Black Scholar.

CULTURE AND REVOLUTION: THEIR SYNTHESIS IN AFRICA

AFTER BROTHER MALCOLM

Malcolm X, as far as Afro-America is concerned, is the father of revolutionary black nationalism. After he separated from the Nation of Islam and repudiated the leadership of Elijah Muhammed, Malcolm came to Africa, and he traveled all over the continent. Egypt, Ethiopia, Tanzania, Ghana, Nigeria, the Ivory Coast, were all stops on his itinerary. The black world burst fully upon him during this sojourn. He was no longer locked by the twisted Islamic world view of Elijah Muhammed. Also, Malcolm was in the great need of reshaping his perspective in order to stand upon his own authority, his own authenticity as an independent leadership figure, because up to that time all that he said and taught was attributed to Elijah Muhammed.

Malcolm achieved the historic tasks of connecting the Afro-American struggle for national liberation with the national liberation and revolutionary struggles of Africa. He was limited, however, by the objective conditions existing in Africa at that time. The high point of action in Africa, at that time, was the sheer achievement of national independence, and the

Organization of African Unity (OAU) marked the apex in the consolidation of organizational forms. No qualitative estimate of the array of African regimes seemed pertinent, except to the farsighted. No distinction was made between revolutionaries and lackies, actual or potential, and the united front concept reigned supreme.

Malcolm was greatly inspired and influenced by the united front concept, and he strove to adapt it to the American scene. He formulated this idea in the concept of the Organization of Afro-American Unity, which was to be a microism of the OAU—Organization of African Unity. This was his guiding image. The idea of an Organization of Afro-American Unity excited American militants because they could see the vanguard relationship and even the potential structural relationship between the OAU and the OAAU. And even at that very primary level of development of the African Revolution, it was very exciting and informative to begin visualizing the Afro-American struggle as being both structured and structurally connected to the African Revolution. Also, everything that Malcolm did at this stage was guided by his major idea of internationalizing the Afro-American struggle by shifting the focus from Civil Rights to Human Rights.

Afro-Americans, following the new direction of Malcolm X, became Africanized overnight. Malcolm taught us many things. He, more than any other single influence, raised our consciousness to a level where we became even more directly proud of Africa and our African ancestry and heritage. We became more directly connected with Africa. Malcolm emphasized our African heritage, insisting that we must become connected with Africa, even though he offed the "Back to Africa" concept. He also emphasized that we must resort to armed struggle and fight for our freedom.

When Malcolm was assassinated, a very important synthesis and unity which he symbolized and which he made possible was gone. And the streams which he pulled together began to diverge. Those who could not relate to Malcolm's message about the utility of the gun but who could relate very heavily to his message about African Culture and Afro-American people taking on African culture and emphasizing their African roots, took advantage of his death as yielding a favorable moment to reject what he said about the gun while raising high the banner of African Culture.

When Malcolm was alive, he inflamed and inspired many people and he also frightened many people. He inspired them by calling their attention again to their Africanness. Many people could relate to that and united around it, but when he talked about the gun the crowd thinned out and he became, once again, "the controversial Malcolm X," or "the enigmatic Malcolm X." Many people were just afraid of the whole subject of guns in the hands of blacks. This was very clear, and this was the part of what Malcolm was talking about that they could not relate to.

But Malcolm was so strong that even though these people did not relate to the gun, they maintained their silence, would not reject it or condemn its use—until after Malcolm was murdered. Malcolm's death left the door open for the public repudiation of that part of his teachings that had already been privately rejected. . . . Now people felt free to select the part of Malcolm that they related to and rationalize the rest away.

So that it was from the death of Malcolm that two large streams began to distinguish themselves and we can see how the Cultural Nationalists split away from what Malcolm had called Revolutionary Black Nationalism. At first the split was very minute, wasn't glaring, and wasn't antagonistic. But the Cultural Nationalist tendency became more and more of a rightist tendency and the revolutionary black nationalist line moved further and further to the left, so that there was a gap created, sort of a forked formation, where the cultural nationalists went deeper and deeper off into cultural nationalism and became more and more separated from any relationship with revolutionary black nationalism and the distinguishing characteristic was the gun. On the other hand, the revolutionary black nationalists moved further and further away from cultural nationalism and became more and more involved with the gun.

At that time, it was not easy to see the mistake involved or exactly where the contradiction lay and just what to do to resolve it. We understood very clearly the contradiction between ourselves and the cultural nationalists. We knew what it was about the cultural nationalists that we didn't like. We could relate to African culture. We incorporated it into our beings. We had no hangups about that. But we even stopped wearing dashikis and emphasizing our Africanness as part of our struggle against the cultural nationalists who had turned African culture into either a fetish or a marketable commodity, and at the same time completely repudiated the gun. We wanted to call people's attention to the gun. So we became extremely related to the gun in a dialectical contradiction with the cultural nationalists who became extremely and totally wrapped up in African culture.

Looking back objectively, we can see that both of these directions flowing from the heritage of Malcolm X contained incorrect elements and attitudes. Both were narrow interpretations of and emphasis of what Malcolm was talking about.

This is why we think that returning to Africa, to the Congo, will help to unite the Afro-American liberation struggle more powerfully than it has ever been united before. We will be able to regain the unity and momentum which we possessed when Malcolm X was alive. To regain that synthesis between the cultural aspects of our Africanness and the revolutionary aspects, because as the revolutionary black nationalist line developed, those who were revolutionary black nationalists went through many changes and one very important thing which many of them did, particularly those who went on to build the Black Panther Party, was to become ideological, adopting the Marxist-Leninist class analysis, which even negated our nationalism.

So there was a problem of beginning to lose our identity in all this development. It did not seem as though we were getting closer and closer to Africa, but that we were getting further and further into ideology, deeper and deeper into Marxism-Leninism, and the other aspects of our African connectedness were definitely downgraded, as a part of our struggle with the cultural nationalists. Now we can see that we got carried away, that some of what we did was incorrect. Perhaps that was all we could do at that time, given the conditions and what we had to work with, but still we can see how it was negative and not the best that could have been done or should have been done.

Returning to the Congo, we find here in the Congo a revolutionary Marxist-Leninist state, with a Marxist-Leninist Party, and a People's Army built along the lines discovered for the formation of a true People's Republic, to deal with safeguarding the construction of a Socialist Society from both the internal and external enemies. This, we see very clearly, will have a profound effect of hurling the Afro-American liberation struggle onto a higher level, making possible an unprecedentedly tighter unity. The whole divergence between the cultural nationalists and the revolutionary black nationalists, in the first place, was based directly on the question of how do we relate to Africa. And the divergence was only possible because Africa was not speaking for itself, or that it spoke with so many voices that much confusion resulted in selecting which voice to listen to. One could refer to Africa and make Africa say anything that one was seeking to prove. Ideologically, Africa was up for grabs.

We recall the host of State Department–CIA niggers who were sent to Africa in Malcolm's footsteps in order to destroy the effect that he was having, to dilute if not destroy his impact. Many Uncle Toms toured Africa, covering the continent in a bootlicking orgy of apologetics, disseminating all kinds of contradictory bullshit misinformation that actually befuddled many Africans as to just what Afro-Americans were all about. The situation was very difficult then because Malcolm was almost all alone. He did not have a well-formed and well-informed cadre to back him up, to help focus the attention of the people on his message. But even without such a cadre and even with all the opposition of the pig media and the bootlicking black bourgeois media, and all the confusion and misunderstanding, Malcolm was still able to have a colossal impact upon the psyches of black people in Babylon, and he turned Afro-Americans around.

But today, we have a situation where we have party cadre and many other black people who have already gone through the process of regaining their consciousness of their African heritage. At the same time, the revolutionary arm of Afro-America also relates to our African roots, and is only separated from the paraphernalia of African culture because of internal conflicts in the Afro-American liberation struggle between the cultural freaks and those who relate primarily to the gun. The cultural nationalists refused to understand that "political power grows out of the barrel of a gun," and this is precisely why it was necessary to wage such a hard and uncompromising struggle against them.

But now a loud voice has risen from the heart of Africa, from the Congo, speaking about a revolutionary Marxist-Leninist state. Not just speaking about it but having actually achieved the consolidation, establishment, and promulgation of the People's Republic of the Congo, under the leadership of President Marien Ngouabi. The historical fact of the existence of a Marxist-Leninist nation in Africa destroys all arguments supporting the perpetuation of the contradiction between the revolutionary black nationalists and the cultural nationalists, which for several years has bottled up and stifled an unestimable amount of revolutionary energy. This energy must again burst forth, on a higher level of consciousness, with cadre already committed to ideology, but firmly rooted in our African heritage and identity. We now have an African model, The People's Republic of the Congo, which is a black nation with a Marxist-Leninist state. All arguments over the synthesis of our history, our culture, and Marxism-Leninism can now be dealt with objectively, because we have an example of where this has already been done successfully.

It is very beautiful that this has been done in the Congo, in the heart of Africa. Of all words, phrases, and statements connected with Africa, even more than the word "Africa" itself, the word *Congo* sets off some very deep vibrations in black hearts, in black souls, in black minds.

I think that encountering the People's Republic of the Congo will enable us once again to call upon our source of strength, our history, and all our cultural aspects—but this time focused into a revolutionary context, for there will be no distinction between our cultural necessities and our cultural heritage. I think that's right on. I think that's fantastic, and I think it's true.

THE PEOPLE'S REPUBLIC OF THE CONGO

The establishment of reactionary, bourgeois regimes throughout black Africa, on the one hand, and the continued domination of large sections of the continent by white racist regimes, such as in South Africa, Southern Rhodesia, South West Africa, Angola, Mozambique, Guinea Bissau, on the other hand, stopped the forward march of the black man in Africa, and also exerted a breaking effect on the liberation struggles of black people throughout the world.

Beginning with the brutal, heartbreaking political murder of Patrice Lumumba, accompanied by the rise of Tshombe and Mobutu in the Congo, the overthrow of Nkrumah in Ghana, and the bewildering succession of reactionary *coups d'état* in Africa, the magnetic attraction which the independent African states exercised upon Afro-Americans faded away. Not even Jomo Kenyatta, the Burning Spear, wrongly associated with the inspiring Mau Mau of Kenya, any longer had magic in his image as far as Afro-Americans were concerned.

For, the major problem in Africa today is not the problem of Colonialism in the old sense of the word, but the new form of neo-colonialism by which the same old slavemasters seek to continue their same old game of exploitation and oppression but using new methods. Instead of occupying African territory outright and openly in the manner of invaders occupying conquered territory, the game of neo-colonialism uses black puppets, such as Mobutu in the Congo, Senghor in Senegal, and Boingy in the Ivory Coast for such domination.

What the bloodsucking imperialists have wanted all along is a free hand in exploiting the riches of the oppressed people's lands. Finding it impossible and too costly, both politically and militarily, to continue maintaining direct control of Africa, the imperialists have come to rely more and more upon their puppets, and they found that these dedicated lackies are able to get the job done for them. They are still able to drain off the fabulous riches of Africa and thereby continue to enjoy a life of luxury and splendor in the mother country at the expense of Africa.

There is no country in Africa that has an independent economy. Those that are not in the clutches of the Western imperialists are dependent either upon the Soviet Union or China. The monopoly which these developed countries have on technology is the key means through which they are able to control the economies of African countries. Also, by blocking their products on the world market, the imperialists are able to force Third World countries to their knees, thus forcing them to capitulate to their economic demands.

By far, the Socialist countries offer the most favorable terms and conditions for the aid that they give to Third World countries, but when it comes to Africa, we again find that the black man is at the bottom of the list, receiving far less than the amount of aid that they need in order to develop independent economies.

We have paid dearly—in lives, riches, and precious lost time—for this situation.

But the tide of history has again turned in Africa.

December 31, 1969, the founding date of the People's Republic of the Congo, marks the turning point. Once again freedom has a toehold in black Africa. The lying propaganda of the imperialists and the colonialists kept the existence of the People's Republic of the Congo a secret. What really has been going on in the Congo has been hidden from us.

What the Soviet Union meant to Europe, what China meant to Asia, and what Cuba meant to Latin America, the People's Republic of the Congo means to Africa and to black people everywhere. For many years now, the Soviet Union, China and Cuba have provided centers of people's power under the red banner of Socialism and Marxism-Leninism in Europe, Asia, and Latin America. Now for the first time, Africa and the Black World have such a center of people's power. And this center of people's power is destined to exercise the same kind of influence upon Africa and black people as the other centers did in their parts of the world and upon their peoples.

This is why what is now happening in the People's Republic of the Congo is so important. The Congo has struck out on the road to true independence. By choosing Socialism as the form of society and Marxism-Leninism for its ideology, the People's Republic of the Congo has challenged the imperialists to a showdown. The government of President Marien Ngouabi has declared war upon neo-colonialism. Backed up by a strong, closely united Party, the Congolese Workers' Party, a powerful People's Army, and with the masses of the people armed and organized into a People's Militia, the Congo is on firm, solid ground. It would take a major military invasion from outside, using a scorched earth policy, to overturn what the courageous Congolese revolutionaries have achieved.

Putting their theory into practice, the Congolese Marxists-Leninists have started nationalizing all of the foreign-owned enterprises in their country. This has brought on a crisis between the People's Republic of the Congo and all imperialist countries. But the Congo has reached the point of no return. There is no turning back for the Congo. This is why Afro-Americans, in their own struggle for liberation, can look upon the Congo as a true, reliable ally in the struggle, for the number one enemy facing the People's Republic of the Congo is the United States of America.

Our revolutionary brothers and sisters in the People's Republic of the Congo have stretched out their hands to Afro-America. We must reciprocate. We must firmly lock hands with the Congo, because the hour is late and the danger is real. Across the Congo River, in Congo-Kinshasha, the United States of America is trying by every means to overthrow the young Socialist regime in the People's Republic of the Congo. Congo-Kinshasha, under the bootlicking control of Mobutu, the worthy successor of Tshombe, is the main base for the operations of the CIA against the best interests of black Africa. There are thousands of American troops stationed in Congo-Kinshasha at this very moment, and many of them are specially recruited black soldiers, mercenaries, who learned their murderous art in Vietnam. Not a day goes by that hostile acts, originating in Mobutu's Congo, are not carried out against the People's Republic of the Congo. And the American military bases there are like death poised and aimed, ready to strike a fatal blow at a moment's notice.

In addition, the arch racist-fascist-imperialist of the twentieth century, Richard Nixon, has pledged the support of the U.S. government to maintain the white racists in power in South Africa and Southern Rhodesia, and he is bankrolling and arming Portugal in its vicious war to stamp out the liberation movements in Angola, Mozambique, and Guinea Bissau. Through the machinery of NATO, gigantic supplies of modern weapons are poured into Africa, into the hands of the racists and the puppets, to be used against the forces of freedom.

It's the intent of the Nixon clique, in league with the other imperialist and colonial governments of the West, to keep Africa and the black people locked in the clutches of neo-colonialism. They intend to accomplish this evil scheme by any means necessary. They have already been hard at work at just this for many years. The meaning of this evil scheme must be crystal clear to Afro-Americans, because whatever the fate of Africa, Afro-Americans will share it. There are no two ways about that. It has always been true.

So we must proclaim our solidarity with the African revolutionaries, particularly joining hands with our Congolese brothers and sisters. We must not sit idly by and watch the white racist-imperialist American government, hand in hand with the French, the British, the Belgian, the South African, the Portuguese, and the Israelis, shackle Africa and the black man in chains once again. *Hands off the Congo!* must become our battle cry, and we must put it into practice.

We must move to help the Congo smash the plots hatched against it by the imperialists in their move to lock the Congo down again by using neo-colonialist techniques. In so doing, we will at the same time be striking a blow for our own freedom, because the enemy is one and the same.

We must *Demand* that the United States withdraw all of its troops from Congo-Kinshasha and cease all military aid to the reactionary Mobutu regime!

We must *Demand* that the United States and all other imperialist countries stop their hostile economic acts against the People's Republic of the Congo!

In this expensive interview conducted in Paris during 1974, Eldridge Cleaver reveals to Henry Louis Gates, at the time a graduate student at Cambridge University in England, the experiences which have changed his views about Cuba, Algeria, and Communism.

"Eldridge Cleaver on Ice," a conversation between Henry Louis Gates, Jr. and Eldridge Cleaver, first appeared in Transition: An International Review, *Volume 7 Issue 3/4; 75/76. Reprinted by permission of the Du Bois Institute, Harvard University.*

ELDRIDGE CLEAVER ON ICE

From *Transition* 49 (1975) and *Ch'indaba* 2 (1976)
Henry Louis Gates, Jr.

HENRY LOUIS GATES, JR.: Were you publicly acknowledged when you came to Cuba, or did you go underground?

ELDRIDGE CLEAVER: I was so far underground it bothered me. It was not generally known that I was there. In an effort to conceal my presence, no announcement was made that I was in the country.

HLG: Did the Cuban government have any particular reason for this, or was it the decision of the Panthers?

EC: We all agreed that it would be best to be cool. I didn't plan to go there and remain underground indefinitely. I just wanted to elude the clutches of the American authorities and then start woofing at them some more, you know? It was agreed that certain things would take place after I got there.

HLG: Such as?

EC: We were supposed to be given a permanent, well-organized facility there. This request was in accord with the atmosphere at that time; Cuba supported liberation movements. We were supposed to have official status, including a program on Havana Radio. Robert Williams did—he used to broadcast "Radio Free Dixie" to the United States from Cuba, he published, he circulated information. All these things were on our agenda, too. But not only did these things not take place, the Cubans never had any intention of allowing them to.

HLG: Did this surprise you?

EC: Well, you have to understand that I believed in international proletarian solidarity. I knew that the support that American leftists gave to Cuba had been very useful to the Castro government. There was a kind of quid pro quo established for progressives: you scratch my back, I scratch yours. We sought to take them up on it. It wasn't as though we went there begging; we went there to get what was ours.

HLG: What happened when you got there?

EC: After the immediate arrival, I was taken to this pad and given all the comforts one could ask for. I was given two policemen, a black one and a white one; they were my constant companions. I was taken on a tour of the island, and I went to every province and had a very detailed rundown on the life of the people and the course of the Revolution. Since this is not a large place, you can't do that for too long before you start getting down to some of the concrete things about Cuba. Some of the things you had been told were obviously not true, especially concerning the racial situation. I began to separate fact from fiction.

I enjoyed talking to the black policeman more than I enjoyed talking to the other guy; he always seemed to inhibit the conversation. I noticed that whenever the white guy was out of the room, the black man would make penetrating comments that seemed more realistic than the things he would say when the white guy was in the room. The white Cuban came by alone sometimes, but the black Cuban never came alone. I asked them about it one day, and I noticed an immediate tension in the room. The white guy answered for him: "Well, he's too busy." Things like that. He also told me I asked too many questions.

Suddenly, my black policeman was eliminated. He stopped coming by completely. By that time, I knew where he lived, which was not too far from me, so I went around to his pad. He wasn't there, so

I left a message for him, asking him to come by and see me. Soon after, he came by and admitted that people had put pressure on him not to see me anymore. He gave me two books, volumes one and two of *Cuban History,* by Philip S. Foner. You can imagine that it's not easy to do that in Cuba; I still have those books. He told me that the answers to my questions were in the books, and that that was the best he could do. He also told me that it was best that we didn't see each other anymore. I understood.

HLG: What did the books tell you?

EC: At that time, I was trying to learn about Maceo. Now and then, you'd hear something about him; you'd hear that this black guy, Antonio Maceo, had liberated Cuba with the sword. Yet they would call José Martí "the father of the Cuban Revolution." Everywhere you looked, you would see statues of José Martí. It looked like they were trying to foist something off on you. You really get sick of seeing him! Little white head, everywhere.

When you tried to find out more about Maceo, you'd run into a block. I once went to the National Library and asked this girl if she had anything about him. She took me to a catalogue: they had essays by Maceo on agriculture, essays on morals, essays on political philosophy, the collected letters, all kinds of things, in volumes and volumes. I asked her where these things were. All these books were locked up in a room where the Cuban people couldn't read them!

HLG: How long had you been there when you discovered this?

EC: I had been there for seven months, and it was the beginning of the end. There were all these people who were supposed to join me in Cuba, comrades from the Black Panther Party. Bobby Seale, David Hilliard, and others were in Sweden, and they all wanted to come to Havana. The Cubans told me that Bobby and the others didn't have time to come, but some contacts in Sweden sent me literature from the Panthers, including a letter from the Cuban embassy that I wasn't supposed to see. The Cuban embassy official, in this letter, was telling other Cubans that the Panthers had wanted to come, but that he had done what he had been told to do and informed the Panthers that it was not possible.

At the same time, there were all these Afro-American hijackers who were coming to Cuba. The Cuban newspapers would list the name of the hijacker, his motivation, and give direct quotes from him. The Cuban officials were telling me to stay away from these people; they told me these hijackers were dangerous. So when I saw them, I'd hide. But I was living right on the main street, and I could see people walking up and down, often through my binoculars.

I started to sneak out regularly. When my cops would go away, I'd go downstairs and walk up and down, look around, try to talk to someone to psych out the situation. I knew a little Spanish from Los Angeles, which made it possible to say a few things. I used to have this uniform they wear in Cuba, a kind of officer's cut, with a pistol holster—the whole outfit. I wore it, with the pistol, when I went out. I think I looked like any other Cuban, except I was tall, which was a little curious and raised a few eyebrows, but nobody said anything. People don't know what's going on in Cuba.

One day I was downstairs, standing in front of my pad, just looking at people walking by—a lot of people do that in Cuba; they just sit around, looking. These cats came by, these Americans, these hijackers. They recognized me, and they went off! I was uptight about that, because I knew the Cubans would know about it.

So the Cuban policeman said to me, "Okay, you saw him? He saw you? No problem. You want to talk with him some more? Since he knows already that you're here, there's no point in hiding it from him." They contacted the hijacker and told him to come over to my pad. When we talked, he told me that he'd been there for a long time. Since he was a member of the Black Panther Party, they didn't put him in prison when he got there; they put him in the Havana Libre Hotel. He was the only Panther who ever hijacked a plane to Cuba.

HLG: Why were they putting other blacks and hijackers in prison?

EC: Security. It's reasonable, I think. Everybody who goes there as a hijacker goes to prison. All kinds of people come to Cuba—you get some kooks, real kooks. It's conceivable that you could get a CIA agent. So this is what they do: they try to find out what you are, then they put you on a special program—cutting sugarcane off in the provinces—and they keep you in prison anywhere from one month to two or three months, depending on the case. They put hijackers in prison to make them happy to be in Cuba when they get out. As for the security interrogation, cats usually give up information about who they are, and give the name of someone who can vouch for them. Through their contacts, the Cuban authorities check this person out. A lot of times, I'd do that: they'd ask me about a person, and I would check it out for them.

HLG: How were these hijackers treated in prison? Were they beaten?

EC: No, it was psychological brutality. All the hijackers said the same thing: they had been to prison in the States, but they had never seen anything like Cuban prisons. What made it worse was that most people didn't feel that the Cubans would lie to them. We went there very naive.

After prison, they sent everybody to Camagüey Province, which is the southernmost province in Cuba, next to Oriente. Out in Camagüey Province, ain't nothing happening. But you can't just get on a bus or train and move. The government has to agree to let you do this. Before you can get on a bus, government officials check your ticket! Tickets are checked regularly throughout the ride.

HLG: What are they afraid of?

EC: People are trying to leave Cuba, lots of people. The government says it's not happening at all, but I found it to be pretty understandable, especially when you consider how large the world is and how small an island is. But you see all these people swimming, trying to float away on a coconut. The government says they're trying to leave "for counterrevolutionary reasons"; they say that these people are *guzanos,* "worms," counterrevolutionaries. But it's not true! I started calling it a Robinson Crusoe Complex, because I had that feeling, too. You really feel that you are standing on a little piece of land—it's a physical feeling about being on an island. Traditionally, the Cubans—those who could afford it—have always known that they could leave and go somewhere, and come back. It's a safety valve—it might even be a psychological necessity to know that you can go somewhere, you know? I find it to be a very strong impulse there.

HLG: Because of the severity of the regime?

EC: Actually, I think that's irrelevant. People wanted to do it under Batista, and they want to do it under Castro. I think they would want to do it under anybody. If there was no government, I think they would want to try to get out. A girl told me once, "You know, I'm like Che Guevara. The Revolution has conquered Cuba; I want to go somewhere the Revolution hasn't conquered—like Paris or London. You know what I mean?"

That's how they have to talk: they have to say that they want to do it "like Che," that they want to fight a new battle. They can't just say they want to go to another continent. I always thought it was wrong and really counterproductive to call everybody who tries to leave a *guzano*. It doesn't work, because the people know better.

Once, a guy told me about a man who was the first Afro-American to hijack a plane to Cuba. He had been in prison a year, whereas these cats I had been hanging with had been there for a couple of months. So I went around to this guy's pad, and he started saying all sorts of things. He said, "People here will tell you it was bad under Batista, but not this bad." I wasn't prepared to hear this kind of shit. He was so cynical about Cuba that it was impossible to talk to him. He was totally, completely negative. He was down on socialism, down on the Cuban Revolution, and he spoke insultingly about Fidel.

HLG: What were his criticisms?

EC: He said that the Cubans were running a game, that they were not sincere, that they were racists. His big argument was that the black Cuban people thought that their government was racist. This guy was married to a Cuban woman; he had a ration book and he was living as a Cuban. He had to stand in line to get his rations, and he had the same regimen that other Cubans had. Most of his criticisms centered around his personal experiences, especially the way he was treated in prison. He used to mutter, "I'm going to go crazy."

In prison, they told him that he was a CIA agent, and that they were going to off him. Pretty terrifying. He had hijacked a plane with another man, and this man had his wife and children with him. But from the time he got off the plane, he never saw this man again. He thought the man was dead; the Cubans told him that they had offed him—and they told this other man that they had offed the first man. The two never saw each other again. At first, he used to be able to scream through the ventilator at this other man. But by separating them, and running all this shit on them, the Cubans began to turn the one against the other. They didn't know each other that well, anyway; they had just hooked up on this flight. And the Cubans told the one, "Do you know you came in with a CIA agent, motherfucker?" He didn't know much about the other dude, so he said, "I didn't know, I didn't know, I didn't know what he was." He had pure faith in the Cubans. They kept him in Camagüey Province, away from Havana, and he really wanted to be in Havana.

So this guy called himself Mosiah Kenyatta, and he kept insisting he wouldn't go along with any program; he kept trying to run away. So they let him go to Havana, where he was installed. He had a little apartment in Havana, and that's where he was when some guys took me to his house. He was completely bitter about his experiences in Cuba, and full of little stories about what the Cuban people would say. He was married to a Cuban, he had a lot of Cuban friends, he was a member of a Cuban family, and all these people were full of Antonio Maceo; they were part of the Cuban anti-racist struggle. Having been through the whole thing himself, Mosiah knew where the camps were, and he knew where they kept the other hijackers. We found a black Cuban girl who was the girlfriend of one of these guys. She was willing to go down there and contact this guy, the hijacker. So she went there, and eventually found him, and gave him my address, and told him to start asking to see me.

At first, we didn't tell him to run away. But he started asking the government, and they started refusing. They wouldn't let him come. Mosiah's wife was from Oriente, so they went on the pretext of visiting her family there. He found this cat, and made contact with him, and told him that the best thing to do was to just run away to my pad, where it was cool.

So this cat ran away and got to my pad, where we had a ritual. Other hijackers started doing this, too. And whenever anyone got to my pad, I would baptize him in the name of the Father, the Son, and the Holy Ghost, and make him a Black Panther. I told the Cubans that I was authorized by the Black Panther Party to induct Afro-Americans into the Black Panther Party anywhere, anytime as I saw fit, and I took these people in. The Cuban government may not have agreed with this procedure, but they were forced to say, "If you want to run your struggle this way, that's your business. No one can tell you what to do; it's an internal affair." You see? So that is how we did it, and the word passed around to all these cats, and they were all trying to make it to my pad. About eight of them made it. Some never made it. It was during this time that the whole thing hit the fan, when this Reuters reporter found my pad.

HLG: How did that happen?

EC: There was this white girl, from Georgia. Her name was Bunny Hearne, and she was a friend of Fidel Castro. When Castro was in the mountains, this girl used to write fan mail—"Come on, champ! I'm rooting for you!" She did this for years, and after the Revolution, she was one of the people that was invited to come. So she went down there, and I think that she was in love with him; of course, he had no intentions of marrying her. She'd done a stateside TV program about why a girl like her, who had worked on the Kennedy campaign, approved of the Cuban Revolution. I think it was on NBC. This was her big shot, where she gave support to the Cuban Revolution. So she went there with stars in her eyes.

It was a couple of years later when I got there, and by that time, she had become bitter about the fact that she wasn't getting married. But she was full of inside information about Cuba, because she knew all the big wheels. She's the one who, for her own reasons—which had more to do with her conflict with the Cubans than with me— gave my address to this Reuters guy, blowing my cover.

At that time, we were really jacked-up in this conflict with the Cubans over the hijackers; the Cubans were trying to decide what they were going to do about us, since we had some guns in this pad—a pistol and two AK–47s. We were in that siege frame of mind, that Afro-American, "Custer's Last Stand" frame of mind. People were dying, and you could see the threat of getting offed. These other cats felt more vulnerable than I did, so we were all in this together; we would go down together. Then this shit started happening over the case of Raymond Johnson, the last hijacker to run away and make it to my pad. This was the last showdown: we told the Cubans that we were not going to let them take Raymond, and that we were going to resist. We made our last will and testament on tapes, and sent them to the States through some Puerto Rican who was from New York. The other

Cubans were talking about storming the pad, but they didn't know about these guns. So he had to tell them about them! The whole thing blew up, then, because we were in the middle of Havana, and it wouldn't have gone over too well, from their point of view, if there had been some sort of violent conflict.

HLG: When all this was going on, did you get a clearer sense of how racism functioned in Cuba?

EC: Well, I told you about how I had felt driven to study Cuban history. What we discovered was the history of Cuban racism—and the problem of racism in the Cuban Revolution. For example, the highest-ranking officials were called *commandantes,* and out of forty-two *commandantes,* there were seven or eight blacks. This goes to the core of the population: some white Cubans will tell you that Cuba is maybe 20 percent black, whereas black Cubans will tell you that Cuba is 30, 40, 50, even 60 percent black. You end up with the impression that most of the people you see are black or mixed; a lot of the people they consider to be white, we wouldn't. But when we asked specific questions about the composition of the mainly white government, we heard the old arguments: there aren't enough educated black people, or, "They ain't ready yet." That's what it came out to, and I consider this to be racism.

My security man was driving some hijackers who lived in my pad, and he drove them to the Havana Libre, to get something from the hotel room. When they were in front of the Havana Libre, this black man came around the corner with three or four rifles over his shoulder. He started shooting, but only at the people in uniform; they were shooting at him and he was downing them. This man was after a specific man in the hotel; he went in there and shot him in the chest. Then my security man shot this dude. The cat had about three bullets for each gun—that's the issue for guard duty; they are issued with a few bullets apiece—which is why he took all those rifles.

So the security man came back to tell me about this shootout, and one thing he mentioned was that the gunman was wearing a very striking powder-blue, silky-looking shirt, with a big red symbol emblazoned over his left breast. I asked what that was about, and the security man said that this was some crazy sect, whose members believe that when the stars and the moon are in a certain position, they're going to be liberated! He said it like it was a joke! I tried to press for more detail, but he wouldn't talk about it. We asked some Cubans about this sect; they went out and did some research and told us that the red symbol on the man's chest had to do with a religion called Santa BaBa. BaBa was a man who led a slave rebellion centuries ago in Cuba, and now there was this mystical sect of blacks who felt oppressed by the whites. The figure of BaBa had been merged with St. Barbara to form this syncretic religion, Santa BaBa, and we found a few examples of rebellions led by these people. In fact, what we found was a whole crawling network of secret societies plotting against Cuba. We began to call it Voodoo Socialism, because we couldn't say anything else about it.

HLG: Are black Cuban workers still the least privileged members of Cuban society?

EC: I certainly got that impression.

HLG: Castro claims to have eliminated racial discrimination.

EC: He shouldn't say things like that. That's an extreme statement which is just not true. This is just propaganda.

HLG: The Cuban journalist Carlos Moore, writing in *Présence Africaine,* has argued that this is done to play Afro-Americans against the United States government. Is that true?

EC: Yes, the Cuban government definitely aims propaganda at specific groups. When Castro left his hotel in downtown New York City and moved uptown to Harlem, he was definitely playing to blacks. He always invited blacks to come to Cuba. The idea was that American attacks on Cuba were the actions of a racist country, attacks less against the ideology of the Cuban Revolution than on the substantial progressive changes in the society.

HLG: If a crucial element in the success of a revolution is the elimination of discrimination based on race, then would we have to say that in Cuba, no revolution has taken place?

EC: No, we couldn't say that. The Revolution has definitely taken place, although discrimination has not been abolished. Black people are undoubtedly in a better position in Cuba now than they were under Batista. But when you judge a revolution, you have to consider its shortcomings.

HLG: In Cuba, you spent most of your time away from your wife. Why was that?

EC: Kathleen was supposed to come to Cuba right away; she was very pregnant. As it turned out, by the time I caught up with her, it was just in time to catch the baby! There were constant difficulties in her path. It was after the incident with the Reuters reporter that I was sent to Algiers—to see her, and also to deflect publicity from Cuba by surfacing in Algeria.

HLG: That was the official reasoning?

EC: That's what they told me. There was a Cuban government operative who came and explained this to me. At that time I didn't know anything about Algeria. I didn't know that liberation movements from all over the world were there, operating the way I had wanted to in Cuba. The Cubans told me that Algeria would be a perfect place to surface, and that I wouldn't have any trouble returning to Cuba. They told me about the great future in Algeria, which was only supposed to last for a week or two.

HLG: Did this order come from Fidel Castro himself?

EC: I wanted guarantees that this wasn't a double-cross, because by this time our confidence in the Cubans was zero. So I had a talk with Castro's representative, who gave me Fidel's personal guarantee. I couldn't really go on my own terms, of course, but I didn't want to go an unknown.

HLG: You went directly to Algiers?

EC: Yes, Morocco to Algiers, with some official Cubans.

HLG: How were you greeted? What was the Algerian government's re-action?

EC: I was really uptight. When I left Cuba, I thought everything had been arranged. And when I landed in Algiers, the Cubans were wait-ing for me to get me through customs. But while I was in the air, the Algerians had "changed their minds"; I was told that they didn't want me there. I met Kathleen, and we had an opportunity to talk. I be-came even more apprehensive when I had a chance to compare what she had been told with what I had been told: she was told that I did-n't want her to come, and I was told that she didn't want me to come. The next day, the Cubans came to me with a plane ticket to Amman, Jordan. They said that the Algerians wanted me to go to a Palestine Liberation Organization camp, so I could surface there, instead. It just sounded incredible—I knew they were lying. "Amman plane," they said, "leaving in two days!" Kathleen was eight months pregnant. I didn't think this was a reasonable suggestion. They wanted me to travel by myself. I thought this must be the ultimate double-cross.

Then the Cubans asked me if I knew a girl called Elaine Klein. I said no. They said to stay away from her, that she was an American and that she was dangerous. When they said that, I immediately thought that this was somebody I should make contact with right away. We had the phone number of Mario Andrade, who was the rep-resentative of the MPLA in Angola. He came to see us, and I told him I wanted to see people from other liberation movements. So Charles Chickarema, from Zimbabwe, came up. He turned out to be very perceptive. I asked him if he knew Elaine Klein, and he said yes, that she was a nice person. I asked him to send her around. It might seem like it would be difficult to find people in Algiers, but it's not. The phone rang, and she came over.

She was on the committee for the 1969 Pan-African Cultural Fes-tival. I hadn't known anything about it. She had helped draft the in-vitation list, and she had included the Black Panther Party and me, in particular, because of my book *Soul on Ice*. She had no idea we would actually come; she had just been making this list at her desk, with nothing else to do. So it turned out that I had a legitimate invitation and a legitimate reason to stay. When I told her what the Cubans had said, she didn't believe it: she got in touch with the Algerian official responsible for this sort of thing, and discovered that the Algerians didn't even know I was there. They didn't know and they didn't care. So I told the Cubans that I had an invitation to stay for the festival. But they still wanted me to go to Amman; then I could return for the festival. I didn't get it: if their intention had been to get rid of me, they could have killed me then; why this insistence on Amman? Then I talked to an Algerian official who confirmed that what the Cubans had said was a lie, and that I was welcome to stay. Next thing I knew, Elaine introduced me to representatives of the Viet Cong—and they knew all about us; they were extremely well-informed. The next day, one of their representatives was scheduled to have lunch with President Boumedienne of Algeria. He said he'd tell Boumedienne that we were okay. The next day, the Cubans disappeared. I never saw them again. It was very strange.

HLG: What was the significance of the festival?

EC: That's hard to say. It was originally organized by the Organization for African Unity. Each member nation sent a delegation to Algeria to display their culture: poets, writers, singers, musicians, dancers, and the rest of the cultural spectrum. This was the first Pan-African Cultural Festival in the history of the world. Each delegation had a pavilion; there were liberation movements from South Africa, South-West Africa, Rhodesia, the Portuguese colonies—they all had pavilions. The Palestinians, who really aren't Africans but who had the support of their African brothers, were able to come as well. There was such a good spirit involved that they gave us a pavilion.

I sent Emory Douglas back to the United States to put a delegation together, and to bring back information, art, and propaganda—everything we had to offer. He brought thousands of our newspapers and a huge delegation of people. It all came at a good time, because almost all of these people were on trial. I was surfacing for the first time, really—I had refused to talk with the Reuters reporter, so he had to put out an unconfirmed report; he had no photos and no corroboration. I surfaced at the festival opening, at a Black Panther press conference. The American press sent television crews. The Algerians were happy, because this was free publicity for their festival; the Western press had tried to ignore the festival, at first. The American press freaked out at our press conference: there were Algerian officials, Yasir Arafat's Al-Fatah, representatives of African governments, representatives from liberation movements around the world. They covered the whole thing. And to cover us, they had to place us in the context of the festival: Miriam Makeba was there, Nina Simone, even Stokely Carmichael. That was actually the first time we had a chance to talk to Stokely since he resigned from the Panthers and renounced the Party.

HLG: What was behind his resignation?

EC: I make a distinction between his public letter of resignation and the disagreements and conflicts we had with him, which had to do with both power structure and ideology. In public, there is this line that Stokely runs about Nkrumahism and pan-Africanism, his absolute rejection of any kind of working relation with whites. He resisted— tried to sabotage—the working relations the Party had with whites all along. Once, when I was in prison, he tried to carry off a little coup against Bobby Seale to take over the Party; Huey was in jail. It was only when he couldn't control or dominate the situation that he began to formulate all these criticisms. Before that, he was right there with us.

He used this thing about white people in a very demagogic way. I traveled with Stokely as a journalist on his first tour of northern college campuses in 1967. We went to the University of Chicago and Penn State, as well as Detroit and New York City. He would make his standard speech, pushing hard that white people work in the white community, and that black people work in the black community. Then, in Chicago, he went to this white doctor's pad for dinner. So I said, "Why are you here, man; how can you be?" And he said, "This man has been a longtime SNCC supporter." You see, instead of associating with white people openly, he was doing it sneakily. He would do those kinds of things. And this was a malady of that movement: running heavy lines about white people, then sneaking around fucking white girls. We used to deal openly. We'd say it was okay to do that, and they would attack us. But they were doing it themselves, and because they were sneaky, they didn't have to deal with criticism. I thought that this was both immoral and not useful.

HLG: Did any sort of ideological developments occur during the festival, between Stokely Carmichael, Don Lee, Amiri Baraka, and the Black Panthers?

EC: Baraka wasn't there. But something had happened in the U.S.: the McClellan Committee came up with a so-called Black Panther, a man named Powell, whom no one had ever heard of. He described a lot of horrible stuff that supposedly went on in the Party: sexual abuse of children, other things. At the same time, Stokely published his letter. Can you imagine the effect it had on the McClellan Committee? That's why I thought his action was shaky. So when Stokely showed up in Algeria, all the members of the Panther Party were there. He and the nationalist clique were living in the Hotel St. George, the biggest hotel in Algiers. He was there only because of Miriam; he hadn't been invited. In addition, he had bad relations with the Algerians and a lot of other Africans by then. He was nervous and intimidated. Nathan Hare, Don Lee, and Ted Joans were there, and they were trying to get us to sit down together and talk, but Stokely would not do it. Finally, that became untenable. So we decided he would come down to our hotel, and he did come down—with a little baby in his arms! He was scared, because he thought we would really vamp on him; he figured that in Algeria we could do whatever we pleased to him and no one would stop us. He felt vulnerable, but we ain't that petty. No one vamped on him physically, but there was some loud talking. He said he hadn't known about the McClellan hearings—but everybody knew about those hearings! He said he had no intention of embarrassing us in front of Congress. So he agreed that I could write out a statement and he'd sign it and read it; that's how shaky his objections were.

HLG: In retrospect, do you think you were being used by the Algerian government to play off the Panthers against the interests of the United States? Or did they look at you as a likely or serious nucleus for a government?

EC: I think they took us seriously when they found out what we were about. You will recall that this was 1969 and 1970. Although the Panthers were eventually eliminated as a serious force within the United States, there was a time when we were *not* irrelevant. The Algerians gave sanctuary and hospitality to liberation movements. Algeria was the hub of all of these movements, including the various African liberation movements. Each movement had facilities, each movement had money, and each was full of political refugees, so it wasn't a dishonest use of valid political movements as propaganda against the

United States. Algeria waged what was probably the most admirable war of liberation in Africa, and this has something to do with their traditions.

HLG: But hasn't there been a post-revolutionary shift away from radicalism, away from Frantz Fanon?

EC: I did get the impression that they have put Fanon to the side; in fact, the whole first generation of revolutionaries has been put aside. But the liberation movements weren't. I have talked with a lot of people who were there during the transition, and they said that they were afraid that this would end up like Chile, where liberation movements were rounded up and shipped back to their countries.

But in Algeria, it was the country's policy to house all of these opposition movements; it was a policy they maintained and defended. People give various interpretations. The militant students who were opponents of the regime said that one of the primary motivations was domestic: by having a very progressive foreign policy, the Algerian government was able to show the students that if they make problems inside the country, then they will sabotage the struggle of the noble Vietnamese people.

The policy that the Black Panther Party adhered to vigorously was to guard against any intrusion into our internal affairs, and stay out of the internal affairs of friendly countries, particularly our host countries—unless, as in Cuba, that became impossible. None of us went to finishing school, but we were very effective and impressive, in the way we moved, in the way we dealt with sovereign governments, with foreign leaders—the way we exchanged points of view. I think the Black Panther Party was ahead of its time in terms of being useful in the United States. If properly used, it could have been very powerful, in terms of being able to take its case into various international arenas. But in any case, we dealt with heads of state and liberation movement leaders, all across the political spectrum, ending with Yasir Arafat, who asked specifically to visit us in Algeria.

HLG: Was this internationalization Malcolm X's concept?

EC: Precisely. We were all looking to internationalize our struggle. I think this strategy had a lot to do with the Yankees' decision to hasten integration; they knew the damage that would arise if they continued that foolish, repressive attitude. We wanted to get the United Nations to hold a plebiscite in New York—inside the United States—to allow black people to go on record for the first time in history, as to whether they wanted to be part of the United States or whether they wanted their sovereignty and liberty. We wanted U.N. observers stationed in various crucial places, to help check the brutality against black people. The U.N. has the machinery for that, and all we had to do was stand in the General Assembly and make a motion. We were in a position to do it, and the American government knew it.

We were preparing to start the process at an OAU meeting in Dar es Salaam. We didn't think it was going to pass, but we wanted the opportunity to put it out there. It would have placed the U.S. in a ridiculous position. We weren't about to declare ourselves independent; we were just trying to put pressure on Uncle Sam.

HLG: Why did you decide to leave Algeria?

EC: Well, it had to do with the developments in Asia. After Nixon showed up in China in 1972, it became very clear to us that there was a new day dawning in international politics. A lot of people who had been wanting to talk to the United States, but hadn't done so for fear of criticism, considered this the green light. The U.S. had been looking to reestablish diplomatic relations with the Arab countries, but they held back because of the Palestinian situation and Vietnam.

Algeria already had a lot of economic ties with the U.S., and people were saying that the Black Panther Party was going to be cooked in six months, that we were just living on borrowed time. There was a constant atmosphere of menace. We knew that we could be offed at any minute, with any turn of events, because we had seen this happen so many times with other people: after the change of regimes in a country, the whole situation would be turned around. So with something as momentous as a complete realignment of political forces on the international level, we saw that the days of the Wild West Liberation Movement were over, or at least numbered. We knew Algiers wouldn't last forever.

From time to time, we would be invited to official receptions. It was largely a question of fashion, and if one country's representatives saw us at some other reception, we would be put on the list next time they had one. But we never received any invitations from the Soviet Union—they made a point of not including us. So then one day the Russians send us a big invitation: "Come to this *big* reception in this *big* hotel."

We thought, "What is this, some kind of double-cross?" The invitation was sent personally by the ambassador, and he asked us to please be there at a certain time. We thought that maybe there had been a coup in the Soviet Union or something, and they were improving their politics. In the wake of Nixon's trip to China, we thought that maybe they were going to start backing other revolutionary movements.

So we show up, and we see the Chinese. The Chinese didn't participate in Russian receptions. Everyone was there! Then, in walks this white American—the head of the American Interest Section at the Swiss embassy. We understood, then, why they had invited us: this was the first time that this man had been invited to any reception. He was being reintroduced on the diplomatic circuit. The whole thing was so callous, so cold-blooded and calculated. They used the Black Panthers to soften the shock of the American's return, and after that, each time there was a reception, he would be there. We could come if we wanted to, but soon people started forgetting to put us on the list.

At that time, we started making plans to leave. Some of us had already departed when, to our surprise, people started hijacking planes to Algeria—one plane, three men, two women, and two children; on another plane, a man and a woman. None of them had passports, and all of them were broke. This created a situation that had to be dealt with. By the time all this had happened, the Black Panther Party had split. The Panthers in New York became fragmented; then we became factionalized in Algeria. The result was that I resigned as the head of the thing, and Pete O'Neal took my place. I was supposed to have no more organizational responsibility, but then Pete O'Neal and all those other cats split. They were saying that it wasn't their responsibility to deal with these hijackers. And maybe it wasn't, I don't know. But I felt I would be able to get out of Algeria safely even if I waited long enough to look after these people.

HLG: Was it sad to resign, or did you feel a sense of relief?

EC: Well, at the time I resigned, I had been thinking about expelling all those cats. The International Section had become a sinking ship, and the so-called "Progressive Black People" had reverted to a real scurvy level of every-man-for-himself. Everyone was just trying to get money, and any way they got it was all right.

Kathleen was not a fugitive, but I was. We were the only two left; everybody else had gone. And there were all these hijackers with no passports. We didn't have enough money; we figured it would cost at least two or three grand per person to get a passport, and we didn't have enough bread for all those people. We had enough to get a passport for one person, who then went back to the U.S. and got some more bread. I used advances from my second book, too, and it all worked out; we were able to get passports for everybody, and everybody got out. When I look back at what happened, I see the writing on the wall. Now the United States has reestablished diplomatic relations with all the Arab countries, including Algeria. There is no place for an Afro-American liberation movement.

HLG: You seem to have found a comfortable and remarkable amount of freedom of movement in France, more than you found in Cuba, and perhaps even more than in Algeria. Does that strike you as strange?

EC: There was a time when it would have, but it seems perfectly logical now.

That's why I came here: I began to understand the whole thing about a Third World Revolution—it's a skin game, man! From the point of view of Afro-America, it's a skin concept; it has nothing to do with economic or social factors. When our program began to go wrong, I started talking to people to see where we went wrong. I was at a meeting one time, with serious people—I won't mention who they were, but they were from liberation movements. They were suggesting tactics that we could use, and one guy stood up and said that he thought we should develop an atmosphere where any American could just be killed on sight—*any* American! I said, "Wait a minute, a lot of Americans are okay." He said, "Oh no, man, Americans are American." He said that black Americans were okay; I told him that a lot of black Americans *weren't* okay. And he said that I was trying to confuse the situation! I said, no, I'm trying to make some distinctions. It was impossible to communicate like that. The other people I talked to weren't particularly opposed to that suggestion—just off the Americans! But it wasn't something I could endorse.

HLG: Do you think a revolution in the United States is necessary—or possible?

EC: It depends on what you mean by "revolution." When I speak of revolution, I mean reorganizing the society—nationalizing the system of distribution. The system of distribution we have now has its roots in some sort of frontier society and some sort of *laissez-faire* economics, neither of which is relevant to the highly complex society in which we live now. This is acknowledged in the United States, but only to the extent that people accept welfare or Social Security. American people look upon Social Security as a good thing, a vital thing. If you tried to take it away, you would probably *get* a revolution. Yet it was resisted as being contrary to the nature of a capitalist system—which it is. In the end, it was a compromise that the ruling forces were willing to accept. They realized that they had to do something to get a larger part of the national product into the hands of more people, in order for the people to allow this system to keep functioning. The people who are able to make big profits from the present system always resist changes that would be beneficial for more people. It forces people to take strong action, in order to get these changes brought about.

HLG: One of the things that Americans have feared about Marxism is the hampering of individual freedom. Do you envision the sorts of changes you advocate for American society as necessitating limitations on individual freedom?

EC: I have only come to understand this issue after seeing how vulnerable the individual is in this world, and how subjected he is to the arbitrary use of power. I have developed a very healthy respect for the concept of individual freedom, and for the American tradition of respect for that freedom, although it is sometimes not applied to black people. Still, we have to make some distinctions. Everybody can agree that the individual's rights should be secure. The individual should be respected. But then, some people extrapolate from that that the individual should have the right to own all the steel mills in the world—and if you try to interfere with that, you are interfering with individual freedom. That's bullshit. It's one thing to speak of the right of an individual, but it's another thing to speak of the rights of all those individuals taken as a whole. And that's when the word-men who serve the capitalist system—William F. Buckley, and all those jackanapeses—come in to weave skillful arguments to deceive people. This whole line of thought needs to be unraveled, and the proper distinctions need to be made, because I don't envision any kind of change in the United States that would hamper the just rights of individuals. But these *other* rights that people claim . . . yes, I see how they could be eliminated. That's what it's all about!

A short reflection on a somber topic lightened by Eldridge Cleaver's irrepressible sense of humor.

EXILE AND DEATH

After his outraged fellow Athenians convicted him of corrupting the morals of the youth, Socrates was offered two forms of punishment: a choice between exile and death. That he opted for the hemlock over the lonely road has been an incitement to martyrs and a reproach to fugitives down through the ages. In high school, I remember marveling at Socrates' choice. It took my breath away just like Patrick Henry's words, "Give me liberty, or give me death!" I recall thinking, some years later, that maybe Socrates was playing to the galleries of future generations, or, perhaps his choice was that of a senile mind seeking an honorable cover for the cravings of his decrepit flesh.

One sweltering afternoon in Havana, I was standing in line with a pregnant French girl we called "the Stranger," to buy an ice cream cone. She had flown over from Paris expressly to have her child born in Communist Cuba. This was the Stranger's second visit to Cuba. Her first had been six or seven years earlier, shortly after the Revolution.

A tall, blonde beauty with a Prince Valiant hair cut, and bright blue eyes, the Stranger was more charismatic to Cuban men than Fidel Castro. Fluent in English, Spanish, and French, she had many of them wrapped around her fingers. As a writer, she had interviewed many of the top dogs and was full of inside facts, figures, and lies, about "La primera territoria libre en Las Americas." But now the Stranger was so bloated by the baby growing in her belly that she felt sorry for the whole world. I felt sorry for her, or rather fear, because she had grown so large so quickly, and was obviously still growing, that I thought perhaps her body had gone mad, and would continue to inflate until it exploded, splattering the Stranger all over this Communist Island Paradise.

A rotund, swaggering man walked by. The Stranger gasped, shrinking behind my shoulder, to make sure he didn't see her.

"Eldridge," she said, "I'm so afraid you might end up like Eduardo." She indicated the chubby man who'd just passed us.

The Stranger went on to explain that she'd met Eduardo on her first trip to Cuba. Then, he'd been a dashing revolutionary freshly exiled from Columbia, thin as a blade, full of ferocity and fire. In fact, the Stranger averred, Eduardo had been her lover, for a season. Now he was a fat poet, writing tired, plump rhymes and jingles about the glory of his suffering land, the heroic proportions of his own contribution to the struggle of his people, and the dangers of Cuban rum.

"Oh, Eldridge," the Stranger said, seized by an attack of pity, which I associated more with what was going on in her belly than with was going on in either her head or her heart, "Don't become like Eduardo!"

I wanted desperately to not end up like Eduardo, if only I knew how.

After spending seven years in exile myself, I developed a respectful understanding for Socrates' choice. Exile can be worse than death. It can be a form of living death. One can become socially, culturally, and politically dead, while remaining biologically alive. The classic analogy is that of the fish out of water, flopping hopelessly around on some foreign, alien, shore.

Exile actually threw me back into my "normal," "familiar" relationship to America: I was out of it again. I was reduced to experiencing America from a distance, through the media. But this time, instead of confinement within the rigid limitations of San Quentin or Folsom prisons, I found myself locked outside America, at large—living inside strange and alien Communist, Third World, and European countries.

The State, clearly, wanted me dead, wanted to take me in its hand and give me the iron lock of years extracted from the soul. But I have never believed that I need die, either to prove my enemies wrong or myself right. I've preferred to kill my enemies. Nor have I ever felt that I'd rather be dead in America than alive in Paris. In choosing exile, my intention was to escape being returned to San Quentin Prison, and the death I believed awaited me behind those walls.

THE AUTOBIOGRAPHY
OF ELDRIDGE CLEAVER

CHAPTER SEVEN

Soon after moving to Paris, I remember going down to a French television station at the time the Americans were pulling out of Vietnam. I remember sitting there in a chair watching the unedited video signals coming in from Vietnam, showing the Marines and G.I.s leaving. There was one especially patriotic image of the U.S. ambassador to Cambodia leaving with the American flag tucked under his arm. There was a lump in my throat.

I was sitting between the editor of Germany's *Der Spiegel* magazine and a man from a very prestigious French newspaper called *Le Monde Diplomatique*. As the scenes of the helicopters leaving and soldiers waving were flashed before us, the men beside me were just laughing. The more they laughed, the more I resented it. They started talking about the U.S. Marines as nothing more than Boy Scouts who couldn't win a fight against an old ladies club.

I had had enough, and without any forethought said to the Frenchman, "You know what man, there was a day when you were mighty glad to see the U.S. military liberate you from him." I nodded toward the German sitting on the other side of me. I could hardly believe the change that was taking place inside me. More and more comments like that just seemed to pop out of my mouth.

The German and French journalists were shocked and angry with me. I just got up and went home.

I began to feel a real sadness at being a fugitive. I wanted to go home, and couldn't.

We had to be careful where we went and who we talked to. We had to be very secretive about where we kept our children, often keeping them in hiding at places separate from where we were staying.

One of the problems with children is that it's hard to teach them to lie. You can't trust them to help you keep your cover.

Like when I would try to tell my children that for a while my name was Henry Jones, not Eldridge Cleaver, they'd say,

"No it's not. You're Eldridge Cleaver."

We kept the children in hiding for an entire year.

At the time my lawyer was Roland Dumas, who today is the foreign minister of France. I liked the man, but to see him appointed foreign minister of a major Western power is an indication to me of how much the world has changed. His colleague, Georges Pompidou, who is now president of France, sponsored my petition for political asylum.

When Richard Nixon and Spiro Agnew resigned, it appeared changes were taking place in the United States, and I began to think it was possible for me to return home.

I began contacting my old friends in the United States, asking them to help me come home. One of them, Mervyn Dymally, had become the lieutenant governor in California. An old friend, Ron Dellums whom the Black Panthers used to protect, was now a congressman.

Both of them were good friends with Jerry Brown, the new governor of California. I thought they could help arrange for me to come home.

They kept putting me off, like telling me to wait until after the next election was over. Then one of my friends came over and told me that whenever I would send a message expressing my desire to come home, everyone would just laugh. After what I had done, they just thought there was no way I could ever come home without spending the rest of my life in prison. My friend's advice was that I learn French real good because I was probably going to spend the rest of my life in France.

That was the last thing that friend should have said to me. I was under a lot of strain, feeling like I was being pushed down a path to some kind of extinction.

When Socrates was faced with a choice between suicide or exile, he chose suicide. I was beginning to understand why he did it. To the new Eldridge Cleaver, exile was a form of death.

At that time Paris was full of American exiles. Some of the black ones we would call French-fried negroes. There were all kinds, just getting away from America, for all kinds of reasons. When you would talk to these people you could see they were frozen in some kind of time frame, reflecting the period when they had left the United States.

If you ran into a black who said, "Hey Daddy-O," you knew he had left in the fifties. Then there's the cool school, "What's happening, man?

What it is? Cool, man." You knew this fellow had left in the early sixties. Then you had the angry guys, my generation, the ones who left in the late sixties.

I could see myself becoming like them, my language, even thinking, everything frozen in time. I was a fish out of water. I was concerned and homesick, especially the day my children came home from school and told us not to speak to them in English anymore because it hurt their ears.

They were in the French school system, doing all their reading and writing in French, and it was confusing to them when they came home to English.

When they said English hurt their ears, I was hurt. I could see my children becoming French, and I wanted them to be Americans, not just on paper, but to really know what it meant to be an American. I was sad.

I became more and more downcast, particularly the day my son came home playing soccer. He called it football. I had been a football player, my favorite sport. I idolized American football players. I wanted my son to be a real football player, not a soccer player.

I felt we had to get out of there, and I just didn't know what to do, since my friends said they couldn't help me come back. I don't think they wanted me to come back.

I began to feel that my life wasn't worthwhile anymore, that it had become meaningless. I began to think that maybe I should just eliminate myself. If I took my life, my wife and children would be free to return to the United States.

I became possessed with the idea of committing suicide, and decided to do it. I knew that I could do it, once I made up my mind. It seemed to be the best way out of the whole mess.

My family lived in Paris, but I also had an apartment down on the Mediterranean near Cannes where they hold the film festival.

All my papers and file cabinets were there. I went there whenever I wanted to write, and as I became more and more depressed with my situation, I spent more and more time in the south of France at this apartment. It was there that I made the decision to kill myself.

I went back to Paris to see my family for one last time, to say goodbye to them. I didn't tell them what I was planning to do, but in my heart I just had to see them one last time.

We had a little dinner that night, and I remember there were candles on the table, and we had turned out all the lights. To me the evening seemed symbolic of our life in France, lots of darkness, very little light, a miserable existence in which we were just marking time and not going anywhere.

I looked at my wife and children, and said goodbye to them for what I thought was the last time.

The next morning I flew back down to the south of France. I was determined to do it that night. Upon arriving at my apartment I just sat around, waiting for a certain feeling to come over me.

Whenever I had done anything drastic in my life, and this was certainly going to be the most drastic thing I had ever done, I couldn't do it until a certain spirit came over me. And when that spirit would fill me, no matter what it was I was about to do, I was gung ho to do it, no matter the consequences.

I was trying to work myself up to having that spirit in me. Soon the whole day had passed and it was getting dark.

I was sitting on the balcony, the thirteenth floor of the building. I had a pistol in my hand. I just felt the spirit would come over me at any time and I would raise the gun to my head and pull the trigger. It would all be over.

As I sat there, just staring out into the night, I began to notice the moon, almost a full moon. It looked so big. I was really fascinated with the moon that night. The brilliance captivated me. It was like I could almost see it moving above the horizon.

I began to see the shadows on the moon's surface. Pretty soon something very strange started to happen. I was feeling kind of excited anyway, but as I continued to stare at the moon, it began to flicker and change.

I began to see images of people. First I saw myself in the moon. In the flickering, my face was hard to recognize. Then I saw my former heroes in Communism, the people who at one time had become gods in my eyes. Fidel Castro, Mao Tse-tung, Karl Marx. Their faces would flicker and go away.

Suddenly I saw the image of Jesus Christ. When I saw that, I just fell apart. I was shaking like a leaf in the wind. I was shaking everywhere, inside and out.

I started to get a feeling of panic about the pistol. Something told me to get that pistol out of my hand. I put it down on the table.

Then I fell to my knees and started crying. Inside, I just exploded: shaking, crying, hanging onto the balcony railing.

I felt like I was going to disintegrate and physically fall apart right there on that balcony.

When suddenly into my mind came the Lord's Prayer, and the 23rd Psalm. You talk about going backward in time. I hadn't thought about the Lord's Prayer since I was a child, or the 23rd Psalm since my mother had read it to me while sitting on her knee. I found I could remember them, and I began to repeat the words to myself. As I did so, the trembling and crying gradually went away. I repeated the words over and over.

Pretty soon the shaking stopped completely. I jumped up and ran into the room to the bookshelf where there was a Bible. It was a family Bible my mother had given me.

When I left San Francisco, I hadn't even thought about bringing it along, but my wife later told me that when she was leaving, just abandoning our house, taking just what she could carry, that just as she was going out the door, that Bible seemed to say, "Hey, take me." She picked it up and put it in her bag. Afterward, we had always kept it among our books.

I opened it and started looking for the Lord's Prayer. I didn't know where to find it. I couldn't find the 23rd Psalm either. I was thumbing through the pages, over and over again.

Suddenly I was overwhelmed with a spirit of peace and total exhaustion at the same time. I set the Bible down, right next to the pistol. I collapsed on the bed and fell into a deep sleep.

The next thing I remember I woke up with a start as if someone had shaken the bed. It was morning. I jumped straight up, the things that had happened the night before flashing before my eyes. My whole spirit was quickened.

I saw myself looking down a path of light that led to a prison cell and came out the other side. It was suddenly very clear to me what I must do. I had received a spiritual message that I must surrender to the authorities, go into that prison cell, and I would come out the other side. There was no fear. I just knew I would come out the other side.

I felt like a new person. My attitude was changed. I felt energy, a liveliness I hadn't experienced in a long time.

I thought over the things that had happened the night before and wondered if perhaps I was going crazy, but a peaceful feeling in my heart told me everything was fine. I had no telephone in the apartment with which to contact anyone, so I folded up my stuff and ran downstairs, and caught a plane back to Paris.

I had to talk to Kathleen. Nothing like this had ever happened to me before, and I had to tell someone about it. It was very clear in my mind what I had to do.

That evening I waited until after dinner and things had quieted down. I was watching her closely, wondering how she would react to what I was about to say. I began to fear that she would say I was crazy, and that would devastate me.

"Kathleen," I said, looking at her very closely, "Something very strange happened to me last night."

I told her what had happened on the balcony, that I was going to surrender to the authorities and we were going home.

Her eyes lit up and she actually jumped, like she had been shocked.

"Are you sure?" she said.

"Oh yes," I said.

We started making plans right then. We were going home.

On November 18, 1975 this article was published on the op-ed page of the The New York Times.

WHY I LEFT AMERICA, AND WHY I AM RETURNING

The writer—poet, essayist, the Black Panthers' information director—has been in Cuba, Algeria and France since he fled the U.S. He was paroled in 1968 after serving nine years of a 14 year sentence for a 1958 California conviction for assault with intent to kill.

I am often asked why I want to return to the U.S. This question never fails to bowl me over, and I find it impossible to answer. I feel it is an improper question. Most people who ask are not really interested in that question. What they want to know is what will I do if they allow me to return.

I always explain why I left in the first place. Lots of people believe I left because I preferred to go live in a Communist country and that now, several years and many Communist countries later, I find the grass not greener on the Communist side of the fence. So now, here I stand, locked outside the gates of the paradise I once scorned, begging to be let back in.

History shows that when the American political system is blocked and significant segments of the population are unable to have their will brought to bear on the decision-making process, you can count upon the people to revolt, to take it out into the streets, in the spirit of the Boston Tea Party.

During the 1960's, the chips were down in a fateful way, uniting the up-surge of black Americans against the oppressive features of the system and the gargantuan popular opposition to the Indochina wars. It was left to the Nixon Administration to bring the issues to a head. The system rejected President Nixon and reaffirmed its own basic principles.

With all of its faults, the American political system is the freest and most democratic in the world. The system needs to be improved, with democracy spread to all areas of life, particularly the economic. All of these changes must be conducted through our established institutions, and people with grievances must find political methods for obtaining redress.

Each generation subjects the world it inherits to severe criticism. I think that my generation has been more critical than most, and for good reason. At the same time, at the end of the critical process we should arrive at some conclusions. We should have discovered which values are worth conserving. It is the beginning of another fight, the fight to defend those values from the blind excesses of our fellows who are still caught up in the critical process. It is my hope to make a positive contribution in this regard.

PART FOUR TRANSITION

From left: Maceo Cleaver, Thelma Robinson Cleaver, Joju Cleaver, Eldridge Cleaver, and Kathleen Cleaver in Altadena, California, August 1976. Photograph © Nik Wheeler.

THE AUTOBIOGRAPHY OF ELDRIDGE CLEAVER

CHAPTER NINE

Missionaries from various denominations would come to the Alameda County Jail and hold Bible classes. Most of the prisoners would taunt them, laugh and call them names. When the missionaries would close their eyes and hold hands with the prisoners who had joined them to pray, the other prisoners would throw salt shakers, bars of soap, and wet toilet paper at them.

I had been studying the Bible, and felt I wanted to join the missionaries in their study classes, but I didn't want to get hit with any of the stuff that was being thrown. Finally, I decided to join them anyway. I didn't think anyone would throw stuff at me, afraid I would punch them out. I just had to join the study group.

I sat down with them, and when they got ready to pray, I joined them. The other prisoners seemed shocked to see me involved in anything religious.

"Eldridge is getting soft," they began to chant.

Nobody had ever done anything like that to me before. I felt bad. They were just young guys, and I remembered myself at that age, and I could see they were going the same way I had gone. Thinking where they were headed made me cry. And the last thing in the world I wanted was for them to see Eldridge cry. In jail they just take that for weakness, opening you up to all kinds of abuse. They couldn't understand that I was crying because I had already been where they were going.

Someone told a reporter that Eldridge Cleaver had turned to Jesus Christ. When my lawyer came to see me one day, he was furious. The *Los Angeles Times* had published an article mentioning that Charles Colson, Charles Manson, and Eldridge Cleaver had turned to Jesus Christ. The article mocked me, the latest born again Christian to come down the pike.

"This is the last nail in your coffin," said the attorney. "No one will try to help you with this stuff going on."

I began to realize that all my old friends, the Communists, the Black Panther Party members, didn't want me to get out of prison. They laughed at me. They wouldn't visit me. My wife would ask them to help me, and they'd tell her to go away. I realized I didn't have any friends any more. Except for my family, I was isolated. In that jail, the days and nights got very long.

One day a strange lady came to visit me. She had read the article about me turning to the Lord. She said, "Eldridge, get ready to come out. I'm going to pray and ask God to tear this wall down, and you are going to walk out. Do you believe it?"

"Go ahead and pray," I said, not knowing what else to say. I didn't know if the wall was going to fall down, or not. I hoped it would.

She was talking to me through a telephone, while she looked at me through a little window. She started praying a fervent prayer. I backed up a little just in case something happened—I didn't want any bricks falling on my feet.

Finally she stopped and looked at me through the little window, saying, "Eldridge, your faith isn't strong enough." She hung up the phone and walked away. She didn't even look back.

My father had died while I was in France. When I read about it in a newspaper, I called my mother. I wanted to help her with the funeral arrangements, to get a burial plot somewhere so we could all be buried together. If we couldn't be together in life, at least we could in death. By that time, however, my sister had already had my father cremated.

At the time of his death, my parents had been divorced for 25 years. I always thought they hated each other. Then my mother told me over the long distance line that she had the urn with his ashes and was going to have them buried with hers. She said there was only one thing left in life she wanted, and that was to see me.

"But that can't be," I said. "If I come home I'll end up with a 75-year prison sentence." I told her I would never see her again.

She said I was wrong, that she had prayed and received an answer that I would one day walk through her door.

A wealthy man in Philadelphia, named Arthur De Moss read that *Los Angeles Times* article too, and sent his lawyer to California to bail me out. On Friday the thirteenth of August, just before they were going to close the jail for the weekend, a guard came to my cell and said, "Cleaver, let's go." I was free.

As soon as I got out of prison I went directly to Los Angeles and walked through my mother's door just as she knew I would. There is no doubt in my mind but that my mother's prayers cleared the way for me to come home. I certainly wasn't praying for myself all those years I was gone. It was a joyous reunion.

Arthur De Moss, after putting up the bail, arranged for me to visit Billy Graham. I told him my experiences, and we prayed together.

Then, with my family, I visited Arthur De Moss at his home outside of Philadelphia. We stayed there about a week, just thawing out. I was still in a state of shock, realizing that a complete stranger had put up $1,000,000 to get me out of jail. I thanked him, telling him I thought it was awful big of him taking a chance on someone with my record, having jumped bail before.

"The day you got out, Friday the thirteenth, is my lucky day," he said, "because that is the day I found the Lord. Secondly, I am not betting my money on another human being. I am betting on the Lord. I know the Lord can change anybody because he changed me."

He told me about his life, how he had been a gangster of sorts, a bookie in New York. When he found the Lord he switched from being a bookie to insurance. I told him many people didn't think there was that much difference between the two professions, and we had a good laugh. He said the insurance man bets his money on the dark horse of death, and the man who buys the premium bets that life will outrun death. He felt he had become an honorable and ethical businessman.

Some of my former friends asked me how I could let a rightwing fascist put up my bail. I said the man had never talked politics with me, just religion. He thought politics were of the devil. This kind man died in 1979, and I often thank God for what he did for me.

Once free, I found myself in a situation where no one trusted me. Everyone was suspicious, wondering what I was really up to. No one believed that I was sincere in my conversion to Christianity. People thought I was playing some kind of game, or was doing something undercover for the Communists. Some thought I was playing Christian just to get out from under my legal problems, then that I got so good at it I just couldn't stop.

In spite of all those who doubted my sincerity, I began receiving invitations to speak and bear testimony at churches all over America. I spoke in hundreds of churches, and people were always telling me I needed to find a church to call my own. But I really didn't feel like joining anything. I had joined the Black Panther Party and didn't want to ever join anything again.

This poem captures one of the most painful, disillusioning experiences of my entire life. Upon my surrender and return to the United States, the Black Panther Party unleashed a fury of negative propaganda against me, branding me a turncoat, a snitch, and every other disreputable thing they could think of. The unkindest cut of all came when I placed a collect call to my old office, the Ministry of Information. I placed the call as a public relations gesture urged upon me by my then-wife, Kathleen. The man who answered the phone told the operator that a meeting was in progress and he would check to see if they would accept a collect call from Eldridge Cleaver. At first he had expressed astonishment bordering on disbelief that Eldridge Cleaver was actually on the phone. After a couple of minutes he returned and announced: "Operator, we refuse to accept this call."

It hurt me to my heart. I was calling collect from a federal prison and my call was refused. After that, all the other mud slung my way by my former comrades-in-arms was anticlimactic. Later, when minor poet Marvin Jackmon and a couple of other nonentities hijacked the Black Men's Conference, for which I had been the main organizing force, my heart was already hardened against necrophiliac opportunists and hangers-on who were trying to squeeze the last drops of blood from the turnip of the corpse of the Black Panther Party. My epithet for the event was my poem "The One Excluded from the Conference."

THE ONE EXCLUDED
FROM THE CONFERENCE

I am the one excluded from the Conference
For improvising words
To the Party's tune.

But I can't sing their song of songs

And I can't carry their tune of tunes.

So what if I hate the State,
As my fathers did before?
Am I less than all the rest?
Must I leave all this undone
Which they passed on to me
Bequeathed to them by fathers
Who received it from their own?

Must I break this chain of blood
By a generation asleep
Bringing forth no gain
In our fight to free the land?

I will hurl a mighty stone
Up this steepest hill to climb
Against this poison State that kills.

I will bury all the dead
Dig their graves with my own hands
Giving orphans loving homes
And gently cradle hoary heads
Gently calming ancient fears
And heal or comfort broken hearts.

I will relight all the dreams
Of a better day to come.
I will call upon the youth
To cast away these golden chains
And defy the Party Line
With a program for the poor
That empties all the jails
And jails the crooks who are the heads
And bans oppression from the earth
By putting bankers in a cage
And paying work an honest wage.

By the time Eldridge sent this letter to Bobby Seale, former chairman of the Black Panther Party, neither of them were connected to the party, which had had finally collapsed.

Seale had moved away from his home in Oakland to Denver, where he had a radio program and was writing a book. This letter, written with an ink pen in Eldridge Cleaver's distinctive large handwriting, was found in Eldridge's papers at the Bancroft Library at University of California Berkeley. No answer was included. However, Seale and Cleaver did eventually reconcile, participating in a lecture tour together. In the week before Eldridge passed away, he and Bobby had talked by telephone about the intricacies of using e-mail.

LETTER TO BOBBY SEALE

July 14, 1982
Bobby Seale
Atlantic Avenue
Aurora, Colorado

Dear Bobby:

I have tried many times over the last few years to make contact with you. My impression is that you've more or less spurned these approaches. Yesterday, I read an article about you in the *Oakland Tribune*, which yielded the address which I am sending this letter to. I hope you receive it.

Knowing how treacherous the media is, I am reluctant to blame you for the little shit-shots which are aimed at me and which afterward appear in articles I've seen about you. In so far as you have any control over it, I'd appreciate it if you'd stop putting me down. Of all people, you're one of the best placed to know what I have and have not done. I have changed—so have you and everyone else. I have not sold anyone out, informed on anyone, or anything like that. I am not an FBI agent, CIA agent, or connected to the local police—as some Black Panthers alleged in the past, thus effectively putting the bad mouth on me.

I realize that my surrender and return to the U.S.A. came as a shock to many people, but there were no dirty deals involved, and I conducted myself in an honorable manner.

When I began to move in a different ideological direction, it was because I recognized that what we were into in the BPP and "movement" was exhausted, had run its course; and I was looking ahead—way down the line, and I was positioning myself for the future—which is now.

When I returned to the U.S.A. in 1975, I was not interrupting any great revolutionary war—but you would have thought so from some of the squeals and howls that went up. As a matter of fact, I returned with the attitude of picking up the pieces of our movement, after it'd been smashed by the F.B.I., Nixon/Reagan, COINTELPRO, etc.

I watched you run for mayor—and almost win. That was the last thing that happened that I could relate to. I heard that "those rats" ran you out of town to make way for Lionel Wilson. I watched greasy snakes like Ron Dellums and his cowardly friends systematically take over, while those who had sacrificed were swept aside. In short, I watched them establish a black neo-colonialist regime.

By being in exile (and I'm sure you know that Huey *ordered* me to split to Cuba: David Hilliard, Melvin Newton, and Charles Garry brought me that order. Big Man, Pat Hilliard, and a few others know what my plan was) I was spared; I was preserved from the destruction that was meted out. I felt it was my duty to return, to pick up the pieces, and to chart a new direction. If Elaine Brown and her crew of freaks hadn't called press conferences and hung a FBI-CIA label on me, I believe it would not have taken so long (seven years) to get something going. It is not in me to give up the struggle. I'm writing this letter to you because I believe that neither is it in you to give up. I am appealing to your sense of fair play and justice and integrity.

We still have brothers and sisters in prison and on the run, squashed and scattered all over the Place. Geronimo, Dharuba, Bro. Rice and many more have been in prison for ten years or more. How can we just forget about them? We can't! We've got to get them out.

Bobby, it is time for us to regroup, to forge another unity, on a higher level. We can do it, if you and I unite, and create a nucleus that others will rally around. The need for such action is more pressing now than at any time in our history. The capitalistic system is in a state of general crisis and black people are being sacrificed on the altar of national recovery. The police departments are preying upon the people and are poised to crush them. The very food supply of the people is in jeopardy. There is no organized force to represent the people. We can—and must create such a force.

I am going to run for mayor of Oakland in the next election—1985, just 33 months from now. Just enough time to organize for victory. I am asking you to join with me and we can win. Then we can bring a whole new political climate to the entire nation. We hold the keys to victory in our hands.

I am sending you, along with this letter, a copy of a document entitled *A Comprehensive Monetary Reform Proposal.* I want to call your attention to the analysis and indictment of the banks. Our people need money, and this analysis shows where the money must come from.

Bobby, I'm appealing to you to at least sit down and talk with me. We have fabulous resources available to us, if only we unite.

I have rented a piece of land at 28th and Magnolia in Oakland—which is where we had that shoot out. The brother and sister who rented the land to me also own the house in which Lil Bobby and I holed up during the shoot out. Lil Bobby was shot dead in the front yard of that house. The house is on the same acre of land that the lot which I have rented is on. The brother and sister who own that property want to make some kind of memorial out of it. I want to erect a monument on the spot where Lil Bobby fell murdered, and turn the house into a memorial museum to the people who died in the Black Panther/Police War. This would be a great success and a powerful symbol to inspire the people. It would be a national memorial museum, filled with relics and memorabilia from all over the country. People will come from far and wide to see it.

I am establishing my campaign headquarters on the land at 28th and Magnolia. There is a lot of power in that relationship!

I hope that you will be agreeable to meeting with me. A lot depends upon your decision. We have brothers and sisters all over the nation, and in the prisons, who will unite with us. We can liberate Oakland and with that base, liberate the entire country.

Please let me hear from you as soon as possible. I am, and shall remain,

Yours for Freedom,
Justice, and Equality.
Life, Liberty, and the
Pursuit of Happiness,
Eldridge Cleaver

cc: Geronimo

While living in Berkeley, California, where he grew deeply concerned with the environmental destruction underway, Cleaver wrote Toxic Waste and Acid Rain, *which he published in a chapbook of his poetry in 1984.*

TOXIC WASTE AND ACID RAIN

I lived near a mountain
On the bank of a winding river.
The north bank of the river
Met the foot of the mountain
Just out back of town.

We were a close-knit Company Town
Built during World War Two,
In very great haste
On a landfill site
Stuffed with toxic waste.

By 1972
Our town resembled a zoo.
We all really got pissed
When a lady had a baby
That wiggled like a snake and hissed.
Another baby looked like a frog.
On the other side of the river,
A lady gave birth to a dog.
One baby had two heads.
Many sported extra thumbs.
Eyes out of line in their faces.
Normal kids were few.
It blew your mind
When one walked up
And paid respects to you.

We had PCBs in the milk,
Dioxin in the bread.
At the rate we were dying

We all knew
In a year or two
The whole town was gonna be dead.

The State filed another report.
The Company told another lie.
Nothing improved at all.
Things were really bad.
Everybody was so sad.
We thought things couldn't get worse
Until the rain began to fall.
The rain was greenish yellow,
Sticky, slimy, and stunk.
The hint of sulphur made you gag and puke,
And Dioxin made you drunk.

Too slippery to walk or drive on;
Impossible to lie in.
And the assorted chemicals
In the high-tech water
Burned and bruised the skin.
The window panes became opaque,
With a crust too hard to break—
    Not for air,
      Cause it was bad out there—
But to let some sunshine in.
First the flowers died,
Then our hair fell out,
And then our teeth decayed.
Our eyes began to fade,
Fingernails started to wither,
And then the trees.

Soon the small birds died,
Then big ones began to fall.
An eagle fell out of the sky one day
And landed on City Hall.

The chickens died a horrible death,
Flopping around on the ground
With their heads still on
Like they do with their heads cut off.
The children got to eat the cow.
My father ate the cat
And then the dog.

First the little fish died.
The big ones it did not spare.
Bodies floated up
From the bottom of the river
Science didn't know were there.

That's when my lungs collapsed,
Then my kidneys went.
I had a quadruple bypass on Medicaid
And then a heart transplant.

My life has been extended
By dining through my veins.
I have a plastic tube
And a pneumatic pump
To keep my juices flowing.
A hot plate warms my blood,
An icebox cools my sweat.
It's all being done at Government Expense
And they haven't raised taxes yet.

There's nothing left to tax
Except my vaudeville act
Which I developed to carry me through
After the lights went out.
I'm known throughout the world,
As the Original Toxic Clown.
I glow in the dark
And my breath is so bad
I can blow a stone wall down.

Maybe they can tax my breath
If I can't find a breath tax shelter.
Maybe there's a breath loophole,
If I put my breath in a bottle.
Maybe I can send a bottle
To the head of the IRS,
As my full share
Of what it costs over there
To protect our environment.
And as my final contribution,
Before at last they lay me down,
I bequeath to you the body
Of the Original Toxic Clown.

Written during the first war against Iraq initiated under the first President Bush, this article was never published, but Eldridge had included it in the manuscript of the compilation of his work prepared prior to his death in 1998. It retains an eerie relevance to the contemporary war under the second President Bush.

THE BUSHWHACKING
OF AMERICA

When President Abdel Gamel Nasser of Egypt seized and nationalized the Suez Canal, British Prime Minister Anthony Eden, boy wonder and protégé of Winston Churchill, invaded Egypt with a powerful expeditionary force to take back the canal. Precisely this same scenario came into play when President Saddam Hussein seized and annexed Kuwait, providing President George Bush with a plausible pretext for dispatching one of the most powerful armadas ever assembled in the history of the world, to take back Kuwait.

Not Nasser but Eden was ultimately destroyed by all the huffing and puffing emanating from No. 10 Downing Street. Nasser went on to become the most powerful, most highly revered leader of the Arab world in modern times. Will Saddam Hussein survive all of the wolf tickets now being sold by 16 Pennsylvania Avenue, and go on to inherit the mantle of Nasser and Saladin the Magnificent? Will George Bush, like Anthony Eden, get swept into the dustbin of history?

After only a few weeks of war, Saddam already has achieved hero status throughout the Arab and Islamic worlds. His resolute, implacable stance in the face of overwhelming odds stokes the deepest fires in the souls of true believers everywhere.

Setting our Jewishness and Zionism aside for a moment, picture this: thousands of Palestinians on rooftops in the occupied territories, cheering deliriously as Saddam's Scuds streak by overhead, destination Tel Aviv.

Now, picking back up our Jewishness and Zionism, let's look beyond the question of who will control the oil of the Persian Gulf after the war is over, even beyond the question of the security of Israel. The burning question is: Can the West, descendents of the Crusaders, accept the idea of a free, wealthy, united, powerful, respected Arab/Islamic nation, stretching from the Urals to the Rock of Gibraltar—from the captive Islamic Republics now imprisoned within the Soviet Union, through the Islamic Republics of the Middle East, to the Islamic Republics of North America?

It is a tragic error—a blunder of historic proportions—for Bush to align himself with the putrid remnants of feudalism, in opposition to the legitimate aspirations of the Arab/Islamic nation. Kuwait, Saudi Arabia, and the petty Emirates of the Persian Gulf are not sovereign nations. They are nothing but artificial rogue devices carved out of the heart of Arab lands by British imperialism to steal Arab oil for the benefit of the West, enriching a handful of Arab traitors while dispossessing, oppressing, and exploiting the Arab masses. The desperate attempt by Saddam Hussein to rectify this situation is amazingly vicious, but also heroic and just. The oil of the Persian Gulf region belongs to the people who live there—for better or for worse—period! U.S.-based multinational corporations—Texaco, Exxon, Standard, Chevron, Arco, Shell, ad infinitum—can no longer control Middle Eastern oil by propping up a handful of antiquated royal puppets. The very existence and rule of these running dogs of imperialism is the number-one obstacle to Arab unification, resurgence, and renewal. U.S. Middle Eastern policy is number two.

There is a new world order being born, but it will emerge over the dead body of the Bush administration. And there is no place in it for kings and sheiks and other political freaks, like the military dictatorships and one-party dictatorships that now dominate the rest of the Middle East and many other places.

Israel should welcome a united Arab/Islamic nation, for such a nation will be most unlikely to nitpick over the details of its borders with Israel. Let's face it: Israel needs the West Bank and a portion of the Golan Heights for its integrity and security, not to mention geographical symmetry. A united Arab/Islamic nation could afford to let them have it. After all, the Arabs are among the biggest land-grabbers in the history of the world. If all the land that they have taken from other people was taken from them, they would all be cooped up on the Arabian Peninsula. I'm sure that if the world would begin to acknowledge the claims and aspirations of the Arab/Islamic nation, this nation, in turn, would be willing to recognize and accommodate the problems of the rest of the world.

The merciless, cowardly bombing of Iraq, criminally massacring thousands of innocent men, women, and children, already has eclipsed whatever crimes Saddam Hussein may have committed—including killing Kurds with poison gas.

But the biggest crimes that a government commits are always those against its own people. What the Bush administration is doing to Iraq is nothing compared to what it is doing to us here at home. After only one year in office, Bush already has put us in a deeper hole than the one Ronald Reagan managed to put us in during eight years of vile endurance.

It is unforgivable of Bush to dispatch our beautiful sons and daughters to a horrible slaughter, to die unnecessarily in the barren desert sands of foreign lands, served up as sacrificial lambs on the altar of oil.

The muzzling of the media to conceal the revolting horror of this war is but a dress rehearsal for the muzzling of the media to conceal the coming repression of the American people to cope with the social, political, and economic chaos that will inevitably flow from the atrocious machinations of the Bush administration.

There should be a Nuremberg-type tribunal set up to try journalists and news organizations for misinforming, misleading, and brainwashing the American people into blind support for the Bush administration's catastrophic Desert Shield and Desert Storm policies of ruthless, genocidal slaughter of the Iraqi people.

This letter to Timothy Leary, who was celebrated during the 1960s for his admonition to "tune in, turn on, and drop out," was written years after most of Eldridge's former radical friends and coworkers had repudiated him for his Christian conversion and conservative politics. Briefly after his prison escape engineered by the Weather Underground, in 1970, Timothy Leary joined Cleaver in his sanctuary in Algeria. Subsequently in 1975, after Cleaver had surrendered and Leary had been apprehended, they met again inside a federal prison located in San Diego. From the tone of the letter published here, it seems that they remained on friendly terms.

LETTER TO TIMOTHY LEARY

Eldridge Cleaver
P.O. Box 5075
Berkeley, CA, 94705

January 6, 1995
Timothy Leary
10106 Sunbrook
Beverly Hills, CA, 90210

Dear Timothy:

I was deeply moved and encouraged by your phone message in response to the card Linda and I sent you. I have been thinking about this move for a long time. I am very excited—what I am proposing will be the consolidating undertaking of our struggle. I want you to join me in GODFATHERING AN IDEA WHOSE TIME HAS COME. The accompanying cassette tape and these pages will clarify what I propose we do.

THE JANUARY LEARY/CLEAVER PRESS CONFERENCE

You and I should hold a press conference during the month of January 1995, either two weeks before the President's State of the Union address or two weeks after. Right now I think we should do it a couple weeks prior—but the timing is open for discussion. As to the subject, the press release announcing it will disclose only that it will be a matter of historic importance to the people of the USA and the entire world. This will heighten interest.

At our press conference, we will call for a movement to begin organizing now to ensure the election of a woman president of the United States for the 2000 election. The United States must enter the new millennium with a new birth of freedom. The present political situation in Washington and throughout the country is a prescription for disaster. We will call upon all unregistered voters to get themselves registered to vote. We will release a position paper to set forth, without getting bogged down in detail or rhetoric, our argument and forecast a great victory at the polls for a woman in the year 2000. The platform will be for National Salvation, Truth in Politics, Saving the Earth, Gender Justice and Healing, and Freedom and Justice for All—including Economic Justice, and the putting at the center of our politics the Loving Heart of a Mother. We need to root out of our national life the misogynistic, infanticidal, racist zeitgeist of the Old Boy Network.

At this press conference we would invite a list of key women to meet with us in Washington, D.C. on April 4, 1995, the 35th anniversary of the assassination of Martin Luther King Jr. At this point I would suggest the following women, but the order of the names of these women does not signify their importance. They will be equal members and it will be up to them to determine their structure, by laws, and officers, etc. Here is my working list:

1. BETTY FRIEDAN
2. MAYA ANGELOU
3. GLORIA STEINEM
4. EX TEXAS GOV ANN RICHARD
5. DELORES HUERTA
6. BERNADINE DORN
7. ANITA HILL
8. JANE FONDA

Please look upon this list as food for thought. We must discuss it, and consult others. The purpose is to assemble movers and shakers, realizing that the women we select will be subjected to an intense spotlight, so we need to have women who can handle it.

We will ask them to become the Board of Directors of an organization which they will form, and have exclusive power to add other members, male and female, to the Board. They will name the organization, whose purpose would be to spearhead the election of a woman president of the United States of America in the year 2000. The organization should be called something like WOMAN PRESIDENT 2000, and it shouldn't dissipate its focus by supporting other issues or candidates. The organization must be non-partisan.

At the April meeting in D.C., we will ask these women to issue a call for a very large meeting on the 4th of July, 1995. This meeting will be the first meeting of the enlarged Board of Directors, at which point it will issue its first paper, to set out in great language, the purpose and goal of electing a woman president in the year 2000. It should put forward a five-year plan structured around a calendar. The Board meeting will take place hopefully during the morning between 7:00 and 12:00, to be followed by a mass rally at a symbolically appropriate location in D.C., with speakers who will affirm this purpose and goal. The rally should feature great music by groups who will help establish the soul of the movement, and raise funds throughout the five years.

We have to decide whether just you and I do this press conference, or whether we include a woman, or anyone else. Think about it. We must send out a powerful and appealing image.

A dynamite event. Imagine, our message would be spread to every part of the world. We can make some deals with CNN or other media to do an exclusive document. We have to consider whether we hire a professional firm to organize the press conference for us. We probably should let the hotel where we hold the conference cater the event, or we could hire an outside caterer. I favor using the hotel to cater it, for security reasons.

During this press conference, we'd have to be on guard not to allow ourselves to get sidetracked with bullshit about the past. We can't allow the press to trivialize matters. We are not ashamed about the past. We fought the good fight, during a very difficult time, and we served with distinction. We will announce our mailing address and our 800 phone number, and welcome volunteers and contributions.

We would call upon the Democratic Party and the Republican Party both to nominate a woman candidate for president in the year 2000.

That way we can guarantee a woman's election. We predict that the party that refuses and fails to nominate a woman will be defeated at the polls.

Let's get together soon to brainstorm and fine-tune the details. Please play your cards close to your chest and I will do the same. We don't want to let the cat out of the bag prematurely. This can really capture people's imagination. If you agree to do this, then I will come to L.A. and huddle with you for several days to jointly work everything out.

Your Brother,
Eldridge Cleaver

The short essay "Reflections on the Million Man March," drafted for publication in Rap Pages, *shows Eldridge Cleaver reaching out to the younger generation of blacks—expressing both his criticism and his understanding of their predicament.*

REFLECTIONS ON THE MILLION MAN MARCH

for *Rap Pages*

The Million Man March was the defining event of the post–Black Revolution generation. This generation looks back with admiration at the generation of the sixties, measures itself against the giants of struggle and finds itself lacking, losing ground, shackled with a failure of heart, inspiration, and imagination. It has no great ideas. . . . A complexed, do nothing, guilt ridden generation whose major contributions are break dancing, dreadlocks, and rap music. A generation that has watched black communities from coast to coast transformed into moonscaped, bombed out battle grounds under the onslaught of the holocaust of drugs. This is a generation up against the wall, with a sense of being pushed backwards by the racist counterrevolutionary backlash. A generation with a foxhole mentality, paranoid at being the sentry on duty when the thieves (the Newt Gingrich gang et al.) break in to steal our freedom, like those who were on duty when the slave catchers snuck in, captured our ancestors, and sold our people into 400 years of slavery, suffering, and death. Rocked by attacks against the gains of the Civil Rights movement, disguised as attacks against affirmative action for being unfair to whites. They have an accurate perception of the malicious nature of the white backlash, and have lived in fear of what it might do next.

Into that vacuum stepped Minister Louis Farrakhan, without peer, a better man than most of his critics.

In this era of skin heads, militias, large scale white male terrorism, and church burnings, we have the weakest leadership in the history of our freedom struggle here in the Hells of North America. This post-Rodney King era, with its tell tale sign of large scale killing by cops, indeed is a new era, an era of the classification of Black Males as an endangered species.

Coming 30 years after Dr. Martin Luther King's Great March on Washington, Farrakhan's Million Man March offered the first chance for this generation to do something big, black, and significant. An opportunity for black men to flex their muscles, to sort of say, "Don't fuck with us!" The Million Man March was also a message to the so-called *Model Minorities*. We, the Afro-American people, have been joined in hand to hand, nose to nose combat with this white man for 400 years. Now that we have overcome and the table is set for the freedom feast, we are not prepared for you to elbow us aside, occupy our chairs, and then join in with the die hard racists to tell us that there is no place for us to sit at the table. We have had so many wars lately, that we have produced a huge population of black veterans with front line experience, afraid of no foe, able to cope. We see ourselves as a mighty race of overcomers, survivors.

Historically our struggle has fallen into three categories:

1. We have struggled against segregation and the evils flowing therefrom. Separate But Equal is a segregation doctrine that robbed our people of the quality of their lives.
2. We struggled against our exclusion from the political arena. Rejected, despised, we were unable either to hold political office or to vote in elections.
3. We struggled against being exploited and oppressed economically. We were kept in poverty and dependence. We were the last hired and the first fired.

In 1954, the U.S. Supreme Court, in *Brown vs. the Board of Education of Topeka, Kansas*, outlawed segregation, and the walls thereof came tumbling down. Martin Luther King started his movement in Birmingham, in 1955. Under the Kennedy, Johnson, and Nixon administrations, Congress passed civil rights laws that opened up the political arena.

But virtually nothing has been done to redress our economic grievances. We have been tossed a few crumbs from the Master's table in the form of Welfare. But we need an infusion of billions of dollars to assuage our economic pain and place us on a level playing field.

When the political arena opened up to us, our protest leaders, the most visible and best known and therefore the most electable folk around made a bee-line for the available political positions. They took our protest organizations, which were the only viable machinery in the black community other than the church, and transformed those organizations into their own electoral machines. This process stripped the black community of political organization. Therefore, the number one need in the black community is a coup d'etat against the present leadership, which is the worst leadership we've had since slavery.

We must not be afraid to pose the hard, impolite, undiplomatic questions. We are involved in a struggle for freedom that goes on from generation to generation. Everything we do, every move we make has relevance. What relevance does a Million Man March have? That there exists a power command among the Afro-American people that can move a million black men to act in concert. What is going on here? What is the message and who is sending it?

We have to examine what damage potential Farrakhan and his friends, in concert, hold for the U.S.A.? Through terrorism, total war, or sabotage? The Million Men coming forward was the manifestation of a Fifth Column. But fortunately for the U.S.A., the Afro-American people are American first.

The agenda put forward at the Million Man March reflects the real problems and needs of the black community. Give Farrakhan credit for focusing the spotlight.

Now, Let's Move It!

From the get go, the Million Man March had a deficit. There was no shortage of people eager to cut Minister Farrakhan down. But Farrakhan's most formidable adversary was the history of the Afro-American people. Of all the fruits of our history of struggle, survival, and overcoming, the most powerful is a thoroughgoing antiracism. Having been victimized by racism for over 400 years, we have learned both to understand it and to oppose it. General Colin Powell said it best, during his commencement address to Howard University. "After all we have been through because of racism, we are not now about to take a detour through the swamps of hatred."

Every time I hear the name "Farrakhan," I think of Malcolm X. I am not one of those who blame Malcolm's murder on Farrakhan. I have no evidence to that effect. I do blame Farrakhan for the mean and nasty things he has said about Malcolm X.

I consider the assassination of Malcolm X the Number 1 domestic crime committed against the Afro-American People since the end of World War II.

The assassinations of J.F.K., R.F.K., M.L.K., and Malcolm X arose from a strategy to sabotage the consolidation of a political dynasty that would have ruled the United States for the greater part of the 21st century. Without these murders, Malcolm X might be President of the United States of America by now.

The most crippling international crime committed against all black people was the overthrow and murder of Patrice Lumumba, the murder of Dag Hammarskjold, and the sabotage of Kwame Nkrumah and his plan to establish a United States of Africa, brainstormed by W.E.B. DuBois, Jomo Kenyatta, George Padmore, Sekou Toure, Modibo Keita, and the other Pan African giants of their generation. This is a work that still must be accomplished, that sees Ghana, the Congo, Nigeria, Guinea, and South Africa united to form the nucleus of what is destined to become the super power of the 21st century, the United States of Africa.

The Million Man March gave voice to those who oppose the killers and the killing of the dream. This was the voice of the Field Niggers, the Soul of Black Folk. The March is over. The voice is silent. But the genie is out of the bottle, and a mighty work has begun. A colossal event is going to occur in the U.S.A. Over the next twenty years, the American Revolution shall be completed. The American Dream shall be realized. And a black man shall be elected President of these United States.

"A Love Letter Writing Butterfly" reveals a silly, flirtatious side of the typically reserved Eldridge Cleaver, who never lost his fascination with women.

A LOVE LETTER WRITING BUTTERFLY

I'm a love letter writing butterfly
I'll write a love letter
To any girl I see
I'll tell her how much I miss her
And beg her please, please hurry write to me.

I'll tell her I dream of her every night
And see her face in the moonlight
I'm a love letter writing butterfly

All I need is her address and zip code number
And she'll soon be hearing from me

I'm a dreamer looking for a dreamgirl
A love letter writing butterfly
All a girl has to do is catch my eye
If I can get her address and zip code number
She will soon be hearing from me.

I spend all my extra money on stamps
I don't smoke, or drink, or go to the movies
I pick up the pennies others leave on the ground

I write love letters to movie stars
And at least once a year I write to the President's wife

I don't care how beautiful they are
I don't care if they live near or far

All I need is their address and zip code number
I don't care if they are big or small
That doesn't matter at all
Just give me her address and zip code number
And she will soon be hearing from me.

I don't care if she's off the wall
I don't care if she plays football
She can drive a Mack Truck
Or pluck a funky duck
She will still get a letter from me.

Speaking to the congregation of a black church in Los Angeles on February 8, 1998 during Black History Month, Eldridge Cleaver presented a concise review of the dramatic twists and turns his life had followed, leading to his renewed faith in God. Less than three months later, he died of heart failure in a Pomona hospital. In keeping with a request he had made to his daughter, his tombstone was inscribed with the words, "A Loving Heart and A Helping Hand," which is how he wished to be remembered.

BLACK HISTORY MONTH ADDRESS

TO GRANT AFRICAN AMERICAN EPISCOPAL CHURCH, LOS ANGELES

I want to express my appreciation to Pastor White for allowing me to stand in this hallowed pulpit, and to say good morning to our Heavenly Father, who has brought us through so much! That young man, who came up to read the scripture, he reminded me of myself when I was his age.

My mother told me that up until the time that I was twelve years old, I was a little angel, but then I became a little rascal. As I look out at your faces this morning, it takes me back to when I was making decisions about what I was going to do with myself in life, and I must give credit to my mother. You need someone to help channel your energy, to guide you in the right direction. It will be later on in life when you realize that there is no right way to do the wrong thing. It takes a long time before you get all the results lined up. All of you mothers and grandmothers here, please don't ever stop praying for your children. I feel so deeply that it was my mother's prayers that brought me through—I wasn't praying for myself, but my mother never stopped praying for me.

Looking at you beautiful people, from the youngest to the oldest, makes me remember how much it moved me, back when the civil rights movement was beginning to burgeon up, to see images either on TV or in the printed press about police officers killing and beating our people. Once I saw this big old burly policeman hit a woman in her back with a big billy club, and it brought tears to my heart. I was with a group of other brothers, and I said, "Man if you were there, what would you do?" I knew that I would kill that sucker.

My mother used to point at Thurgood Marshall, who would upset the entire state up when he would come to one of those southern towns. He was a very mighty lawyer, and he systematically made the moves that dismantled segregation in the southern states. And my mother used to say, "Son you got to be like Thurgood Marshall, he's a freedom fighter. You've got to do something to help bring freedom." She told me that on the day that you die, they're going to weigh your soul on the scales of eternity. If you have not done something to advance the cause of freedom, then your soul will not balance two dead flies.

I said, "Mama, that's pretty extreme."

She said, "I'm trying to get a point across to you boy, 'cause you're hard headed."

She'd tell me to be careful about what kind of organizations I affiliated with because she said a lot of organizations are going around here that try to appeal to our people on the basis of race, and want us to become racist. She'd tell me, son, don't ever join an organization like that because if you do, the minute you become a racist, you are a dead man. And I have never done that, I have never been a racist. A lot of people accused me of being one, saying, "man you were a Black Panther." We were not racist. They accused us of being suicidal, saying, "don't you know the police will kill you." We know, they'd been killing us, but we weren't suicidal, we were kamikaze, and there's a difference. I said I will not stand around and allow my people to be abused as they have been, I would rather go down in flames. That's how a lot of us felt. I give my mother her credit for instilling these principles in all six of her children.

My father—I had a lot of problems with my father. My father used to play the piano in his father's church, but he cut the church loose and started playing the piano in nightclubs. He'd tell me, "Son, whenever you get into trouble out there, always try to avoid a fight. A lot of people get killed, just for some dumb fight." He'd say to me, "If some guy wants to talk tough, let him talk tough. Whatever you do, don't hit somebody first, and try to get out of it. But if you can't get out of it and they hit you, take them out." That was my father's attitude.

Then there came a time when he started fighting with my mother—and I went up against him. It ended up destroying our family. The last fight they had I told my father that he could never hit my mother again.

He said, "Well who's going to stop me?"

I said, "I'm going to stop you."

"You and what army?"

I said, "It doesn't require an army, father."

By then I was playing football, boxing, and gang fighting, and I wasn't scared of nobody. That night he tried to make his move, I got in between them, and he hit me. And I kind of slipped. He hit me right here, and I tell you, it still hurts. And that's been close to—it's been about 48 years ago since that happened. I'm glad to say that I had a chance to reconcile with my father.

As I grew up in Los Angeles, and became a juvenile delinquent, started getting into trouble, going to youth authority and all that, getting into more trouble, going to prison, it seemed like my life could not possibly go anywhere good. It seemed like I just made so many bad decisions, that it was impossible to do anything to straighten it up. I was in that condition when I decided that I had to stop doing criminal things.

When I got out of prison, I joined the Black Panther Party. I tell you I never had so much trouble out of the police when I was a criminal as I did when I started getting involved in the freedom movement and hooked up with Huey Newton and Bobby Seale.

When I was younger, and looked at what was going on around me, I used to wonder, "what is this all about?" I wanted to understand why my people were in the position that we were. To understand that, I had to study the whole history of the world, I had to study all the realms of knowledge because this wasn't taught in school. Nowadays you can go to a bookstore and find so many books about black people you could never read all of them, but when I was growing up, there were hardly any books about black people. They would teach us that our history started off in the cotton fields of slavery, but we knew better. I give credit to our ministers, because our folk in slavery were first led by ministers. People try to secularize these guys, like Nat Turner, Denmark Vessey, and Gabriel Prosser, but these guys were called by God, and they stood up for freedom.

I remember when I used to think that people who went to church were soft, and I stopped going there. I used to like being with the tough guys, the boxers and the football players. There used to be a whole lot of bullies around when I was growing up. They used to like to punch out the little guys, you know. I was always a bit taller, so they didn't mess with me, but they'd punch out all the little guys. And I remember once back in grammar school, this guy named Gilbert got his nose bloody during recess, and the bullies told him they were going to wait for him after school and really do him in. So he came and got behind me. See, my name is Leroy Eldridge Cleaver. I had to let Leroy go because I wore that out with the Los Angeles Police Department, but all my brothers and sisters, my father, they all called me Eldridge. But back in those days, Gilbert said, "Leroy will you walk me home so they won't get me?" So after school, I got a couple of my buddies, and we walked Gilbert in the direction he lived. We wanted to get him close enough to home where he could just run the rest of the way, so they couldn't get him.

My mother lived in Altadena, after we moved from L.A., and my other brothers and sisters never moved over ten miles from her in their lives. I'm the one that got up and got out of there. But it was like coming full circle the other day when I was talking to the Pasadena Police Department. I've talked to a whole lot of police in my life but on that day we sat down and I had breakfast with the chief of police. The police invited me to come talk to them because they realized they have a problem with how people look at them, and they wanted me to explain it from my point of view. I explained to them how people feel that they are protecting an unfair system, and that they are there to plug the gaps in a very shaky social policy put forth by politicians. People are in pain, and when the police show up, people see them as agents of a shaky system, and they react to them in that manner. The Pasadena police understand that, and they are trying to make a different move.

I feel that I am called upon to put my shoulder to the plow, because when I look at what is going on in our society today, I can't help thinking that it is 15 minutes to midnight and the clock is ticking. As we move into a new millennium, I know that we have got to go a different way than we have gone. It took a lifetime of banging my head against the wall, trying to go the other way, to bring me to that understanding. I became a Marxist, a Communist because I saw that this system was unfair and I just wanted to do whatever I could to destroy it, and help replace it with something better; that was my idea.

My life was very closely connected with Dr. Martin Luther King, although I didn't like Dr. King because he was going around talking about turning the other cheek, you know, and loving your enemy. I wanted to kill my enemy. I did not understand how anybody could reach that conclusion. I used to look at the people going to church and wonder, "these people, do they believe that?" I used to think something must be wrong with them.

I had a chance to meet Dr. Martin Luther King once; he was getting ready to make a speech at Vanderbilt University. Stokely Carmichael was on the same program with him, and so Stokely introduced me to Dr. King. We shook hands; he was a short man. We had a meeting with Dr. King, and we asked him if he wouldn't take a position against the war in Vietnam, and if he wouldn't say something nice about the people they called black militants, because we felt kind of isolated then. And—this is what I respect about Dr. King—he talked the same way behind closed doors as he did in public. He told us that we had it all wrong. You guys believe in fighting fire with fire. But you don't understand that when you fight fire with fire, all you do is make a bigger conflagration, and we're trying to put out the fire. He said the raging fire that we are trying to put out is the fire of hatred. And you don't return hatred, you put out the fire of hatred with love. Because love is the water that will put out that fire. And he told us that suffering is redemptive. We were kind of hoping that maybe he'd have another dream that night.

So we went to the church the next day to hear him preach. Stokely and I, we were hoping he'd throw us a bone, you know. But in his sermon Dr. King said, "If there's going to be any blood, let it be our blood!" I jumped straight up—and said, "Man you are insane. You're talking about integration, if we're going to integrate anything, let's integrate this bloodshed." But he said, "That's not what we're trying to do. We want to get rid of it, the bloodshed." Dr. King, he never wavered.

I remember the day that he was murdered, a lot of us said "OK, now it's our turn, the man of peace has been taken down by the sword." We did win a larger audience, we did have a lot of action after that. But I began to really to miss Dr. King. I had a heavy responsibility, we had to discipline these guys and control these guys. I remember being in a room with 300 black men, and all of them had guns, and I had to tell them what to do. We were dealing with people whose own families couldn't control them, whom the prison system couldn't control, the police couldn't control, the political, economic and social system couldn't control, and we had to control them because they were under our orders. And we did it, but we did it by being strong, by being forceful, and also by having rules that were clear, and by being just according to those rules. There is no way out.

The day that Dr. Martin Luther King got killed, that was the beginning of the trouble that I got into. They had riots all over the country, people burning and looting and all kinds of things. But we didn't believe in spontaneous riots, we believed in ambushes. Two days after he was killed, I got into a gun fight with the Oakland Police Department. There were 14 of us.

When I went to court I pled not guilty, but we did it, we attacked the police because we were mad. In that gun fight three police officers got wounded, I got wounded. And after the shooting was all over and we were in custody, they shot and killed Bobby Hutton. I was taken to prison that same night—first to the hospital, then to San Quentin.

My lawyers filed a writ of *habeas corpus,* and when we got to court, the judge asked, "why do you have him in San Quentin?" The prison authorities replied that it was because I violated parole. He asked them, "what is the basis for that violation?" "Well, he was in a gun-fight." "How do you know he was in a gunfight?" The police said I was in a gunfight. So the judge said that the police alleged that I was in a gunfight. But that I was innocent until proven guilty, and that it was his job to preside over the procedure to determine whether or not I was guilty. He said, "You are usurping my power and my function, and you're going to come to me with just the word of the police, to make me leave this man in prison." He said, "we're going to have a recess," and told them to come back with "some better information than that, or I'm going to issue this writ of *habeas corpus* and set this man free." So they had the recess, they came back, and that's all they had: the police's word that they saw me in the gunfight. The judge said "that's not good enough. We'll decide that when we go to trial." So he let me go.

I'm telling you, the state appealed that decision to a higher court, the higher court agreed with the state, and so I went before the judge. The judge said, "I am ordering you, in 60 days from today, to show up at your parole officer's office at eight o'clock in the morning, and he will transport you to San Quentin. Do you understand that?"

I said, "Yes sir, I understand that."

"Will you be there?"

"Yes, I will be there."

I went to Havana. I wasn't going along with their program. We had it well organized, you know, we had to think ahead and plan, that's what the oppressor wasn't ready for. We started planning years ahead, thinking years ahead, and that's why I was able to get up out of here.

I stayed in Cuba for eight months. People asked, "man what was you doing, sitting there watching the calendar? How do you know you stayed there eight months?" Because when I left San Francisco, I left behind my skinny little wife. Only the people involved in helping me leave knew where I was going and knew when I was leaving. I didn't even tell my wife what I was going to do, I just did it. Then I sent her word, and she arranged to meet me in Algeria. This was eight months later.

When I got to Algeria, they told me that Kathleen was in this hotel room, and they gave me the room number, and I went there and knocked on the door. The door opened, and there was a fat lady standing there, and she had Kathleen's head on her shoulders. I said, "Hey, baby what happened?"

She said, "What do you mean, what happened? We're going to have a baby."

I said, "Well, when is it due?"

She said, "Next month."

So, I thought, when did I leave? That's why I know I was in Cuba for eight months, no more, and no less. I arrived in Algeria just in time for the birth of my first child, my son. No doubt about it, because it's me all over again. When I first saw my son, I couldn't make out anything, his face looked like a crumbled up dish rag. But my buddy looked at him and said, "man, he looks just like you." The following year, my wife and I had a daughter, she was born in North Korea. I'm telling you, it was these children that brought me to the Lord.

I was traveling across the world, I lived in Cuba for eight months, I lived in Algeria for four years, I lived in France for three years, and I traveled all over the Communist world. As I traveled looking at all these Communist countries, I saw oppression in those countries. I said this is not it. I saw people being abused. And those people would come and talk to me because I was obviously not part of their government. Being a person of color in any of those Communist countries lets people know immediately that I was somebody they could talk to. They'd tell me what was going on in the country, how they felt about the government. It was the direct opposite of what the government said that they were doing. I have never seen one Communist government that was all right, that the people liked. Third World countries, the same thing, it was dictatorship. As a matter of fact, I have never seen one government in the whole world that I like, but I never saw any people that I didn't like.

So I began to disengage from that revolutionary philosophy, that Marxist philosophy. In the midst of all that, I started looking at my children. I could see my wife and myself in their faces. Something just snapped in me; I knew this could not happen by accident. All that stuff that they teach about the big bang theory and all that, forget it, I could see that these children came about as a result of a plan. Something very precise is involved, you plant the seeds and nine months later you get the crop. It's not fifteen months later, or three months later. Anything that controlled, and throughout all creation it's all controlled, you can't tell me that just happened by rolling the dice. I could see the hand of God.

I knew there was a Creator. I wondered what was going to happen to me. I had been running my mouth all over the world, talking atheism. Suddenly, here I am—convinced there is a God. It was about that time when Richard Nixon got busted and kicked out of the White House. You see, I had run for president, on the Peace and Freedom Party ticket, against Richard Nixon when he won. I started seeing all these black men and women getting elected to offices, going to Congress. I didn't get too excited when Mayor Bradley got elected. I knew him, he used to be a lieutenant of the Los Angeles Police Department. I didn't expect him to help me. But Congressman Ron Dellums, he was my cut buddy. I started contacting Ron, asking him to help me come back home, you know. Get in touch with his buddies, Lionel Wilson, superior court judge, tell him to reinstate my bail and let me come back. And Ron Dellums sent me word—man, you better learn French real good, and just stay where you are, everything has changed back here, the whole pecking order has changed, your place has been taken by somebody else. If you come back you'll just go to the penitentiary.

I tell you, that broke my heart, because I knew if Ron wouldn't help me, none of those other guys would. That's when things started coming to a head for me. One day when I was in Paris, I picked up the newspaper, and I read that my father had died. I phoned my mother up, she was in Altadena.

I said, "Mama, I just read in the paper that daddy died a few days ago, maybe I should send you some money so we can buy a plot of ground in Arkansas, so we can all be buried together."

She said. "Eldridge, you know the last thing in the world your father would want is to be buried in Arkansas. Anyway, it's too late because your sister (my older sister Wilhelmina) has already had him cremated."

I said, "Well, what did she do with his ashes?"

"I have his ashes, right here," she said, and described the urn where she put his ashes.

"Mama, what you going to do with them?"

"When I die I'm going to have them buried with me."

I said, "Mama, I thought you hated this guy's guts. Yawl been separated for 27 years and you're going to have his ashes buried with you?"

She said, "The man that I married is not the man that your father became at the end. And the man whose ashes are in this urn, this is the man that I married. And how could I hate his guts? I had six children with this man."

Then she said, "There's only one other thing in life that I'm looking for, I want to see you walk through my front door a free man."

I said, "Well, you must be preparing to live a long time. I'm facing 82 years in the penitentiary, and I ain't coming over there."

She said, "I don't know how long it's going to take or how long I'm going to live, but I know that I will live to see you walk through my front door because the Lord has promised this to me."

The wheels started spinning, and I knew that I had to change my life. It was heavy, because I was a fugitive. My wife was not a fugitive, my children were not fugitives, but because of me they were locked outside of our country. I began to think I should just check on out. Maybe I'd just blow myself away, and then they could be free to come back home. We had a house in Paris, and I also had an apartment down south on the Mediterranean, a place that my publisher had gotten for me to write. I thought I'd just go down there and blow myself away. I felt so sad, thinking my whole life had come to an end.

I remember that night sitting out on the balcony with my pistol, just waiting for the right feeling to come over me. I was looking up at the moon, I could see a man in the moon. . . . Pretty soon something started happening that I cannot really account for, it was like watching a movie or something like that. I started seeing the man in the moon changing. I saw all my heroes of communism, from Karl Marx all the way down to Vladimir Lenin, Joseph Stalin, Mao Tse-tung—I would see their faces, then one after the other, each just fell away. At the end of all that I saw an image of Jesus Christ.

As a matter of fact, nobody was there talking to me, but it felt like I was being told: Here is the answer. The vision told me, "Get that gun out of your hand." I took my pistol and put it back inside the desk, and then went out again to the balcony, crying. I was crying, I was trembling. It was scaring me—you know I've been scared a lot of times in my life, but never like this: I was trembling inside of me. I fell out of the chair, and fell down on my knees. I started thinking about my mother, who always used to say the 23rd Psalm. I used to get hung up where it says, "the Valley of the Shadow of Death"—because I had set my tent up in that valley. Then, I saw a light coming from the moon straight at me. It came and then it curved, and as I looked, I saw a dark spot on that path of light, and when I looked again, I saw that spot was a prison cell. It was absolutely clear to me that I had to walk that path of light, and I had to go into that prison cell. As I looked closer, the light came out of the other side of the prison cell. It was clear. What I was being told was "you don't need these politicians to help you, all you need is me. It's going to be all right. You're going to go to that prison cell, but you will come out the other side."

And I jumped up and I went back to Paris the next morning. Kathleen had already taken the children to the nursery school down the street. I was just getting there when she came back, and I said, "Kathleen, I got to talk to you." I never do anything like that without checking with Kathleen, because a lot of times she has some good input.

"Kathleen," I said, "Something very strange happened to me last night."

"Well, what's that?"

Later on she told me I was looking strange. I told her about the little vision that I had.

I said, "Kathleen, we're going home. I'm going to surrender, and we're going—" I thought Kathleen was going to say "Eldridge that's crazy, you'll go to jail!" There have been many times when I tell her something I want to do, she'd say, "Eldridge don't do that, that's crazy." But it was usually about shooting or robbing somebody, or making some kind of move, and she was always against it, you know. But when I told her that I was going to surrender and we were going back home, she jumped straight up, and clapped her hands, she said she was going to start packing. That's all I needed.

I went to visit my lawyers, and told them, "Look, I want you to contact the American government and organize my surrender. I want to go back home." But they said, "Eldridge, all our clients are people like you, political exiles. . . . If the word got out that we surrendered you to the American government, it would destroy our whole practice. We don't want anything to do with that." So I said, "Ok, I'll contact you and tell you where to send my file." I knew another lawyer in Paris, but when I went to his office, they told me that he was out of the country and would be back in four days. They told me to call him on that day.

At that time, France had just elected a new president, and this lawyer had gone with the president on a visit to Auschwitz, the Nazi concentration camp. This man, a Polish Jew, had been the youngest survivor of Auschwitz. He was 14 years old they day they took him, his sister, and his mother off to the gas chambers. . . . His mother told him, "Samuel, you see that flower bed over there, you go over there and you lie down in that flower bed and pretend that you're sick, like you do when you don't want to go to school." So Samuel went over there and pitched a fit. He told me later how they took his mother and his sister through a door and he never saw them again; they gassed them. About a week later, when the Soviet Union and the United States seized Auschwitz, he was still alive. An American GI had brought him back to the United States and raised him, and educated him and he became a lawyer. By a special act of Congress that was put through by President Kennedy, he became a citizen of the United States, and the French government made him a citizen of France. He's the lawyer that designed the contracts that allowed for trade between the Communist countries and capitalist countries, and he has law offices all around the world. So, after he came back from Auschwitz, I went to see Mr. Pisar.

He told me that when he was at the concentration camp with the president of France, the place where the microphones had been set up for the speeches was the spot he had last seen his mother standing. He said going back to Auschwitz, and all the memories that flooded back, staggered his soul.

He asked me if I was I sure that I wanted him to organize my surrender. I told him I was. And so he wrote out a little thing, and he gave me a copy of it. Like a card, commemorating his return to Auschwitz. The card read, "From one ex-convict to another."

I said, "Mr. Pisar, I didn't know you were an ex-convict. What were you in prison for?"

He said, "For being a Jew."

He contacted the American government and organized my surrender. That's how I came back. It took another four years of going to court . . . and one day, in court, the Alameda County district attorney said to me, "Eldridge, there's somebody who wants to talk to you, wants to meet you."

I said, "Who is it?"

"Lieutenant Hilliard."

I recognized his name from my grand jury transcript—this was a man that we had surrendered to, following that gunfight in 1968. He told me that the reason that they were not rushing my case to trial was because of him and 13 other Oakland police officers. They were mad about how the police had killed Bobby Hutton after we were in custody. He said, "that's first degree murder, and if you go to trial, we'll testify against you but we will also testify against them and they don't want that. That's why I don't think they're going to take you to trial." And they didn't. I ended up with a plea bargain, where I was to serve 2,000 hours of community service; that's eight hours a day, five days a week, for a year. That's how my case was settled and made me a free man—and I'm glad to be free.

I have to point out just one thing. I have to point this out because I acted on the promise of that vision, that I would come back home, and I would get out of that prison cell. When I got back to Oakland, they locked me down tight. I went before this black judge, whom I was trying to get to lower my bail, or just put it back at $50,000, like it was when I jumped bail, but he had raised it to $1,000,000. The newspapers were laughing at me, people accused me of all sorts of things when I surrendered. But there was a very rich man in Philadelphia who read the article, and he started writing to me. His name was Art De Moss. He came to visit me, then he went before the judge during my bail hearing.

"Your Honor," he said, "I would like to be heard."

The judge said, "And who are you?"

He said, "I'm a businessman from Philadelphia, and the Lord Jesus Christ sent me out here to bail Mr. Cleaver out of jail."

He went up to the judge and he had a million dollars worth of stock in a little blue bag. And the judge looked at the stock—it was in Pennsylvania Railroad or something—and the judge said, "I won't accept this. I don't like the maturity date of these debentures, I will not accept these."

So Art De Moss said, "Your honor, when the bails bondsman gets somebody's bail, he has to go through an insurance company to get a bond to back him up. I own the insurance company that backs up more bail bondsmen than any other insurance company. So all I need to know is how much money do you want and what time do you close this court?"

He said, "I close the court between 4:30 and 5:00, depending on the volume of my business. What I want is $1,000,000."

Art De Moss said, "Eldridge, don't worry, I will be back in time. And all you have to do is decide what you want for dinner because we're going to have dinner together."

The judge said, "I know what you're going to have for dinner (because he had a menu, you know). You're going to have dinner up there in the jail."

Art De Moss left, they took me back upstairs; that was about 11:15 in the morning, it was Friday, August 13, 1976. They were acting so strange, I was worried that they were not going to let me out on bail. The sheriff was acting crazy and the judge was acting crazy. I was watching the clock and it was about 15 minutes to four when they called me to go back to court. When I went back downstairs the judge came out, he said, "Mr. De Moss, do you have something to show me?"

He said, "Yes, I do your honor."

He had a million dollars. He had opened a special bank account, where he put in $1,000,000. He handed the judge the bank book, and told him, "you have control of the account, but when this matter is settled it will all come back to me. In the meantime the interest goes into the account."

I was amazed, because I had stepped out on faith, with that vision. And I didn't know how it was going to work out, but the Lord sent Art De Moss to bail me out. I'm glad that chapter is closed in my life. And I'm here to testify that God is real, and that Jesus Christ is Lord, and he is alive. And he has a program of redemption to save us.

As I grow stronger in the Lord, I base my ministry on the second Book of Corinthians, chapter five, verses 17 through 22. Where it speaks of becoming a new creature, a new creation in the Lord, and that we are called to a ministry of reconciliation as ambassadors for Christ. I take that as my calling, and I travel all over the country. I went to an Indian reservation in Montana. And I asked the Indian people if they could forgive us for what we did to them. They said, "We can."

I went to a black church and asked the Afro-American people if they could forgive white people for slavery—they said they could. We apply the gospel of Jesus Christ to all of our little problems, but then try to sweep the big problems under the rug. We have got to deal with that because we cannot go forward from here like we are. We've got to forgive and we've got to love. That is why I was willing and able to go talk to the Pasadena police or anybody else. We've got to lay our cards on the table, we've got to stop doing the wrong thing, stop causing so much pain. We have to do the right thing for our children and our grandchildren, and for our Lord and for our Creator. Because nothing else matters.

ELDRIDGE CLEAVER, MY RUNNING BUDDY

CECIL BROWN

When I met Eldridge Cleaver in July 1968, I had just read *Soul on Ice* and considered it the new direction in African American literature. I had also heard him speak at a rally in Chicago, where I was studying. In the early summer, I headed out to the Bay Area with a few friends. I had a drive away Cadillac and I took it out to Berkeley. I remember ringing a doorbell in San Francisco and Eldridge leaning out of a window to see who was below.

Looking over at my white companion, he smiled and said, "Don't worry, brother, we don't mind that kind of thing out here in California."

He may not have used those exact words in that order, but his meaning was disarming and clear: he was not a racial bigot. My next image is of meeting Eldridge in his house—we liked each other and trusted each other immediately.

I set up an interview with him for the *Evergreen Review,* a hip East Coast magazine for which I had already published a short story and an essay on LeRoi Jones.

Eldridge invited me to drive around with him to witness his daily routine. I agreed; this would be a perfect way to conduct our interview. It didn't take me long to realize that he was a master rhetorician, not in the derogatory sense but in the original Greek sense: one who uses logic in oral debate.

Cleaver had his own distinctive way of talking and of using slang to make his points. The way he moved his head was unique; when he talked he tilted his head back, then looked at you askance. He liked to use his hands when he talked, often jabbing his forefinger at your face, and then resting it alongside his temple, fusing his words with his gestures.

To someone not familiar with black speech, his answers to my questions might have seemed rambling, but to me they were sensible. I got used to his long explanations, but I wondered if my editors would have a problem with it. (They did.)

We drove over to the office of his lawyer, Charles Garry, who handled all of the Black Panther legal cases. Eldridge was proud of Garry, and Garry was very respectful of him. Only a month earlier, Garry had brilliantly convinced the court to grant Cleaver's release from Vacaville, where he was imprisoned after the shootout with the Oakland Police when Bobby Hutton was killed.

In those days, Cleaver was at the height of his fame as a black American writer; he was lecturing at Berkeley, and challenging Governor Ronald Reagan to duels. One of his friends, the brilliant author Reginald Major, described Cleaver accurately when he wrote: "If there is a political Rosetta stone capable of translating the passion of the Panthers into a philosophical, sound program, it is Cleaver."[1]

At Garry's office, Eldridge threw his heels up on a desk and made a few phone calls, and from there we drove over to his office at *Ramparts* magazine. We spent that day driving around San Francisco and Oakland, I remember him being powerful, funny, and insightful. I was twenty-five and he was thirty-two; we shared an interest in literature and writing. "I was either going to be a lawyer or an economist," Eldridge told me as we began our interview. "I went to junior college, you know, and I was going there 'cause I didn't graduate from high school, but they had this thing where you could take these courses, make-up courses; I found that I didn't like to go to school and be uptight with bread. . . . So I started cutting marijuana, see, like my partners were into that. . . . So I started running with the bag, trying to get the coins right, and pretty soon it became clear to me that I couldn't fool around with that narcotics and deal with the pigs at the same time. Well, what I did, I said, I'll drop out of school this semester, concentrating full-time on spreading this Joy, watching for the cops, and the next semester I'll have a bank roll and I'll go back to school and I can be cool, you know—but in the mean time I got a case; and I got shot in to a nine-year forfeit."[2]

When I asked him how he got caught, he was frank: "They caught me because I whipped some people up on their heads and shot at them and tried to ravish a woman . . . and in the process of doing all that brutalizing, I thought I was a one-man Mau Mau thing, you know. . . ."

This was the same kind of bravado that made his persona in *Soul on Ice* so appealing to my generation—black and white. His honesty about his crime had the same fresh ring that Richard Pryor's comedy had. If we can speak of personalities that define an age, then Eldridge, like Richard, was an icon for the most intelligent, hip audience of the day.

I cannot recall whether the car we were riding in was a convertible or not, but I do remember that the sky was blue and expansive and that Cleaver was laughing, and serious at the same time, while we were riding up and down hills in San Francisco. Together we reviewed the history of black oppression that had been aided by white intellectuals. Cleaver said, if "[a white person] is intellectually honest, I don't have any vested interest in denying [that] particular person if he is saying something."

He was not an intellectual bigot. "Unless it's politics," he added, "then your enemy ain't saying nothing, no way, never. If a cat is using words to persuade people and influences people against something you are supporting, then you are not going to be persuaded by that. You are going to be trying to counter that. But if it's in his neutral realm where people discuss ideas and values and analyze experience, then if a man makes a valid analysis you welcome that, because he's enlightening you. He's adding to your tools for dealing with your environment. So you welcome that. But whites in the past have not wanted to see that happen with black people, because when black people started dealing with the evils in their environment they were dealing with the white man and his activities, so the white man was not interested in certifying an analysis that was an indictment of him and his activities."

"The black writer," he told me, "is in the position to essentially further the indictment of [white injustice], to elaborate the indictment and to keep a wary eye on the white man because he can be counted on to pretend to be changing the situation, to pretend to be doing better and to put a snow-job on us for another hundred years. See? So you gotta watch him so that when we wake up we have to remind ourselves and the people that it's the same old shit warmed over."

After we had lunch somewhere in Oakland on Grove Street, we headed over to see one of his friends. On the way, we spoke of the case of James Baldwin, who was the most widely read and discussed novelist of the times. We talked about Rufus, the character in Baldwin's *Another Country,* a homosexual who committed suicide.

"I think the shit that Baldwin puts on paper he should be telling to a psychiatrist," Eldridge said, "It's not something he should be projecting out as a model for black manhood. You see, he put that shit in his book to try to make Rufus the embodiment of black masculinity in our time. And Rufus didn't have anything to do with brothers that I know. Rufus was like a white boy, a black boy with white mind, castrated psychologically. I couldn't relate to Rufus, man. I have a very hostile reaction to [*Another Country*]. When I read it I just took Baldwin at face value. But I don't want to say too much about Baldwin, because that's been dealt with [one of his essays in *Soul On Ice* repudiated Baldwin's views on homosexuality] And I've met Baldwin and I consider him a friend as long as he keeps his mouth shut."

It was when we got into the specific role he saw for the young black writer, that I understood that Cleaver had really worked out a serious idea about writers and literature. "I think that [young black writers] need a good perspective on the history of literature, the way we got into this shit, you know, where we are now. I think that for a black writer to *really* come into his own he needs to have as part of his working equipment some understanding of what world literature means, what literature means to people, and the part that it plays in helping people cope with life, in terms of explaining what some of the best minds have seen going on in the world."

He paused, and then resumed: "We need a fighting literature; we need to understand ways of using words to expose, and to resurrect, the conscious efforts the white man has made to rob us of our history, to rob us of our dignity, of understanding, of ourselves as a strong and proud people. But not just that. Literature is . . . one of the essential things for survival, like music, dancing, and technology. Literature is just as important as any of the other major categories of human activity, and not just literature—literature is just one way of doing it, putting it on paper—but the whole process of recording one's history and views of life and interpretations of human experience. There used to be a time when they had what we call the oral tradition. That is, history as the memory, the collected memory of a people."

We discussed his own writings, especially his story entitled "The Allegory of the Black Eunuch" which I thought then—and still think now—is one of the great pieces of American writing. I wanted to know if that story was a new form of literature—something between fiction and non-fiction.

"I don't know what that shit is," he confessed, "I'll tell you what happened. I was in Folsom and my cell partner and a couple other cats were having dinner and we got into this argument. This cat, an old motherfucker, talking that pimp talk, you know, and very disrespectful to black women. He was a coward; he was everything we were trying to get out of. We were trying to explain something to him and he couldn't understand it, so I say I'm going to write this shit down, so he can read it—maybe [then] he'll understand it. And I kind of started reconstructing the conversation, you know. Then I just went off into my thing."

I was curious to know if he ever showed the finished story to the man he was writing it for.

"Yeah, but a few weeks later this dude died of some liver ailment. They took him to the hospital. I believe they could have saved him, if they gave him attention, but they won't give you medicine if you talk too much, you know. They let you die, man. . . . That's one of the things I'd be scared of most in the penitentiary, man, is getting a bad illness going. I'd have to go to the pigs." By which he meant he would have to depend on the prison authorities for medical help.

He told me he was scheduled to teach at UC Davis and I asked him what he was going to teach. "As for the name of the course," he said, "I don't know what I'm going to name it, maybe *pigology*. But I know what I'm gonna run down—the same old shit I always be talking."

In my last question, I asked him if there was a contradiction in *Soul on Ice* between what he had written about white lawyer Beverly Axelrod and his "Open Letter to all Black Women," which ends the book.

"I wouldn't go as far as to say that; I would say this: I married Kathleen. I'm not married to Beverley Axelrod, you dig it? I was in the penitentiary, and I wanted to get out. Now Beverly Axelrod was a lawyer who got me out of the penitentiary. When she came on the set, I thought that any reluctance to relate to her would be very unbecoming to me in the condition was in. So, I just blew my soul . . . from the moment I wrote her my first letter—you see I didn't know her, and she didn't know me; she came to see me in response to a letter I had written to her. I wanted to attract her. . . . I only had words, and I used those words . . . and I got out of the penitentiary."

I typed up the interview and sent it in to the editor. I was excited when I saw that Eldridge was going to give a class at UC Berkeley, since I had just started teaching in the English Department there. University graduate students had asked him to teach a class on racism, and it was given the number 139 X.

Ronald Reagan went ballistic. "No tiny faction of malcontents is going to be allowed to tear down our institutions of learning." He declared that the faculty members who approved Cleaver's teaching at UC ought to be fired. The Board of Regents compromised and permitted Cleaver to give only one class, as long as the course also had other teachers.

"The ruling angered the students and faculty," Major wrote, "who immediately organized mass meetings to protest the Regents' actions, while vowing that Cleaver would deliver all ten lectures."[3]

But Governor Reagan was still livid about Cleaver even doing one class. "One of the lectures will deal with negative influences of Grade B movies on the American mentality," Cleaver said, "using Mickey Mouse Reagan's career as a text."[4]

I tried to see Eldridge in his class, but the room was packed and I couldn't get close enough to talk to him. I followed his public dispute with Reagan in the newspapers, and read that Cleaver had challenged him to a duel.

Later in November, I went to hear him speak at Glide Memorial Church. "Don't do anything with the interview," he said, "I'll be back and we can finish it."

He didn't appear for his November 25 lecture. Cleaver had chosen to absent himself from the country rather than obey a court order to return to jail.

A few days later, I read in the paper that Eldridge Cleaver had disappeared. The following July, the news announced that he had reappeared in Algeria, North Africa.

He spent seven years in Cuba, Algeria, and France with his wife Kathleen. In 1975, around Thanksgiving, he surrendered to the FBI. When he finally was bailed out in August 1976, about a dozen people were there when he walked out. I went down to greet him at the courthouse in Oakland.

He looked older, but still cheerful, still charismatic. He greeted us. Somebody poured champagne in paper cups. We welcomed him home.

Fourteen years later I was sitting in the French Hotel Café in Berkeley and Eldridge walks up.

I was surprised that he remembered me. He said, "I told you not to publish that interview [that] I'd be back."

"That was a long time ago," I reminded him.

"Yeah, but I wanted to add something to it," he said. "I read the article and it was good."

From this time on until his death in 1998, Eldridge and I were friends. We spent a lot of time at Café Roma and Café Strada, both on College Avenue in Berkeley. Seated in Café Roma, I would observe him getting off the bus, which stopped across the street from the café. Dressed in dark pants and a flamboyant scarf, Eldridge walked in carrying a couple of briefcases. Once in the café, he would pop open the briefcases and take out his books, his book holder, pencils, and, in later years, a computer.

Occasionally he would already be there when I arrived. He would be sitting alone with his book, his writing accouterments spread out on another table. If he was not alone, writing or reading, then he would be engaged in a conversation with somebody—an old friend or a new acquaintance.

Over the years, we shared many stories. At his table, I heard about the white lady who left Eldridge a house in her will because she felt the Black Panther Party was right. She had heard Eldridge speak, and had been impressed by his truthfulness, and when she died she gave him her house and some bonds. Her will was handwritten, but it was very clear. Eldridge would show it to me, and it looked authentic. I heard about how the woman's children tried to take the house from him.

In 1990, when I was studying for my Ph.D. at UC Berkeley, I took a course by Alan Dundes. Professor Dundes had edited a valuable collection of folklore called *From the Laughing Barrel,* in which he included an article Eldridge had published in the *Negro History Bulletin,* called "As Crinkly as Yours." Professor Dundes told me that the essay was the best thing he had ever read on black folklore and black style in hair.

An hour or so later, as Eldridge and I took our daily cappuccinos together, I mentioned Dundes' admiration for the story. "Thank him for me," he said, "That was the first thing I ever published. How did it happen that I wrote about that?"

I was always asking him details about his stories, so he was anticipating my question.

"Dudes in prison always had their hair cut by the prison barber. So one day I decided that I wasn't going to get my hair cut. I kept it the way it was. They called me up to ask me why I wouldn't have my haircut. So I said. . . ."

What followed was a story about resistance, and the freedom that came from having stood up to the authorities. He was a gifted raconteur, and his narratives were great oral literature.

Eldridge took a keen interest in interdisciplinary studies, especially the oral tradition. Back in 1968, in our interview, he had mentioned how blacks passed their culture along through the oral tradition. He eventually donated some of his papers to the Bancroft Library at UC Berkeley.

In the afternoons, after our cappuccinos, we would make an excursion from the café, which is like theater (with the waitresses as actresses), into the real world. (Usually, I would drop Eldridge off at one of the numerous domiciles he had over the years.) But—if there was a party—then everything changed.

When Eldridge was sixty, a Berkeley poet threw him a party. Out in the backyard Eldridge signed his prison mug shots as souvenirs.

At the opening of his film, *Panther,* the writer Melvin Van Peebles met Eldridge. He invited Eldridge to come inside to watch the film, but Eldridge preferred to stay in the lobby and talk to young people about what was really happening with the Panthers. In the theater, I watched somebody playing the film role of Eldridge, while the real Eldridge was out in the lobby competing with the celluloid.

Later, perhaps that year, somebody hit him on the head and stole his truck. He was taken to the hospital. Cleaver was the victim of a criminal act, and he talked about it as a sort of reversal—somebody had done to him what he had once done to others. The doctors operated on him immediately, saving his life. While he was in the hospital, the police impounded his truck.

I didn't know about the incident until after his surgery (in his brain no less) when he called me from the hospital to see if I would pick him up. Eldridge had a saintly humility when he asked for help. Of course I'd pick him up. I took him to a house where he had his notebooks and a roomful of files.

In 1968, Eldridge had told me he was going to teach "pigology" at UC Davis, but when he actually lectured my class there in 1995, he was talking about "African Revolution." He'd been profoundly influenced after reading the book *African Revolution* by John Hendrik Clarke. My classroom was packed with students, black and white. After the lecture, we went to lunch at the student cafeteria, where students crowded the table, just to get a look or exchange a word with him.

When we finished lunch, Eldridge asked me to drive him to a rental car agency, because he needed a car. He wanted to rent a van, but when the agent needed to see his driver's license, he didn't have one. Nor did he have a credit card. Finally, the manager came out and realized that it was Eldridge Cleaver, the man whose book he had read in college, and he decided to let him rent the van anyway. I only had to give my credit card as reference. As we left the parking lot, Eldridge remarked that the van was perfect for his purposes because he was going to sleep in it.

As we drove back to Berkeley, I watched his headlights out of the back rearview mirror.

Suddenly, his lights went off the road. I didn't know what had happened to him. I tried to phone him when I got home, but nobody answered his phone. I didn't hear from Eldridge for a few weeks. By that time, the rental office had called me and said that the van had not been returned and that they had not heard from him. I was becoming desperate upon hearing this, because they were going to charge my credit card for the van if he didn't return it.

Finally, after doing some research, I learned that Eldridge had driven the van (packed with his belongings) down to Pomona, California. When I got in touch with him, I was angry, but Eldridge coolly explained that he had finally returned the van and that everything would be all right. Eventually, it was.

Later, I spoke with him on the phone several times, and learned he was doing fine back in southern California. He was going to return to Berkeley in a few days, to see Bobby Seale, and we would meet then. We were going to walk up to Berkeley and do another interview on how he saw the campus after so many years since his historical lecture.

But we never got to do that. I heard of his passing on the news. I'd received a postcard from him, signed, "Take No Enemies!" a quote from the speech he gave at an Indian reservation, but I think, more than anything, it defines his attitude towards telling the truth.

May 5, 2005
Cecil Brown, Ph.D.,
author of *The Life and Loves of Mr. Jiveass Nigger*
and *Dude, Where is My Black Studies Department?*

NOTES

INTRODUCTION

1. Robert Scheer, "Introduction," *Eldridge Cleaver: Post-Prison Writings and Speeches* (New York: Random House, 1969), p. xvii.
2. The late Warren Wells, while incarcerated for life in Mule Creek State Prison, in Ione, California, wrote a statement to be read at Cleaver's funeral on May 9, 1998. "I Remember Eldridge Cleaver," was the title he gave the statement, which is quoted here.
3. Robert Scheer, "Introduction," *Eldridge Cleaver: Post-Prison Writings and Speeches,* p. xxii.
4. Ibid., p. xxi.
5. Eldridge Cleaver, "Affidavit #2: Shoot-out in Oakland," in *Eldridge Cleaver: Post-Prison Writings and Speeches,* ed. Robert Scheer (New York: Random House, 1969), p. 91.
6. Lee Lockwood, "Introduction," in *Conversation with Eldridge Cleaver: Algiers* (New York: Dell Publishing Co., 1970), p. 23.
7. Sanche de Gramont, "Our Other Man in Algiers," *New York Times Magazine,* November 1, 1970, p. 31.
8. "Eldridge Cleaver Meets the Press," (printed transcript, undated), p. 3.
9. Jack Olsen's book, *Last Man Standing: The Tragedy and Triumph of Geronimo Pratt,* gives a comprehensive background to the politicized case brought against Black Panther leader Geronimo and its ultimate resolution in 1997. After having his conviction vacated and being freed, Geronimo won a $2.5 million settlement from the Los Angeles Police Department and the FBI for their participation in abusing the legal system where he'd been sentenced to life in prison.

AFTERWORD

1. Reginald Major, *A Panther is a Black Cat* (New York: William Morrow & Co., 1971), p. 143.
2. Cecil M. Brown, "The Minister of Information Raps: An Interview with Eldridge Cleaver," *Evergreen Magazine,* October 1968.
3. Major, *A Panther is a Black Cat,* p. 147.
4. Ibid., p. 147.

INDEX

READING GROUP GUIDE
FOR *TARGET ZERO*

1. The writings collected here are divided into four parts. How would you characterize the tone and subject matter of these four parts? Can you discern connecting, recurring themes or are they completely distinct?

2. Cleaver's best known book is *Soul on Ice.* How do the other, lesser known texts excerpted here compare? How does it differ from his later work, *Soul on Fire,* also excerpted here?

3. How do Cleaver's early life experiences, as told in Part One of the book, inform his later attitudes toward women, particularly as they are expressed in *Soul on Ice?* In Part Four, Cleaver reflects on the possibility of a woman president for America. Given the current political mood, was Cleaver being a visionary or was this yet another form of rebellion against the times? How do you think Cleaver's views on women changed over the years?

4. Do you agree with Professor Gates' statement in the foreword that Cleaver "was far more a writer, an essayist, than he was an activist"? How does Cleaver's politics affect the quality and tone of his prose? How do his politics change over the arc of the book and how does that influence his prose?

5. Based on the main text and the complementing essays, what were some of the contributing factors (aside from the FBI's COIN-TELPRO activities) that led to the splintering and eventual dissolution of the Black Panther Party?

6. From the beginning, it is apparent that Eldridge Cleaver and Huey P. Newton had some basic ideological differences. What were they, and how did those differences play out between them? How, if at all, do you think they led to Cleaver's expulsion from the Black Panther Party?

7. While in exile, Cleaver had the opportunity to travel to places such as Cuba, France, Africa, and Asia and to interact with other

revolutionaries of the time. How do you think his exposure to different cultures and perspectives influenced his own ideas on how the goals of the Black Power movement could be achieved? Why did he eventually come back to America?

8. How did Eldridge's perception of America change over the years and how did America itself change? In what ways was Eldridge right about his vision of America?

9. Discuss the role of humor in Cleaver's prose. Does it deter from the seriousness of his arguments?

10. Three essays bookend this collection. Kathleen Cleaver, Henry Louis Gates and Cecil Brown all met Eldridge when he was in his prime. How do their essays complement Eldridge's own words? What does this say about Eldridge as a man of his times? What do they tell us about how the perception of Eldridge changed over the years?

11. Over the course of his life, Cleaver's ideology changed radically. Were there any signals in his earlier writings that this change might occur? How does the tone of his writing change as his political thinking evolves, how does it stay the same?

12. When put into historical context with other progressive leaders such as David Walker, Nat Turner, John Brown, and other well-known figures in black history, how does Cleaver's life and work compare? Are there any parallel themes that emerge?